SO-ADE-149

LITERATURES OF THE WORLD
IN ENGLISH

LITERATURES OF THE WORLD
IN ENGLISH

Edited by

Bruce King

Professor of English
Ahmadu Bello University
Zaria, Nigeria

ROUTLEDGE & KEGAN PAUL

London and Boston

First published in 1974
by Routledge & Kegan Paul Ltd
Broadway House, 68–74 Carter Lane,
London EC4V 5EL and
9 Park Street,
Boston, Mass. 02108, U.S.A.
Printed in Great Britain by
Cox & Wyman Ltd
London, Fakenham and Reading

ISBN 0 7100 7787 4

Library of Congress Catalog Card No. 73–89197

CONTENTS

			Page
	Contributors		vii
	Preface		ix
	Acknowledgments		xi
	Introduction	Bruce King	1
1	Australia	Brian Elliott	23
2	Canada	Peter Stevens	42
3	England	William Walsh	61
4	India	B. Rajan	79
5	Ireland	A. Norman Jeffares	98
6	Kenya	Douglas Killam	116
7	Nigeria	D. S. Izevbaye	136
8	South Africa	John Povey	154
9	The United States	Bruce King	172
10	The West Indies	Kenneth Ramchand	192
	Notes		213

CONTRIBUTORS

Dr Brian Elliott, Department of English, University of Adelaide

Dr D. S. Izevbaye, Department of English, University of Ibadan, Nigeria

Professor A. Norman Jeffares, Department of English, University of Leeds

Professor Douglas Killam, Department of English, Acadia University, Wolfville

Professor John Povey, African Studies Centre, University of California, Los Angeles

Professor B. Rajan, Department of English, University of Western Ontario

Dr Kenneth Ramchand, Department of English, University of the West Indies

Professor Peter Stevens, Department of English, University of Windsor

Professor William Walsh, Department of English, University of Leeds

PREFACE

Our idea of English literature has changed radically in recent years. A surprising quantity of good writing has come from the newly independent English-speaking countries. As we have become conscious that there are emerging literary traditions with characteristics of their own in the new nations, we have also become aware that the literatures and cultures of the older nations are distinctive and need to be freshly examined for their particular qualities. The new literatures of Africa and the West Indies have helped place in perspective Australian, Irish and Canadian authors as belonging to their own national traditions, in contrast to American or British ones.

With this in mind, it seemed useful to bring together a collection of introductory essays on the more important English literatures. Most of the contributors have had the experience of living and teaching in various English-speaking nations. They have been asked to write on whatever seems helpful towards aiding the reader's response to a particular national literature. The approach adopted by the contributors varies; there are critical discussions of individual works, historical surveys tracing the development of a literary tradition, and studies which show the influence of the cultural situation on a writer. Some of the contributors feel that cultural nationalism is an important issue of our age; other contributors are sceptical of its importance. The essays, while introductory, might be said to examine, if not always define, the particular characteristics of a specific literature. I have written my introduction largely without reference to the essays which follow, in the hope that the reader may find another perspective more useful than consistency of opinion. Since my introduction is personal, and not a summary of what will be said by others, it only touches on writers with whose work I am familiar. I am conscious of having often rushed in with generalizations about the characteristics of a national literature where others have, with more wisdom, preferred not to tread.

While the following essays can be used by students needing a short introduction to a particular national literature, the book

should be read as a whole. It is interesting to see the similarities
and differences between the various national traditions of English
literature. Often the differences make us aware of the cultural,
political and social characteristics of a nation. Perhaps the main
interest of this collection is in the range of literatures presented
and the many books and authors one would like to read.

ACKNOWLEDGMENTS

The editor and publishers wish to thank the following for permission to reproduce copyright material:

East African Publishing House, Nairobi, for Richard Ntiru, 'The notion of modernity in African creative writing', *East Africa Journal*, vol. viii, no. 10 (October 1971) and Leonard Kibera, *Voices in the Dark*; Heinemann Educational Books for James Ngugi, *The River Between*; Laura Tanna for her interview with Okello Oculi published in *BaShiru* (Journal of the Department of African Languages and Literature, University of Wisconsin), Autumn 1970–Spring 1971.

INTRODUCTION
Bruce King

Until recently, English literature meant the literature of the British Isles. The major writers who lived outside England either were not studied or could apparently be assimilated within the British tradition. The United States was an exception in having a long literary history of its own, and writers of world class; however, American literature was usually not studied outside North America, there was no consensus as to who were the important authors, and many of the better American writers preferred to live in England or Europe. Sometime during the 1950s our perspective on English literature changed. It was now recognized that the United States had a literary tradition of its own; Australian writing gained general attention; next, the West Indies and the newly independent nations of Africa, led by Nigeria, seemed to be areas where the most interesting contemporary literature was being written. Almost contemporaneous with the emergence of new national literatures, universities began to offer courses in Commonwealth, African, Irish and Canadian writing. As a result, our idea of English literature has changed and is likely to remain changed. The best books of the year are as likely to be written by Ghanaians, West Indians or Australians as by Americans or Englishmen, and their subject matter, themes and style will often include characteristics that are puzzling to foreigners. Since such characteristics may add to, or detract from, the qualities of a book, they are likely to become an increasingly important concern to readers, students and critics. A reader is now likely to be confronted with English social awareness, American individualism, Nigerian tribalism, Indian mysticism, and the West Indian search for identity. We may need to adjust to English irony, American exaggeration, or that peculiar inwardness common to Canadian writing. Since authors, consciously or not, tend to work within their national literary traditions, it seems likely, at least for the immediate future, that an awareness of the

characteristics of other English literatures may become part of
our reading habits.

Colonialism is as responsible in North America and Australia as
in Africa and Asia for the development of national English literatures around the world. Colonialism, whether as indirect rule or
the exploration and settlement of continents, brought with it the
English language, English literary forms, and English cultural
assumptions. Colonization also brought the possibility of a new
literature emerging once English becomes a vehicle for the expression of local culture. A new English literature may express a culture
which has grown up with the settler communities, it may be a
continuation of indigenous cultural traditions, or it may be some
mixture of the effects of colonization, including the bringing
together of various races into one nation. While the use of English
as a means of literary expression in other nations might be said to
have begun among the settlers in seventeenth-century Ireland and
America, it has only been since the Second World War that the
varieties of English literature have had international recognition.
The recent importance of various national English literatures is a
reflection of such cultural and political developments as: the dissolution of the British Empire, the emergence of new nations, the
weakening of Commonwealth ties, the increased awareness of
independence in former colonies, the importance of the United
States, and a general, if vaguely defined, feeling that the English
cultural tradition is no longer relevant outside the British Isles or
that it supports the dominance of a British-influenced élite. The
break-up of our older concept of English literature, into national
literatures, thus reflects the growing cultural fragmentation of the
English-speaking world. We no longer share the same models of
language, manners, morals or beliefs. It is possible to regret the
passing of a single literary culture which provided a frame of
moral and social reference for the educated of a large section of the
world, while also recognizing that an awareness of the distinctive
qualities of various national literary traditions has become a
contemporary necessity.

It should be remembered that the study of 'English' literature
is itself fairly new, and largely a product of this century. 'English
studies' came about when the classical languages, Greek and Latin,
were no longer felt to be necessary for the education of a gentleman. With the European classical tradition no longer providing

our central source of moral education and superior entertainment, Shakespeare, Donne, Pope and Keats replaced Homer, Virgil and Cicero as required reading. There was a diminution of historical vision, which was made up for by a greater immediacy and sense of familiarity in the authors who were studied. That there was something lost in the process – a sense of the past, the feeling of an education shared by most of Europe – is, I think, reflected in T. S. Eliot's *The Waste Land*, which, among its themes, sees the descent into the emotional limbo of the modern world as a fragmentation and break-up of older, more valid cultures, in which our own feelings and beliefs were rooted. The modern literature of the early part of this century can be seen as perhaps the last expression of the classical tradition which formed our cultural inheritance of the past. The cosmopolitanism of Eliot, Pound and Joyce was part of an international modern style, but the writers held a fixed, timeless, permanent view of man in which the past defined the present.

It is somewhat ironic that the very critical movement in England which did most to defend such writers as Eliot and Pound was also the first to attempt seriously to define the qualities of British literature. English academic criticism, as it had to come to grips with and explain to students the distinctive qualities of their national literature, defined what we have come to think of as English literature: a stylistic balance between the formal and colloquial, a preference for quiet irony, understatement, realistic subject matter, and a concern with man in relation to society. To this list one might add moral seriousness, a distrust of ideas and ideologies, and distrust of cosmopolitan and fashionable values. In the British tradition, roots, fixed values, a sense of place are seen as desirable and to be preserved. British literature is filled with poems and novels celebrating a country home or a family estate as a source of the good life in contrast to the various corruptions offered by the city. Often, as in *Mansfield Park* and *Howards End*, British novels treat the question of who will inherit the estate as representative of who will inherit the best of the nation's culture.

Just as the assumptions and themes of English literature reflect British culture, so the qualities of the writing are an expression of the language itself. The English language, as Professor Walsh shows, can create in its texture, movement and imagery a feeling of actual experience and a sense of life. It is this rather than

3

critical theories or formal literary conventions that is the shared basis of English writing and criticism. English is capable of great variety of movement and texture within a paragraph, sentence, or phrase; sound often appears to imitate meaning. We might contrast this with a language such as French, in which local effects are harder to achieve, and which lends itself to more sustained rhetorical patterns.

As I understand it, our present view of the major English writers grew out of T. S. Eliot's literary criticism and was given its current shape by F. R. Leavis and the critics who wrote for *Scrutiny*. In setting the now accepted canon of English literature in order, Leavis was making both literary and cultural choices. While these choices now seem correct to us, it would be possible to select other characteristics as representative of the great tradition of English literature. A preference for realism instead of fantasy, moral earnestness in place of gaiety of spirit, or the wish for an harmonious society rather than individuals pursuing their own interests, involved discriminations between various attitudes towards life and art which have often competed in England. When Leavis criticized Eliot's magazine, the *Criterion*, as another international cultural review, he was in a sense rejecting the older view of English literature as part of a European heritage, and demanding for it an independent tradition of its own in which national, rather than classical or international values would have the cultural ascendancy. In saying this, I am not attacking Leavis or the writers connected with *Scrutiny*; they created the standards of English literary criticism during a time when it was necessary to make choices. However, one result of treating English as a national literature separate from European or classical literature (a distinction still not made so sharply in European countries) was to bring into currency values which might not be appropriate to English literature outside the British Isles. Leavis, I imagine, was aware of this, since he and such *Scrutiny* critics as Marius Bewley were among the first in England to treat American literature as a distinct and separate tradition having qualities of its own. And it was only after the English tradition had been defined that it was possible for American critics to see clearly, by contrast, the characteristics of their own national literature. An example of this is Richard Chase's *The American Novel and Its Tradition*. A similar process of defining one's national literature by contrast to that of England or the

United States has become common in other English-speaking countries.

It can be said that until recently British English had a position similar to that of Latin during the Roman Empire, and that the growth of national literatures written in English somewhat parallels the development of vernacular writing during the late Middle Ages. A central tradition has lost its unifying force and various regional developments seem likely to gain equal status, while still retaining their roots in the original culture. As with many analogies, this one is perhaps more useful as a starting place for further thought than as an exact parallel. Logically, the analogy would demand that each national English become a separate and distinct language, such as French, Spanish and Italian. While this is unlikely to happen, we are aware that English is used differently throughout the world. Not only do words carry different implications and meanings in, say, London, New York and Lagos, but the structure and rhythm of sentences are likely to be different. Prose cadences in the writing of Mark Twain or Norman Mailer are significantly unlike those we find in the novels of Jane Austen or E. M. Forster; in poetry we are often aware that British and American verse seems based upon different feelings for the movement of speech. While poets in both countries may revert to the iambic norm and common syntactic patterns when consciously aiming at a formal style, their natural cadences are usually dissimilar.

If such a difference has developed between American and British style, greater differences can be found in Africa, India and the West Indies, where other languages influence the use of English. In reading African English poetry, for instance, one is often conscious of the influence of tribal languages upon stress and rhythmic patterns, the influence of traditional oral literature on poetic form, organization, and the way meaning is communicated. In the West Indies there is the importance of Creolization, and the sophisticated playing-off of various registers of English against each other; in a novel we might notice an interplay of standard British English, educated West Indian English, and various popular West Indian forms of speech. A similar significant counterpoint of registers of English can be found in Nigerian novels. The presence of tribal proverbs, pidgins, regionalism, and other forms of non-standard English in literature may be an example of a writer's naïve nationalism or his wish to be exotic; but it can also be essential to the imaginative coherence with which society and its values are depicted in serious writing. Often deviations from standard usage carry cultural assumptions. The following passage from Achebe's *A Man of the People* shows the variations an author can perform on our associations of speech with levels of sophistication:[1]

> 'Look, Agnes, why don't you use my wife's bedroom instead of wasting money,' said Chief Nanga getting back to his seat. 'She travelled home today.' His phonetics had already moved up two rungs to get closer to hers. It would have been pathetic if you didn't know that he was having fun.

If various English literatures reflect national characteristics of speech, they often show unique thematic and formal qualities. The English novel tends towards realistic descriptions of society, an awareness of the different values held by various classes, and is concerned with the morality of human relations. Even when a story is told through the eyes of a central character, the emphasis is on the relationship between the self and society. In the novels of Fielding, Jane Austen, Dickens, George Eliot or John Wain, we see man acting out his destiny in society and we are often aware that conflicting moral attitudes and beliefs are expressed by contrasts of manners and behaviour. In the American novel, the focus is more on character than society and more on the character's consciousness and inner world. Huckleberry Finn, Isabel Archer and Herzog attempt to define their reality through themselves; society, as far as it is important, is a stage upon which the moral sensibility can act. I often have the impression when reading American novels that I am inside the main character and that the story is about that person's experience in a hostile world. The major American writers seem concerned with experience for its own sake, or as part of a pilgrim's progress towards an unobtainable new Jerusalem where the soul could lay down its burden. Many American authors have seen opportunity for personal spiritual development in the newness of their country and in the vast open spaces of the West; other writers have treated with irony such themes as the American as an innocent new Adam in an unfallen Eden, or the idea that the continent made possible the quest for an individual's personal destiny without the inhibitions imposed by European civilization. Melville, Henry James and Nathaniel West are among those who treat the American dream with shades of irony. In

6

American writing, we are often aware of an attack on literary form and formal style, which are regarded as limiting, Europeanized and somehow against the articulation of the individual identity. There is a tendency towards an elaborate style in which the conscious self can realize itself, a tendency towards concrete, particularized descriptions, and a tendency towards highly charged symbolism.

In the process of formulating a national tradition, the literary critics of most English-speaking countries have adopted the concepts which influenced British criticism, especially the criticism of Leavis and *Scrutiny*. We think of a national literature written in English as having distinguishing characteristics in the use of language, as revealing distinct cultural preferences, and as representative of, or having its roots in, influential sections of the community. A national literature also requires a canon of major or significant authors forming a main tradition around which one can place minor or supposedly less relevant writing. In recent decades American critics have no longer inflated every literary reputation, as they so often did in the past; there is a recognition that the country has produced six or seven major writers, and that other authors will need to be judged within this perspective. There is a growing awareness that there are common themes and certain qualities of style and literary form which define at least part of the American tradition. It is realized that the literary tradition has reflected such major cultural influences as Puritanism and the later loss of faith. It is accepted that Rousseau and European Romanticism have been as lasting an influence on the literary imagination as the growth of the country through settling the virgin lands of the West.

If we look at Australian literary criticism, we notice similar tendencies. Where it was once said that Australian literature reflected national vitality, the exploration and conquest of virgin lands, or described the country's non-European landscape, more recent criticism has tried to establish a canon of important authors of enduring literary value and has tried to analyse what the major authors have done with the nationalistic themes of the past. Writers are often aware of the themes of their national literature and use them consciously in their novels. Many contemporary Australian writers, such as Patrick White, contrast the conformity and materialism which prevails in the urban suburbs with the spiritual challenge offered by the open spaces of the interior of the country. The deserts thus become a metaphor of the soul. Perhaps the best example of a modern writer treating commonplace themes paradoxically is A. D. Hope's 'Australia':[2]

> They call her a young country, but they lie:
> She is the last of lands, the emptiest,
> A woman beyond her change of life, a breast
> Still tender but within the womb is dry.
>
> Without songs, architecture, history:
>
> . . . .
>
> Yet there are some like me turn gladly home
> From the lush jungle of modern thought, to find
> The Arabian desert of the human mind,
> Hoping, if still from the deserts the prophets come
>
> Such savage and scarlet as no green hills dare
> Springs in that waste, some spirit which escapes
> The learned doubt, the chatter of cultured apes
> Which is called civilization over there.

I realize that it is controversial to suggest that the acceptance of a critical tradition distinguishing between major and minor writers is a sign that a country has cultural assurance. It could be said that newly independent countries do not have enough shared history or enough writers worthy of foreign attention to claim a tradition. I do not think this is true. English-speaking Canada has had a history of solid, good writers; and yet an outsider cannot help but notice how uncertain Canadians are as to what constitutes their literary tradition, who their best writers are, and, indeed, which of the foreigners who have lived in Canada and which of the Canadians who live abroad are part of their national literature. I think this confusion is itself part of the larger question: what is the Canadian identity? If you assume, rightly or wrongly, that literature is a reflection of society, or of a significant class, or of shared national values, then your important writers will be seen in terms of cultural history. English-speaking Canada lacks confidence in these matters, and it is significant that critics have attempted to define the national literary tradition through such themes as solitude and survival. A recent example is Margaret Atwood's *Survival: a thematic guide to Canadian literature* (which might usefully be read in connection with her novel *Surfacing*). French-speaking Canada, perhaps because it feels itself a citadel surrounded by enemies, seems to have a clearer sense both of its cultural identity and of its literary tradition. I think English Canada has in some ways been unlucky in not having an author of international reputation. Moreover, some of the best known Canadian writers seem Canadian only by chance: Malcolm Lowry, for example, was an Englishman who spent his last years in Vancouver, while Brian Moore, from Northern Ireland, took out Canadian citizenship before moving to New York. Mordecai Richler lived in England for so long that many Canadians stopped thinking of him as part of their culture, although his novels, along with Moore's *The Luck of Ginger Coffey*, give the fullest representation of what it means to be part of the various immigrant and ethnic groups which make up large sections of Canadian society.

Most critics agree that solitude is a basic theme and mood of Canadian literature. This is sometimes accounted for by the vast unpopulated lands to the north and west; it has been said that Canadian novelists fill their work with descriptions and detail to counterbalance their anxiety towards empty spaces. It is sometimes said that Calvinism in English-speaking Canada and a Jansenite Catholicism in Quebec explain the feeling of isolation and joylessness. More recently, critics have tried to explain the greyness of Canadian literature as the result of the colonial experience and the growing fear of American cultural and economic domination. In a cold, harsh, insecure country the literary imagination tends towards portraying failure. Another explanation of this greyness might be the fragmentation of the national community into different regional, cultural and ethnic groups. It is difficult to read Canadian novels without being aware that they often treat of local experiences: the Maritimes, small town Ontario, the Jewish community in Montreal, the older Presbyterian élite of Toronto, the Irish Catholics. Each novel or story seems to depict a small, self-enclosed world, untouched by the outside, or only in contact with other communities through being menaced by them.

Canadians often claim that unlike the Americans they have not historically pursued a national policy of cultural assimilation and have preferred to let each region and ethnic group develop in its own way. If there is much to be said for such a policy, Canadian literature may include a record of some of the problems it raises. It should, however, be mentioned that many of the English literatures record similar feelings of isolation, alienation, and cultural fragmentation. Since the newer nations do not have stable societies built around a long history of shared values and common experience, their literatures often show the individual on his own, fighting to survive or attempting to give some purpose to his life. We can see this in West Indian writing.

The small body of criticism in which West Indians have analysed their own national literature is impressive in its intellectual power and its concern with the texture and use of language. I do not know if the latter is an academic influence, reflecting an English critical tradition at the University of the West Indies; it is more likely a development of the consciousness most West Indians have of the various kinds of English spoken in their islands. If you think of the multi-racial society of the West Indies and the varied cultural influences on it, it is not surprising that a criticism should have developed with an awareness of how social nuances are revealed in the use of language. Since the quality of West Indian writing has been impressive, it is somewhat surprising that a serious attempt has not been made to establish a critical canon of major writers, as distinct from tracing the history of recent literature. No doubt the same awareness of cultural and racial backgrounds which accounts for the vitality of West Indian writing also accounts for the lack of consensus as to what West Indian literature is.

The lack of agreement as to what is the tradition of West Indian literature is partly the result of many different islands, each with a different history and culture, having so recently become independent nations. But even more importantly, the question of who and what is West Indian is, for the present, bound to have political and racial implications. There are some critics who would claim that Jean Rhys is not West Indian since she is white and has largely lived in England, that V. S. Naipaul is representative of the more recently arrived Indian settlers who do not share in the black experience of the majority of the islanders, and that many of the best known West Indian black writers are culturally products of a Europeanized middle class. As often happens, when ideology is given precedence over literary values, the best literature seems to go out the window. Hopefully, this will be a passing phase of West Indian literary criticism.

To an outside observer, it is surprising how much the novels written by West Indians of different races have in common. Recently, after reading Michael Antony's *The Year in San Fernando*, I read once again Jean Rhys's *Voyage in the Dark*. I was struck by similarities of subject matter and theme, and also by similarities in style and technique. In both books a sense of not belonging and being an innocent stranger among those who appear to control their own destinies is conveyed through a conscious neutrality of tone in which objective descriptions are tinged with a tremulous passivity and wonder. In both novels one feels time passing less in terms of sequence than in relation to emotions, events, experiences. The world outside the narrator is treated as stable and fixed, only to be found unreliable and itself changing. One might say that while West Indian writing sometimes adopts the American device of a seemingly immature narrator or central character, the result is often different. In West Indian writing we are not only more aware of others – often as pushing, hustling, demanding individuals trying to make their way – but we also realize that the others are like the narrator in seeking an identity, roots, a fixed place in what is found to be an unstable society. V. S. Naipaul's books show similar characteristics.

One's first impression of Naipaul is that here is a nineteenth-century novelist, working within the tradition of social realism, comedy of manners, and depicting a fixed culture through rich descriptions of daily life. But in fact Naipaul's characters are always seeking a place to rest, a place to call their own, a useful function in society. When the characters are not acting upon each other, aggression and self-assertion give way to the same insecure trembling found in the novels of Rhys and Antony. The world of others which seems so fixed to Naipaul's Mr Biswas is in fact as unstable and fragmented as his own existence. Indeed the ugly lack of taste which Mr Biswas observes is not mere philistinism; people must necessarily employ such defences to retain their small, desperately won privileges. In Naipaul's books we also find a final charity towards those who seem to oppress his heroes similar to the charity towards others found in the novels of Antony and Rhys.

I am not claiming Naipaul, Rhys and Antony as *the* West Indian tradition to the exclusion of George Lamming, John Hearne, Denis Williams or Wilson Harris. Indeed, some of the characteristics I have mentioned will not be found in other authors. My claim, however, is that the better writers of a nation, regardless of their racial stock, often adopt similar themes and styles. There are critics who say the West Indian literary experience must reflect the black experience. Others say that there can be no true West Indian literature until a generation of writers born after independence has come to maturity. My own feeling is that despite racial differences and differences found between writers from the various islands and the Guyanas, the West Indies already has a literary tradition. For example, Vic Reid's *The Leopard* was answered by Denis Williams's *Other Leopards*. That Wilson Harris can articulately define in what ways Guyanese writing is unlike that of the islands, and build his own mythology upon this difference, reveals, at least as far as the literary imagination is concerned, a broadly shared cultural and historical outlook.

A characteristic I have noticed in Nigerian literature is the tendency to see events as somehow beyond the control of the main characters, as if men were caught between larger forces. Wole Soyinka's poems and plays often allude to or show a world governed by Ogun, a Yoruba god who in creating also destroys; thus life is a constant progress of joy and tragedy. In Achebe's novels tragedy continually results from the clash between new and old and the conflicting demands made by a society which is always in transition. In Elechi Amadi's *The Great Ponds* we are led to believe that the villagers are under the curse of gods until the final paragraph of the novel when we learn that the many deaths in the village are part of a world-wide influenza epidemic. While it is possible to see the novel as alluding to the Nigerian Civil War and to the effect of foreign influences, it is similar to other Nigerian literary works in its portrayal of the immense vitality of everyday life and in its assumption that people will be crushed by forces beyond themselves. It is unlikely that the tragic sense reflects the disillusionment which followed independence. The same vitality and pessimism can be seen in Cyprian Ekwensi's *People of the City*, written long before national independence.

It might be said that the tragic sense in Nigerian literature is a legacy of colonialism, which shattered traditional patterns of life without creating an harmonious modern society. While this may explain aspects of Nigerian writing, other African literatures do not show man caught in the grips of larger, uncontrollable powers. There is disillusionment in the Ghanaian novel, but it is angry and conscious of how the hopes of pre-independence Africa were soiled by the Nkrumah era and its aftermath. Where Ghanaian and Nigerian literature often touch is in lamenting or satirizing the turning away from African tribal values, which are seen as spiritual and natural, towards a gross love for European 'things'. Nigerian and Ghanaian writing, unlike that of Kenya, seldom attacks the white race or European culture directly; rather it shows African society losing its identity and becoming corrupted through the desire for material wealth.

If I am right that the tragic sense in Nigerian literature is not solely political in origin, it is likely to have deeper roots in tribal legend and myth. If Soyinka's work is often an allegory of a world governed by Ogun, so J. P. Clark's play *Ozidi*, and Amadi's novels, show how deeply tribal culture is still felt as a living presence. In the novels of Nigeria and Kenya, we are often as aware of the effect of events on the tribe or community as on the individual; the narrator often reflects the community's vision and in telling his story he may use such techniques of oral literature as proverbs, rhetorical questions, allusion to myth and didactic endings. One notices how often the narrator is a modern version of the tribal story-teller. The narrator's firm presence is usually felt in the opening paragraph, and though he does not call attention to himself in the way the narrator of the eighteenth-century novel would, we are aware he is there, making judgments, supplying information, telling a tale. When Amos Tutuola's *Palm-Wine Drinkard* was first published it seemed like a sport, an odd instance of the uneducated folk mind finding written literary expression. Tutuola's stories, with their creative improvisations on Yoruba legends, can now, I think, be seen as a natural starting place in the transformation of Nigerian tribal consciousness into a modern tradition of English literature. While writers may not continue to use the techniques of oral literature, it is probable that for the immediate future Nigerian literature will be concerned with the problems of adjusting traditional African customs to the new situations brought about by colonialism and the subsequent emergence of an independent national state.

In putting this collection of essays together, I have been slightly arbitrary in choosing the countries represented. Nine countries were obvious choices, because of the international reputation of their best writers, their long literary history, or because they seemed to be where the best creative writing is now being done. My choice of Kenya for the tenth country in the collection may surprise some readers. New Zealand and Ghana have claims to be included equal to those of Kenya. New Zealand has given us one minor international classic in Katherine Mansfield, and has several writers who have achieved reputations abroad. New Zealand, with its cultural tradition more British-oriented than Australia, its developing body of Maori writing in English, and the interesting use of Maori conventions in its recent literature, could have provided more than enough material for an essay. Ghana also has claims to be represented in a survey of important national literatures. Although significant Ghanaian writing only began to blossom during the 1960s, its flowers have been among the finest of contemporary writing. I have been struck not only by the richness, complexity and depth shown in the work of Armah and Awoonor, but by how similarly they have given literary form to the disillusionments which followed independence.

My decision to include Kenya in this collection is based on its being representative of so many newly independent nations which face the problem of assembling cultural and literary traditions out of the disorienting effects of their recent history. In Ceylon and Pakistan, writing in English came to an end when the national governments adopted other official languages. Although writing in English continues to flourish in India, its national function is often questioned and there have been repeated predictions of its demise. Writing in English remains alive in Malaysia and Singapore largely through the determination of a few intellectuals, and men of letters, often in the face of government pressure favouring Malay and Chinese. In Tanzania, Swahili has ousted English as the language of literary expression. One might have expected Kenya to move in a similar direction; but writing in English is not only flourishing in Kenya but the country has become the centre for other East African writers working within the language. Kenya also has, in James Ngugi, one of the best-known African authors.

The precarious state of English in East Africa is, I think, reflected in the literature which has emerged from Kenya. Unlike West African literature in which colonial experience is often treated indirectly and as an historical fact, East African writing is directly concerned with the struggle for independence, shows racial conflict, and argues the need to affirm a cultural tradition; emphasis is given to such matters as pan-Africanism, the African personality and the political aspects of culture. Ali Mazrui's *The Trial of Christopher Okigbo* is an example of a Kenyan novel which is more concerned with ideas than most English writing. Okigbo, the Nigerian poet who died fighting for the cause of Biafra, is tried for putting tribalism ahead of his art and thereby diminishing the achievement of African culture. In the writing of Ngugi and Ali Mazrui, I find an ideological purpose dissimilar to the more exploratory nature of West African writing. A Nigerian writer such as Achebe may claim to be a teacher with a responsibility towards his society, but his novels are so filled with ironies and complexities that no single message or point of view predominates. Although Ngugi is perhaps more experimental in his fictional techniques than Achebe, he is also more didactic. His novels show the need for Kenyans to see that tribal ritual is necessary to communal harmony, the need to overcome tribal differences, and the need to be aware of independence as a continuing cultural struggle. Since Kenya, unlike West Africa, has a settler class, the question of who has right to the land is also a central theme. Indeed the multi-racial aspect of East African society may well offer an explanation of the emphasis given cultural conflict and the concern with African identity in Kenyan writing. It is probably too early to speak of a Kenyan literary tradition in the same terms that we can speak of Australian or Nigerian literature. The characteristics which I find in Kenyan writing are, I suspect, indicative of a national literature which is still in the stage of finding its identity. Since the same characteristics and themes can be found in the work of many Ugandan writers, it may be best at present to speak of a developing East African tradition of writing in English.

Language is a part of culture and the use of a language requires accepting certain cultural values implicit in the meaning of words. Since a language carries cultural assumptions, nationalists have often opposed the use of English and advocated using local languages. Thus in parts of Asia and Africa, the English and French languages have been rejected; they have been thought reminders of the colonial period and carriers of foreign values. Such suspicions of former colonial languages should not surprise us since language has often been seen in relation to politics; consider the way the boundaries of political affiliation are drawn by language in Canada and Belgium. After the War of Independence, some Americans even contemplated replacing English with German as the official national language; if this had happened and the United States had formed stronger German ties, modern history might have been markedly different. If language were rigid and unchangeable and its meanings set by one cultural group or nation, it would be right to be suspicious of a language imported from abroad; however, language is flexible and changes itself according to the situations and realities in which it is used. Words carry different implications throughout the English-speaking world; and the history of the meanings of words is also a history of changing cultural values.

Ireland was perhaps the first nation to be faced by the problems that result from English being a language of colonization. It is perhaps significant that an early example of English writing in Ireland is Edmund Spenser's sixteenth-century plan for subduing the natives. By the eighteenth century, colonization had seemingly succeeded and resulted in a brilliant period of writing in English: Swift, Burke and Goldsmith. Part of what we think of as the best Irish writing combines this eighteenth-century English tradition of wit, poise and reason with a more native tradition, rooted in older Irish culture. Many Irishmen, however, do not regard anything written by their countrymen in English as Irish literature. Such writing, although it forms the dominant literary tradition of the nation, is often spoken of as Anglo-Irish to differentiate the language of expression from Gaelic.

Irish writing in English is, I think, uniquely similar to African writing in its ability to incorporate a still living oral tradition within the forms of modern European literature. The oral Gaelic tradition was handed on in rural areas and Irish literature often borrows from the individualism and the speech of the peasant. We are aware of the influence of Gaelic on the cadences of Anglo-Irish prose, the often un-British syntax and the way Irish writers seem rather to be talking than using print for rational, impersonal discourse and narration. In the stage Irishmen of Synge and O'Casey we can see many of the characteristics we are familiar with in the personalities of George Bernard Shaw, Oscar Wilde and Brendan Behan. There is the same stabbing satirical wit, the calling of attention to oneself, the same conscious display of learning and paradox, and the love of telling improbable stories. Irish poets have often attempted to recreate the tradition of song, and Irish novelists from Swift to Joyce and Beckett tend towards assembling a variety of anecdotal stories under the shelter of some larger external form.

Irish writing at least until recently often oscillated between precise accuracy of observation and the mythic, without intervening stages of reality. If the West Indian is concerned with his identity, the American with his spiritual destiny and the Englishman with his place in society, the Irish writer often treats of fantasies and private visions. One thinks of Yeats's *Vision*, O'Casey's *Paycock* and, in Joyce's *Ulysses*, Molly Bloom's monologue. The characters of O'Casey, Joyce or Beckett do not connect and do not expect to connect with others. In other modern literatures this would be lamented as a revelation of alienation, isolation or man's existential condition, and Irish writers are often read as portraying the modern spiritual condition. There is, however, a curious acceptance of personal views of reality in Irish writing, as if the national psyche did not feel there was much to be gained from adjusting to society. As in Yeats's 'The Circus Animals' Desertion' there are the joys of imagination and insufficiencies of reality:[3]

> Those masterful images because complete
> Grew in pure mind, but out of what began?
> A mound of refuse or the sweepings of a street,
> Old kettles, old bottles, and a broken can,
> Old iron, old bones, old rags, that raving slut
> Who keeps the till. Now that my ladder's gone,
> I must lie down where all the ladders start,
> In that foul rag-and-bone shop of the heart.

Perhaps such extremes might be explained by the history of Ireland. It was until recently an impoverished country, exploited by England, divided by religion and language, and its rulers and populace were of different blood stocks. As Joyce's *Portrait of the Artist* reminds us, its writers were conscious of a history of betrayed leaders and of the oppressive influence of the Catholic Church in the nation's politics and culture.

What does one do when the local language and culture seem insufficiently rich or developed to support a writer's aspirations, while the accepted language of art has colonial associations? The classic model in the past for coping with such problems is *Portrait of the Artist*. In *Dubliners*, Joyce shows a grubby provincial society which is spiritually paralysed and culturally dead. It is an essentially colonial society in which excitement, vitality and hope only appear when foreigners enter or when there is a chance to go abroad. Those who have remained in the society and tried to make themselves superior to it are usually shown as pathetic imitators of foreign values and manners. Stephen Dedalus, in *Portrait of the Artist*, sees his country caught up in pettiness, memories and division. To accept the Gaelic language, Irish nationalism or the Catholic Church would be demeaning, a denial of his spiritual freedom:[4]

> When the soul of a man is born in this country there are nets flung at it to hold it back from flight. You talk to me of nationality, language, religion. I shall try to fly by those nets.

But when he speaks to the dean of his college, Stephen uses the word 'tundish' instead of the common English word 'funnel'. This seeming mistake in usage takes on a symbolic importance and raises the question of whether the artist can work in a foreign language:[5]

> The little word seemed to have turned a rapier point of his sensitiveness against this courteous and vigilant foe. He felt with a smart of dejection that the man to whom he was speaking was a countryman of Ben Jonson. He thought:
> — The language in which we are speaking is his before it is mine. How different are the words *home, Christ, ale, master*, on his lips and on mine! I cannot speak or write these words without unrest of spirit. His language, so familiar and so foreign, will always be for me an acquired speech. I have not made or accepted its words. My voice holds them at bay. My soul frets in the shadow of his language.

Faced by the inability of his country to provide suitable nurture for art, Stephen leaves for Europe where in exile he will attempt 'to forge in the smithy of my soul the uncreated conscience of my race'. A similar pattern of exile followed by the literary recreation of the essential quality of one's national culture can, I think, be seen in many Irish writers. We also find it in other countries where the quality of life, or the discrepancy between cultural ideals and reality, drives the writer into exile. The Ghanaians Armah and Awoonor, the Canadian Richler and the West Indian Naipaul are examples of writers who usually live abroad and yet continue to write about their country, analysing it, probing it, trying to understand the underlying patterns behind the apparent chaos.

I think Professor Walsh is right in seeing national English literatures as part of a broad spectrum of English literature. One cannot escape history by an act of will; most of the national literatures written in English will continue to share in and draw from British literary and cultural traditions. It is significant that Stephen learns that 'tundish' is in fact an English word which the Irish continue to use long after it has been forgotten in England:[6]

> That tundish has been on my mind for a long time. I looked it up and find it English and good old blunt English too. Damn the dean of studies and his funnel! What did he come here for to teach us his own language or to learn it from us. Damn him one way or the other!

In other words, the Irish heritage shares in the English. The same can be said of American, Australian and Indian writing. Even Amos Tutuola, whose work is closely related to oral Nigerian literature, has been influenced by the Bible and Bunyan's *Pilgrim's Progress*. Another Nigerian, Chinua Achebe, shows the breakdown of Ibo culture as a result of English colonization in *Things Fall Apart*; but the form of his novel is influenced by nineteenth-century English fiction and he seems to share the historical vision of Yeats's poem 'The Second Coming', which is alluded to in his title.

Often the other national literatures gain part of their effect by answering or replying to the English literary tradition. Thus Achebe's rich use of proverbs in *Things Fall Apart* is consciously and ironically set against the stilted standard English used in the first chapter and at the novel's conclusion. Mark Twain's *Huckleberry Finn* is a conscious outrage against the standards of British English, and European values and manners in general. Twain especially mocks Sir Walter Scott's romantic novels, which were at the time influential in the United States, Canada and Australia; he uses uneducated Huck to show what real moral adventures are available within the New World, in contrast to Tom Sawyer's romantic European notions of adventure. More recently, the South African writer Nadine Gordimer has, I think, shown in *The World of Strangers* the impossibility of living by the values of English liberalism in her country; her subsequent novels have explored the conflicts which develop when a liberal sensibility is faced by situations in which it is necessary to choose sides and accept ideological commitments.

Sometimes a nostalgia for, or an ideal of, a long-established English tradition finds direct expression in the various national English literatures. It is this ideal of a more ordered, settled, complex society which presumably led such Americans as Henry James and T. S. Eliot to live in England, and which caused the American Agrarians to speak of the Southern states as the last European country left in a modern world of individualism and industrialism. For many Americans, Australians, Canadians, and some Indians and West Indians, England is the promised land where it is possible to live more finely and fully in a sophisticated, settled society. If Henry James's novels explore such possibilities and trace some of the resulting ironies, the many West Indian novels treating of immigrant life in England usually show the promised land as a place of disappointment.

The recent development of so many national English literatures will have a long-range effect on university studies. We can no longer assume that there is a fixed subject called English; we can no longer assume that most students of English will be familiar with the established classics of our language. The British literary tradition has become one among many. Students not only want to study their own national literature, they are also attracted towards what appears as exotic foreign writing. It has become increasingly impossible to fit everything into a fixed syllabus, and as more options are offered more of the British literary tradition goes out the window. In England this may be seen as an extreme view of what is happening; however, even in England the proliferation of options has led to some curious courses of study in which major authors and important literary periods are neglected.

If we are to put the current confusion of English studies into some kind of order, it seems necessary to begin by recognizing that there are different national literary traditions with values and histories of their own. But we must also remember that each literature is a part of world English literature and each is a development, and shares in the heritage, of British writing. Criticism must insist that contemporary or local relevance is not always of enduring value. Cultural nationalists can be simplistic and levelling in their tastes. Local colour, dialect, and facile optimism are sometimes preferred to the serious and profound. The universities, where modern literary tastes are often formed, will especially need to be responsible for separating what is of value from writing primarily of historical or momentary interest. It is perhaps only by comparing and contrasting the literatures of the English-speaking nations, and seeing them as growing out of the past, that we can regain the liberal, rational vision of the world which readers once achieved by studying the classics. If we do not find a way of integrating traditional English studies with the study of other national English literatures, there will be an increase in provincial, specialized or incoherent visions of the world, which is exactly what the study of literature is presumed to prevent.

CHAPTER ONE

AUSTRALIA
Brian Elliott

All Australian literature of the nineteenth century (since the first settlement in 1788) relates broadly, or at any rate most comfortably to the imagery of bush life. There are exceptions but this is mainly true. In the nature of the case pioneering development had to occupy the main part of the colony's attention in those early days when there was nothing else to think about. As soon as there was a community – a common if scattered interest – it was the impulse of the people who shared it to express their acquired experience. So almost before you know where you are, you are bound to have some pretty crummy poetry:[1]

> When Sol has commenc'd his diurnal career,
> And the bright spangled dewdrops from buds disappear,
> With my dog and my gun to the forest I fly,
> Where in stately confusion rich gums sweep the sky.
> Then anxious, my eyes each direction pursue,
> Till the fleet-footed WALLABA rises to view!

The need is to describe. In Australia, it was environment that dominated – and daunted. The place was unlike Europe: that had to be got used to before anything else. It was a vast image: the vastness itself was overwhelming. Man was a pin-point; Sydney was a dot. Oddly in a settlement so cut off from every civilized contact, so dependent for all amenities upon what was brought from outside, there was little disposition to look back and almost none to hug the coast or look sentimentally at the sea. The gaze of the young nation turned inland, sustained, in the early days, by hope that here might be another America ever unfolding treasures to the west – but when that hope faded, still the western image thrived, albeit coloured with a melancholy which, poetically speaking, was probably only the heritage of a bypassed romanticism; derived rather from Thomson or Cowper or Gray, the late eighteenth-century nostalgics, than the more sensual romanticism of Wordsworth or Keats.

Undoubtedly, though, a certain romanticism did underlie the earliest Australian efforts to be poetical. As in Europe itself, the preoccupation with landscape accorded with the spirit of the times. The difference was that in Australia the landscape was new and strange; it seemed grotesque and had to be learned in order to be lived with at all. So there was a double reason for the Australian landscape-obsession which, after the course of a century and a bit, came eventually to clog all the channels of poetic invention. At school we youngsters learned to chant:

> I love a sunburnt country,
> A land of sweeping plains,
> Of ragged mountain ranges,
> Of droughts and flooding rains. . . .

Dorothea Mackellar's *My Country* epitomized that stale romanticism as it had lived on into the early years of the twentieth century – survived or atrophied.[2] Earlier it seemed to mean more, or had a little more warmth and colour – less 'literariness' – as in the balladry of the 1890s:

> The roving breezes come and go, the reed beds sweep and
>   sway,
> The sleepy river murmurs low, and loiters on its way.
> *It is the land of lots o' time along the Castlereagh.*

That is Banjo Paterson, 'The Travelling Post Office'. The same lazy, sweet mood, which is very true, very recognizable and very conformable to the inland landscape is also in Henry Lawson's 'Reedy River':[3]

> Ten miles down Reedy River
> A pool of water lies,
> And all the year it mirrors
> The changes in the skies.
> Within that pool's broad bosom
> Is room for all the stars. . . .

In the end, though, the late-romantic Australian intoxication with landscape left lyrical poetry tired and listless. The trouble was that everybody had been working too hard all that time to accommodate Australian experience (landscape, nature, life) to standard English stereotypes. This question of the stereotypes is not a trivial one. It is not too much to suggest that the major task of any emerging literate community is to create and establish its stereotypes – its definitive clichés – and, having set them up, continually to revise them and keep them active. In Australia this was the principal task of the colonial or pioneering period, and it may be said that only with its completion – with its effective initiation as a system in working order – could that phase be considered over. It is, I believe, mainly achieved now, though this confidence could be a little uncertain . . . in the main, the game seems to fit on the board and all that remains is to manipulate the pieces. But we are only just in time, perhaps; for in the advancing conformity of the patterns of living throughout the western world, all the new countries run some risk of being ignominiously swallowed up. Australia's patterns possibly don't yet all clearly show; the stage is still tentative. But roots have gone down and eventually the tree must take shape. Enough has been achieved to ensure that.

The Australia – New South Wales – of 1800 was a convict outpost, a prison romantically (from one point of view – often very unromantically when seen close at hand) remote but still a prison. Until the end of the century it was still the prevailing local picture in spite of the fact that an analysis of the population then showed that, since the 1850s, natural increase and immigration together had left the penal settlement far behind. The first Australian novel was the disguised autobiography of a convict, Henry Savery's *Quintus Servinton* (1830).[4] The part of it which is set in Hobart describes with fair plausibility the life of a convict at that time – what is pathetic in it is rather Savery's own personal self-deceptions and small hypocrisies than any disguising of the general facts. Savery would like his hero to be accepted as a picaro full of potential goodness who is buffeted by a heartless world. But the book never 'took', partly perhaps because it was too early, yet too belatedly eighteenth century in outlook. The convict was felt instinctively by several writers to be the inevitable symbol on which to build an Australian fiction and from time to time other writers tried it: John Lang in some stories and in a novel, *The Forger's Wife* (1855); Caroline Leakey in *The Broad Arrow* (1859); and finally, Marcus Clarke in *For the Term of His Natural Life*.[5] Clarke's convict established an acceptable form. To begin with, he was innocent and suffered in silence for a noble motive (in itself unimportant to the narrative, since in revising the work for republication Clarke substituted a different and unrelated one). The story becomes a catalogue of heroic sufferings whose only concession to realism was to introduce into the pageantry instances of factual horror, in themselves historically authentic but highlighted extravagantly by selection and emphasis, such as a flogging from which the victim dies, and an episode in which an escaping prisoner survives for a time by practising murder and cannibalism. While details of the plot can be verified the picture as a whole is romantically distorted. But this was the image which satisfied the colonial sense of the appropriate. Until recent scholarly studies of the convict records put the picture into a truer proportion, *His Natural Life* represented the truth about the Convict System. When William Hay, in 1919, published his *The Escape of the Notorious Sir William Heans* (*and the Mystery of Mr Daunt*), the national preoccupation with convictism had changed though it had not yet disappeared.[6] Hay's Sir William is a gentleman convict and the portrait is a moral and psychological study, still faintly melodramatic, but with little physical violence, and offering even less to factual probability; such suffering as Sir William undergoes is more inward and mental than applied. In the end he achieves a symbolical but believable escape.

The convict was probably the most potent of the colonial social stereotypes. Another, less sinister, is the honest, lean, sunburnt bushman. Alexander Harris, writing in the 1840s in *Settlers and Convicts* (a kind of novel but also something of an emigrants' handbook), was even so early prepared to generalize about the Australian character, meaning primarily the settler:[7]

> There are very few Australians that one can dislike. A general manly spirit and fairness of feeling characterize all except a few bullies of the very lowest class, and a few pampered half idiots of the very highest.

Henry Kingsley, in two novels set in Australia (*The Recollection of Geoffry Hamlyn*, 1859; *The Hillyars and the Burtons*, 1865), had differentiated the types sufficiently to distinguish between the gentleman-settler and the new proletarian.[8]

> Both Major Buckley and Captain Brentwood made it a law of the Medes and Persians, that neither of their sons should hold any conversation with the convict servants . . . and indeed they both, as soon as increased immigration enabled them, removed their old household servants, and replaced them by free men, newly arrived: a lazy independent class, certainly, with exaggerated notions of their own importance in this new phase of their life, but without the worse vices of the convicts.

This is the new young Australian of the people, a type with some sterling qualities – self-reliance, adaptability, energy and initiative; but he refuses to touch his cap to the Buckleys and the Brentwoods. When Joseph Furphy, in what must be considered the most consummately (if not comprehensively) representative of all colonial Australian writings, *Such Is Life* (1903, but begun a decade earlier), refers with confident contempt to 'the slender-witted, virgin-souled, overgrown schoolboys who fill Henry Kingsley's exceedingly trashy and misleading novel', it was this kind of social distinction principally that he had in mind.[9] The realism of *Such Is Life* was beyond anything yet experienced in Australia and the humour too deflating to be found immediately acceptable; it took another fifty years, more or less, to sink in. *Such Is Life* has now become recognizable as a work of national definition; a work, that is, of native humour and genius. The book describes and contains (without any obvious concern about plot) an epic view of life in the Riverina, the country north of the Murray and west of the Divide, a country inhabited (as the book shows it) by a scattering of sheep stations and a main community of drovers and bullockies (carriers) whose humble occupation is to keep going the vital life-lines of the country. The range never extends to a city or to any town larger than Albury, Hay or Deniliquin – or that thriving metropolis, Echuca, on the southern side of the Murray, the principal link by water with the distant civilization beyond. Here is a world where a man is a man (for a' that) and where, except among themselves, squatters of the Buckley–Brentwood type enjoy scant prestige, though there may be here and there a good fellow among them.

In the 1890s the Sydney *Bulletin*, a popular weekly magazine, set out to pursue a frankly nationalist policy and was so successful with it as to become known as 'the bushman's bible'.[10] Its main importance was social and political, but it also maintained a deliberate programme of encouragement to local, hitherto unpractised writers, and out of this bias developed two strongly-flavoured local literary institutions in verse and prose: ballads and short stories. A solid foundation for this material (broadly proletarian and egalitarian in sentiment) was provided by the social phenomenon known as 'mateship', derived from the fact (not uncommon in pioneering communities, but particularly marked in a hard and primitive country like Australia) that working-class society, in town or country, was male-dominated. The *Bulletin* articulated the voice of the Australian masses – if Australia could be said to possess masses. And the masses believed in solidarity against the oppressor (i.e., government, or the growing industrial machine). The masses stuck together. In the bush, men stuck together. So everybody was mates, and that defined the ethos. Henry Lawson was the best of the writers of this group and in his Joe Wilson stories really animated the arid bush landscape with genuine human figures.[11] But his literary resources were confined to short forms and he never produced a major work.

Joseph Furphy summarized his attitude to the world and to literature in a phrase: 'Temper democratic, bias offensively Australian.'[12] What he achieved in that line (in his three books which are really one book, *Such Is Life, Rigby's Romance* and *The Buln Buln and the Brolga*) was more distinguished and more richly representative than anything brought off by any of his contemporaries; but his words might equally well serve as a motto for the *Bulletin* tradition, which was vigorously nationalist. A. B. (Banjo) Paterson wrote:

> And it may be that we who live
> In this new land apart, beyond
> The hard old world grown fierce and fond
> And bound by precedent and bond,
> May read the riddle right and give
> New hope to those who dimly see
> That all things yet shall be for good,
> And teach the world at length to see
> One vast united brotherhood.
>
> 'Song of the Future'

By and large, enthusiasm dominated criticism and the period tended to dwell on symbols of sanguine expectations: the bronzed, the brave and the matey, and in landscape motivations, on a lyric scene that had been sourly described forty years before, by Marcus Clarke, as *'toujours gum'*.[13]

Reaction was due and it followed. To what extent it could be traced to a single influence – to one poet of genuine gifts, with great natural talent and learning to back it, Christopher Brennan – may yet merit inquiry; but Brennan, whose major publication was his *Poems 1913*, was not a popular figure in his day or indeed much known beyond a small circle until years later.[14] He may nevertheless have provided a spark which others fostered, since it was in Sydney and in activities centred about him that the literary regeneration of poetry in Australia was attempted. Brennan produced a distinguished volume of verse which, for the first time in the history of the country, was literary without being visibly provincial – in fact appeared so little so, as to be felt to be out of touch. So far as Brennan derived his substance in any clearly traceable way, it was from the French symbolists in respect of style and technique; from German philosophy, especially Nietzsche, in ideas. He was, however, in many ways more scholar than poet and *fin-de-siècle* in mood, at all times a writer for the connoisseur rather than the people. But in moving the subject matter of poetry away from local lyrical landscape, in introducing standards of sophisticated reference, he put it into the minds of a younger group to attempt something less ambitious but similar, that would reach a wider audience. The first moves in this direction were associated with the journal *Art in Australia* which from about 1916 performed a useful function by throwing open its columns to poetry and to criticism. This movement gained from the enthusiasm and initiative of the painter Norman Lindsay, himself no poet but an encourager of poets; what he wrote was criticism, plus a few entertaining lightweight novels – all designed to underline aesthetic and not merely nationalistic principles in all the arts. Lindsay was for emancipation, without being too lucidly clear from what oppression. The manner of his approach was bohemian and Rabelaisian or Dionysian or Hyperborean – terms he was fond of indulging.

Heady as this was, impenetrable nonsense at times, it was fresh to the Australian intellectual scene, and in fact, provided stimulus (in the magazine *Vision*, four issues in 1923) for several poets, then young men in an experimental stage of development. It was the first Australian poetry that was independent, sophisticated and intellectual. When it first made its appearance it was, as it were, intoxicated with itself, youthfully, extravagantly, absurdly voluptuous (intended to be beautifully sensuous). Kenneth Slessor wrote:[15]

> When to those Venusbergs, thy breasts,
> By wars of love and moonlight batteries,
> My lips have stormed – O part thy mouth above,
> Lean down those culverins twain, and bid me spike
> Their bells with kissing. . . .

But these boy-scout bacchanals exhausted themselves in due course. Neither Norman Lindsay nor Hugh McCrae, who assisted the movement, were as young as the youngest of the contributors, but they were young – sometimes skittish – at heart. The younger men – notably Kenneth Slessor and Robert FitzGerald – matured after their baptism here in literary trivia, to write, in 'Five Bells' (Slessor) and such poetry as 'The Face of the Waters' (FitzGerald), some of the most impressive modern verse, which will not require apology in any company of its own generation.[16]

> Why do I think of you, dead man, why thieve
> These profitless lodgings from the flukes of thought
> Anchored in Time? You have gone from earth,
> Gone even from the meaning of a name;
> Yet something's there, yet something forms its lips
> And hits and cries against the ports of space,
> Beating their sides to make its fury heard.
> 'Five Bells'

> For eternity is not space reaching
> on without end to it; nor time without end to it,
> nor infinity working round in a circle;
> but a placeless dot enclosing nothing,
> a pre-time pinpoint of impossible beginning,
> enclosed by nothing not even by emptiness –
> impossible: so wholly at odds with possibilities
> that, always emergent and wrestling and interlinking
> they shatter it and return to it, are all of it and part of it.

It is a hand stretched out to touch your neighbours,
and feet running through the dark, directionless like
darkness.

'The Face of the Waters'

Just before the Second World War a young South Australian
poet, Rex Ingamells, tried to think out for himself the combining
rationale of his poetical and national feelings. He took them, as
many still did at that time, to be two faces of the same thing.
Ingamells was deeply impressed by the responsiveness to Australian landscape shown by D. H. Lawrence in *Kangaroo* (1923),
and then by some other local and more political persuaders. Blending this new perspective with an awakening interest in the art, the
mythology and the hitherto unexamined cultural life of the Aborigines (a subject now opening up with the appearance of several
scholarly studies of Australian Aboriginal ethnology), he invented
what he called the Jindyworobak programme for poetry. It introduced a new respect for the literary and artistic ecology of the
country, treating all imported idea-systems as antagonistic to or
even destructive of the true, native spirit of Australia. His attempt
at an accommodation between Aboriginal and white principles
never quite came off – how could it? – and yet there were some
interesting results and Ingamells gained a notable following. He
introduced into his vision of Australia the 'ancient and original'
Aboriginal myth of the Dream-Time or Alcheringa; it was a beautiful, timeless idea, a pre-Creation concept in which all existence
was more potential than actual: a mythical identification of men
with their totemic animal or vegetable ancestors, visualized in the
original condition from which all creation came, and to which it
must finally return – an idea, in other words, which combined the
concepts of heaven, earth, chaos and eternity. The trouble with the
Jindyworobaks was that, while their theories were interesting, they
themselves appeared more dogmatic than practical, and there was
unfortunately not among their number any writer of sufficient
stature to establish them as having permanent poetic value. One
survivor, Roland Robinson, has made interesting and beautiful
verse out of the programme, but little of Ingamells is remembered
at present. The Jindyworobaks were, however, not negligible
in their influence, even if, in the end, the effect was only
to give another twist to the same old nationalistic impulse. Even

an accomplished modern poet like James McAuley shows an
occasional trace, more particularly in his early work – but that
includes some of his most striking pieces ('Terra Australis',
'Envoi'), in which several of his symbols have a quasi-totemic
impact.

A certain precious, remote quality marks the performances of all
but a very few Australian poets, especially, I should say, of the first
(which is also in most ways the strongest) of the three distinguish-
able modern generations of poets since the Second World War.
For want of more precise terms they might be called Modern,
Recent and Contemporary. Kenneth Slessor and Robert Fitz-
Gerald have been mentioned earlier. Fragments of their Modern
style were seen in a snatch from Slessor's 'Five Bells' and Fitz-
Gerald's 'The Face of the Waters': these poems are highly organized examples of literary sophistication which far transcend the
methods and aims of the *Vision* movement in which both poets
first came to articulate expression. In the mature work of both, the
preciosity of the *Vision* treatment, with its roots in French symbolism *via* the *Yellow Book* and English turn-of-the-century aesthetic-
ism, has been sensibly modified towards a plain man's thoughts
about life. But still the concept of poetry as 'poetical' prevails.
FitzGerald may be quoted again in a whole poem, illustrating his
skill, control, the sensitivity and the intellectual trenchancy of his
thought, diction and imagery. But this poem, 'Edge', is still 'difficult', élitist, not for the common reader. Indeed there is no reason
why it should be. But it remains 'remote', and, strong as it is in
effect, somewhat uncomfortably 'poetic' for a concept that is so
essentially rational.[17]

> Knife's edge, moon's edge, water's edge,
> graze the throat of the formed shape
> that sense fills where shape vanishes:
> air at the ground limit of steel,
> the thin disk in the moon's curve,
> land gliding out of no land.
>
> The new image, the freed thought,
> are carved from that inert bulk
> where the known ends and the unknown
> is cut down before it – at the mind's edge,
> the knife-edge at the throat of darkness.

Writing of this quality puts FitzGerald, at least in my opinion, at the head of Modern Australian poets. He did not write a great deal, he has not always managed to maintain the same excellence, but at his best he is superb and never for merely literary reasons. All the others who might be considered rivals to him fall short, a little, of the magnificent and metaphysical seriousness which his best work possesses: their conscious literariness reduces their price, though I am speaking still of distinguished poetry. Most impressive after FitzGerald, I believe, is A. D. Hope, a true intellectual and a man of great learning, an academic who has always done his best to throw off the contamination of his ingrained academic habit of mind, but who nevertheless even at his best – and his best is excellent – remains a University wit, a brilliantly bookish poet. He has been prolific, and in his later work has achieved not merely greater complexity and weight, but also a greater poetic freedom. In his earliest poems is found a persistent impulse to shock the bourgeois which is not well understood: it was a protest against a certain ugliness and illiberality of mind which he found in his Australian audience and which he detested (as Patrick White detested Sarsaparilla) because he found it present also in himself. Hence his poem 'Australia'; hence such pieces as the (not very successful but here and there brilliant) 'Damnation of Byron' and 'The Return from the Freudian Islands', in which phrases sometimes appear of telling if perhaps unnecessary virulence:[18]

> But cactus or euphorbia here and there
> Thrusts up its monstrous phallus at the sky.

and sometimes also of memorable wit:[19]

> Here the saint paused, looked modestly at the ground
> And waited for their plaudits to begin.
> And waited . . . There was nothing! A faint, dry sound
> As first a poet buttoned on his skin.

In his mature work, 'Soledades of the Sun and the Moon' (a poem addressed to the Canadian P. K. Page) or the yet later 'Epistle: Edward Sackville to Venetia Digby', there is no more question of mere clevernesses of that kind, and the element of the poet's disgust both with his own mind and with his unhappy intellectual ambient is turned to philosophical reflection. As a literary artist – a technician – he scarcely has a rival. It is a weakness in Hope, though – the weakness of a very good poet, it might be the strength of a lesser one – that his world of reference is almost always too bookish, too constantly and heavily responsive to the schools. He has suffered unfairly from criticism which fails to distinguish between works of serious endeavour and many light and entertaining poetic frolics, satirical gambols and squibs. Only a poet very confident of his powers plays such games; it is the public, not Hope, who is responsible for that confusion.

Among the Moderns must also be included James McAuley, Judith Wright and Douglas Stewart, who represent a descending order of academicism. McAuley, like Hope, is a professor of literature; his poetry has a splendid but perhaps too dominating academic precision. His earliest work was electric and memorable:[20]

And I am fitted to that land as the soul is to the body,
I know its contractions, waste and sprawling indolence ...

In his later work he has become both a Christian (Catholic) apologist and a more gentle humanist, but always, literary and precise. Judith Wright has had more vogue than discerning appreciation; she has written too much and attempted too wide an appeal, but a little of her work will survive among the eternal things, not only her early and superb 'Bullocky', but many later pieces in which her motivation is tenderly emotional, humane, nostalgic and sweet. She is not the first Australian woman poet but she is perhaps the most womanly of them. Douglas Stewart keeps, like all of these 'first-phase' Moderns, a close hold on poetry as a conscious art, a gesture of Davidian defiance against the philistines: poetry is a sling with which to slay Goliath. What is pleasant about him is his simple, lyrical unpretentiousness, his liking for rhythms and song, for pictures and images and agreeable sensations. He is not averse to wit and an occasional scamper. He retains, very amiably, from an older Australian period, a sense of poking about in the bush and seeing things, and is still something of a romantic. He has a lively mind and clear perception, and for a few very vivid pieces, like 'Rock Carving', 'The Snow Gum' and many of his small lyrics on very small things, animals, birds and flowers, is a memorable companion to the other Moderns.

For the second (recent) phase of post-war poets I shall have to content myself with reference to a collection of *Twelve Poets 1950–1970* (Jacaranda Press, 1971; the editor is Alexander Craig), of whom all but, I would say, the last two are solid representatives of Recent poetry: Francis Webb, Vincent Buckley, R. A. Simpson, Chris Wallace-Crabbe, Bruce Dawe, Gwen Harwood, Peter Porter, Randolph Stow, Rodney Hall, Les A. Murray, Michael Dransfield and Richard Tipping. I would class the last two as Contemporary; the rest all fit in. There is a mixture here of literary-academics and independents; the drift, clearly, is back to independence, which is the natural Australian order; academicism can never be anything but a (temporary) blight in this country, albeit an inevitable and in small or transient doses a handsome one. The most earthy and in many ways the most reassuring of these writers is Bruce Dawe: a plain man writing with complete honesty for a plain reader. Webb, who is perhaps the nearest to a genius, is not an academic but he affects an academic obscurity. Les Murray stands comfortably in the middle. But as you move on to Dransfield and Tipping clearly the indication is for a decisive return to direct, natural perception and spontaneous sensation; the 'literary' skills become secondary.

The poets of the third phase may also be approached conveniently in a published collection, unsatisfactory as such books inevitably appear after a time – contemporary work is always embarrassingly difficult to assemble. But with a few reservations the anthology *Australian Poetry Now* (ed. Thomas W. Shapcott, Sun Books, Melbourne, 1970) can be recommended. There are too many poets in the collection for individual comment. Dransfield and Tipping may represent them. Both apparently rebels yet activated by a direct concern for those experiences of revelation (however inspired) which lie within the compass of the poetic intelligence, they are concerned to reshape poetic expression itself and relate it in new ways to the general experience of living. It is the less necessary to analyse their performances because at this level they merge with the activity of young poets everywhere. It is possible with some asseveration to claim these young (and sometimes revolutionary) writers as an Australian vanguard. But their advances are the common possession of youth. With them, poetry, in merely expressing its natural urges, becomes both signally national, personal and characteristic, and equally and at the same time international.

Prose is another matter. Disregarding minor writers, not a great many novelists really stand out. However, standards are relative; if we had never known Patrick White, perhaps there would be many whom we are now inclined to class as minor who would have seemed to have more importance. The presence of one giant reduces the rest of the community to dwarfs. The first post-colonial novel to make a really solid impression was Henry Handel Richardson's *The Fortunes of Richard Mahony* (a female author in spite of the *nom-de-plume*). Women have always had a dominating influence – or at least a notable presence – in Australian fiction. *Richard Mahony* (a trilogy completed in 1929) was probably the first novel to demonstrate the capacity of an Australian subject matter to reach proportions of literary weight under modern conditions, and in competition with imaginative works from outside.[21] It is a work of both historical and psychological interest, concerned with a colonial settler who is unable to accept the conditions of life in Australia, and whose career closes with a painful and tragic death. It was the forerunner of a spate of novels on historical subjects, not exactly similar but themselves all in a pattern, which occupied attention in the thirties and forties. In these the general plan was to follow the life story of a pioneer taking up new country; it came to the same thing whether he began as a convict or a gentleman (the levelling effect of Australian life); this pioneer-hero triumphs after long struggles with various kinds of adversity (drought, floods, fire, fever, the Aborigines . . . the whole packet of clichés), but exhibits the patriarch in his old age destroyed by the generation which followed – his pride reduced, his possessions broken up, mostly by the inevitable march of development and the modifying effects of change in the advance to modern times. The moral of this was that heroism (the pioneering patriarchs) must cede to democracy (commerce and urbanization). The vogue for historical narrative was extended in several works by Eleanor Dark, whose *The Timeless Land* (1941) was the first book to give serious attention to the Aborigines in a historical perspective (it carried certain echoes of a Jindyworobak point of view). But the Aboriginal subject matter was not altogether new, as a work of some sensitive interest had been produced earlier by Katharine Susannah Prichard in *Coonardoo* (1929) – a study of black and white relationships, not, however, historical in intent, in an outback station setting in Western Australia.

Among the names of modern Australian novelists that of Martin Boyd, recently deceased (1972), stands out. His work exhibits the qualities of a passionate imagination allied to a subtle sense of the variety of human character within, it is true, a relatively limited scope of human types. His historical perspectives, based upon a rich personal inheritance of family records and impressions, are sound in no merely bookish way – they are derived from real events and people, presented in terms of fiction in such a way as to carry both historical and psychological conviction. He is at his best in a series of stories which relate, always from an intimate, never a pretentiously public point of view, the events and characters of the Langton family over the course of several generations. The location is Melbourne, and the emphasis is upon the niceties of upper-class Australian society – much of it snobbish, though in the long run Boyd's treatment of the issue presents him in the role of a subtle and ironical anti-snob. Two outstanding books are *The Cardboard Crown* and *A Difficult Young Man* (1952 and 1955). The closeness of the material to Boyd's own personal and family experience is illustrated by the broad similarity of the content of an autobiography, *Day of My Delight* (1965). In the last issued of his Langton novels, *When Blackbirds Sing* (1962), Boyd takes an impassioned stand against imperialistic war and war-politics.

There has not been space to comment on the extent to which the Australian stock has benefited from expatriate writers. It was as though, for some at least, it was necessary to go abroad if only to acquire the perspective which would enable them to describe objectively and with detachment the social facts they could never quite see from close up. Hal Porter has travelled in and written of Japan, but the bulk of his writing is locally accented. He made his name first with short stories, sometimes of an exquisite and filigree delicacy. His later writing is of a more marked robustness, one novel, *The Tilted Cross* (1961), being placed in a historical setting in Tasmania and building to a considerable atmospheric tension, although it relies too much, perhaps, upon a certain intriguing grotesquerie of style. The best of his writing, taken all together, is reminiscent and autobiographical; his study of his own childhood and early youth, *The Watcher on the Cast Iron Balcony* (1963), is as rich and sensitive a record of such a subject matter as can be found anywhere among Australian writers.

Randolph Stow is not a prolific writer and he has for many years now no longer been a resident; but he writes with an Australian imaginative commitment and great sensitivity. It is possible that he has not yet written his best book, but in what has appeared two works are pre-eminent: a poetical study of Aboriginal and white relationships in *To the Islands* (1958), and something closer (if one may guess) to autobiography – a study of country life and a child's attachment to his own early landscape and to the people who filled it, including friends and members of his family – *The Merry-Go-Round in the Sea* (1965). Stow is also a poet, and the same delicate sensitivity which marks his prose appears equally in his verse. A children's book, *Midnite* (1967), though a trifle, is interesting in a charming and whimsical way.

The best of Thomas Keneally appears, in the view of most readers, in *Bring Larks and Heroes* (1967), a novel which recurs to history and the convict system – or the mythology it engendered. Keneally treats his subject with a refreshing, modern, lyrical imaginativeness which shows that that mythology is still capable of some contemporary regeneration, though it is doubtful if it can ever again be fully brought back to life; it is now poetic and remote, artificial and nostalgic. In later books some of his personal motives and preoccupations come out, which relate to his traumatic guilt for having left his seminary just before ordination as a Catholic priest.

The work of Patrick White has been left until last. It clearly stands above the achievement of every other Australian writer. And yet one doesn't want to preach a sermon on it. He is the first clear example of a writer of genius to identify himself with an Australian social and intellectual outlook. He is highly critical of Australia, more particularly of the shams and shames of petty bourgeois Australian philistinism. Some day someone will make a study of Australian philistinism: it may contain some surprises. It has been a target for attack since the first Australian consciousness (Melbourne in the mid-colonial period: *vide* Marcus Clarke), and more vehemently since Norman Lindsay's rather joyous and innocent harlequinades with their abuse of Uncle Jobson and all parsons. White's onslaught gains force and persuasion from the depth and darkness of his abhorrence. He attacks not only the suburban masses (Sarsaparilla), but everybody else who combines low intellectual development with high, stupid prejudice. His verbal virtuosity allied to the deadliness of his observation of people's habits and characteristics (especially their unpleasant ones) renders him capable of such destruction and devastation as emerges in his portraiture of Mrs Flack and Mrs Jolly in *Riders in the Chariot* (1961). It is wrong, however, to look in White only for the destructive principle. There is, sustaining and animating all his writing from *The Aunt's Story* (1948), a double concern for spiritual and at the same time for more mundane human insights which sets everything he writes apart from the substance of all other modern novelists I can think to compare him with. His Theodora Goodman (*The Aunt's Story*) and Miss Hare (*Riders*) are two pure representatives of certain aspects of transcendent human insight (a Blakeian concern with an experience of innocence) which approach close to insanity; while in *Riders* the symbolism of the chariot – and the insights of those who get to glimpse it – signifies the potential of spirituality in the common mind, which is his continued preoccupation. Some readers are prepared to see in the series of his novels after *The Aunt's Story* through *The Tree of Man* (1956) to *The Vivisector* (1970), a progressive pattern of religious thought. If that is true (and it needs closer analysis yet), it will no doubt be revealed to have its parallel interest on the human plane intimately integrated with it.

Something still remains uneasily to be said about Australian literature in general. It will appear from the drift of what has gone before that the literature of Australia, as a whole, tends to dwell upon easy stereotypes and has not yet developed to the point where it can comfortably and competently rest on recognizable truths. But if that is the case, it is hardly a remarkable fact. It takes more than three or four generations to evolve the kind of simple community self-knowledge which can support a Jane Austen. It may be that while the nineteenth-century prose-norms still obtained, a few Australian writers came a little nearer than later writers have done to representing ordinary and unexceptional people in simple daily situations. Henry Lawson is no Austen, but in stories like *Telling Mrs Baker* or *Water Them Geraniums* we have glimpses in intimacy of certain personalities and circumstances which recommend themselves to a reader more by their directness and truth than by anything that is peculiarly local in their emphasis.[22] In the same way but with many changes it could be said that Furphy's *Such Is Life* tells the truth about the lives of the people it depicts (life, under the conditions described, is clearly *such*): there are few women and those who appear exhibit no great grace, but among the men who form the community of the road there is not merely a representative variety, but the individuals are portrayed with wit, humour and a penetrating intimacy of insight. Among more recent writers Martin Boyd possesses one of the richest talents in the portrayal of women, and it is perhaps a fair criterion to adopt that the young nation whose writers have at last learned to portray women well is fairly on the way to achieving sophistication. But while the presentation of female characters and the depiction of social forms in which women take their place is now considerably more widespread, it is still not a very positively developed Australian talent. The most intimate and detailed female study which occurs to mind among modern Australian novels is possibly Teresa in Christina Stead's *For Love Alone*, a portrait which by no means depends on any element of psychological exoticism for its effectiveness; but here is by no means the quiet, simple kind of social character we are permitted to observe at such close advantage in that other young woman whose uneasy passage from girlhood to maturity was earlier placed before us, Emma Woodhouse.

In the course of a natural evolution over two hundred years (which, nationally speaking, amounts only to extreme youth), some progress has been made in Australian national self-awareness, and the literature expresses it. But that progress is chiefly, until recently, discernible only in one main direction. In Australia, a country which posed problems from the very beginning because of its antipodean reversals and its general topsy-turvy images (those scraggy old gum trees, the hopping kangaroos, the anomalous animals that laid eggs), the whole of the colonial period was taken up, absorbed and obsessed, with exploration of the physical environment. And the job was so well done that you can take that part for granted now. Between the Australian people and their landscape there exists now a firmly understood relationship – loving, hating, love-hating – that needs no further demonstration and no apology. What remains, then, for the literature to achieve is a new picture of Australian society and the individuals who make it up, as comprehensive and as authentic and convincing as what exists already in terms of landscape. In its time the landscape image had to fight its way through the same sort of tangle of stereotypes; what we see in the picture of society today – the insistence on the coarse beer-swilling image, the saccharine mateship, the unfeeling slighting of women, the all-male exclusiveness with its sunburnt horsiness, the riotous humour and the cranky non-conforming and (nowadays) sometimes rather lecherous ego-centricity – all these amount to equivalents, yet to be conquered, of the droughts and floods and bushfires which provided the first drafts of the early landscape awareness. In a community where everything is new, where all the norms have to grow from their own uncertain roots, it must naturally take time to effect a result, and all the first impulses are bound to be expressed with extravagant exaggeration. So that, in literature at least, is how we stand: a people which has yet to discover itself in detail and in particular, but has at least learned to see itself in its proper setting. That is a fair beginning.

CHAPTER TWO

CANADA
Peter Stevens

Canadian historian William Kilbourn, in discussing one of the patriarchs of British North America in the nineteenth century, Bishop Strachan, expressed a dominant trait of Canadian political life: 'Ours has been a politics of the extreme centre.'[1] In another context Kilbourn has put Canada forward as a viable nation straddling the opposing forces of absolute authoritarianism and chaotic political division.[2] Certainly Canada is often presented as an alternative society to the stultifying ways of Europe and to the brashly aggressive life of the United States of America.

Through the nineteenth century Canada was so busy establishing itself at a political level that it produced little writing uniquely Canadian. Its writers depended on forms and ideas drawn from English Romanticism. Nor did this country produce any critical visions in literature about the ideal life that might take shape in this country. Only one utopian novel of note, *A Strange Manuscript Found In A Copper Cylinder* (1888) by James de Mille, has been written in Canada because[3]

> by the time Canadians had become urbanized enough to lose the spaciousness and freedom of frontier life, which in itself constituted a kind of unacknowledged utopia, the literary utopia had lost its meaning in the recognition that rigid planning produces only the utopia of a nightmare. But Canada was never near enough to the totalitarian world of the 30's and 40's to make even that a meaningful vision, and so we have gone entirely without a utopian literature.

Yet this one utopian novel gives rise to interesting speculations about the nature of the Canadian character.

The novel tells the story of Adam More who is stranded with a companion in the Antarctic. His companion is killed in gruesome circumstances, and More is carried by boat into the world of the Kosekin, a people whose lives are organized on the basis of a reversal of what are considered normal values. They worship the dark and poverty, and believe that the real reward of human love is separation, for then the lover can act out the lover's boast of complete selflessness in the face of love. The Kosekin are generous but their generosity has ulterior motives: by giving up possessions and wealth, they become paupers, considered to be the highest class in their society. The ultimate search is for death, so in their hunting of treacherous sea serpents many of them perform negative heroics, that is, they attempt impossible feats against their animal enemies in the hope of being killed in the process.

Adam as representative 'normal' man reacts against such negativism, but the satiric intent of the novel is directed against the hypocrisy of contemporary materialism which governs men in spite of their expression of moral ideals and virtues. Under the Kosekin's surface selflessness is pure selfishness: by showering gifts on other people, they prevent the receivers from rising to the highest goal of pauperism, while the givers by this means elevate themselves to the Kosekin highest class. The ultimate paradox occurs at the end of the novel as Adam by a show of strength becomes for the Kosekin a god of light they can worship, thereby showing the shallowness of the Kosekin's beliefs. Not only that. This ending throws in doubt Adam's stance in the novel: he has been horrified by the land of the Kosekin but in the end he becomes their emperor. Thus, his normal values are to some extent questioned by this turn of events.

The theme this paradoxical novel expresses is that all extremes, whether they be selfishness or selflessness, prosperity or pauperism, are equally pernicious. The middle course is best. In Woodcock's words the novel is 'cemented by a moral vision that is perhaps not peculiar to the author so much as characteristic of Canada'.[4]

Moderation and the refusal to make a commitment can of course lead to mediocrity, but the middle course can be reached by assessing both sides in order to gain a balance in a tension of polarities. Indeed, two recent critics of Canadian literature see this tension of opposites as a main staple of much Canadian writing. W. H. New

43

in *Articulating West* (1972) maintains that a tension exists between an Eastern and Western attitude in Canada. Such a split, without being limited to a purely geographical concept, explains the struggle for a viable literature in both form and content in the twentieth century. Eli Mandel sees many opposites functioning in both life and literature in Canada:[5]

> We may put it that the tension in Canadian life is between vulgarity and gentility. Or we may choose other pairs: American as opposed to British influences on Canadian writing; colonialism as opposed to nationalism; social realism as contrasted with abstract design; originality as opposed to traditionalism.

Another fundamental tension in Canadian life not mentioned here by Mandel is the bilingual and bicultural split between French- and English-Canadian. This concept of two nations within one makes one of the marked differences between Canada and the United States of America. Another essential difference is the achievement of independence without revolution. Northrop Frye also differentiates between the Canadian experience of the frontier and that of the Americans. According to Frye, the American frontier and journey of settlement moved from one sea coast to another in an irregular but steady line, whereas the Canadian movement was originally by water through the maw of the St Lawrence with the land encroaching on the ships sailing up-river till only small canoes could traverse the waterways to reach the great inland lakes. The first explorers of Western Canada went from the lakehead via the vast network of rivers and lakes. 'To enter Canada is a matter of being silently swallowed by an alien continent.'[6] The early settlers were surrounded by the frontier rather than confronted by it face to face, so the settlers tended to wall themselves in against nature. In another essay Frye sees the unique pastoralism of Canadian literature emerging from a response to nature as a totally new impression on immigrants with artistic pretensions:[7]

> It is a country in which nature makes a direct impression on the artist's mind, an impression of its primeval lawlessness and moral nihilism, its indifference to the supreme value placed on life within human society, its faceless, mindless

unconsciousness, which fosters life without benevolence and destroys it without malice.

Our nineteenth-century poetry is certainly full of descriptive detail about nature but our poets do not appear to be really seeing the landscape before their eyes, except on a few occasions. Poets such as Charles Sangster, Charles Mair, William Kirby and Alexander MacLachlan give some sense of the landscape, but too often their view is coloured by the traditional forms they try to use in treating nature. Most of them model their poems on the Romantic responses of the English poets of the nineteenth century, and such responses are not viable in the new world. The emphasis in many narrative poems of the nineteenth century shifts to the settler as epic hero, carving out a living space for himself, digging in, driving off the Indians. Yet the settlers fall short of epic stature simply because they become merely domesticated in trying to reproduce a little bit of England within Canadian nature. But the usual polarities occur in ironic tension in much nineteenth-century writing about settlement, and Susanna Moodie's experience provides a prime example.

Mrs Moodie came to Canada in 1832 with her husband to live in the backwoods north of Peterborough, Ontario. They had no experience of farming and encountered many difficulties, which Mrs Moodie records in *Roughing It In The Bush* (1852). This book has been called 'an unpretentious, highly literate account of an heroic if not always intelligent struggle against a hostile environment'.[8] Certainly Susanna Moodie came to Canada full of expectations that her cultured mind and her literary interests would enable her to cope with this new country. She is ready to praise what she sees in Romantic terms: she gushes fulsomely about the grandeur of Quebec City when she views it from the St Lawrence, but when the Moodies approach the city they find it is racked by cholera. Throughout the book this contrast between expectation and reality recurs. Although Canada is the land of her hopes, she is constantly disappointed. She cannot deal with the new classless society she finds, there is no literary life to help her, particularly as she remembers the English countryside in genteel poetic terms and finds no consolation in the land that surrounds her. Her first Canadian winter subdues her spirit and produces a depressing melancholy in her. Nature around her causes her discomfort, economic trials and depression but she tries continually to accept the landscape, though she recognizes that isolation in nature and inexperience in dealing with the land have caused the crushing poverty of the first years in Canada. The summary of those years speaks for itself:[9]

> For seven years I have lived out of the world entirely; my person had been rendered coarse by hard work and exposure to the weather. I looked double the age I really was, and my hair was already thickly sprinkled with grey ... I was no longer fit for the world.

Yet when she leaves her 'dear forest home' she sheds 'regretful tears', and writes of her admiration of the landscape. The record of the disasters and how she copes with them is left to stand as a warning to deter settlers in a situation similar to hers in England from coming to Canada. She sees this warning tone in her book as its principal merit, for in the last sentence of the book she describes the book as 'revealing the secrets of the prison-house'. (It is possible to see in this phrase an ironic reference to Wordsworth's 'shades of the prison-house' in 'Ode On Intimations Of Immortality'.) This seesaw between romantic hopes and disillusioning reality is the dominant structure of her book, and one critic has even suggested that perhaps her hold on artistic ideas was the only viable means by which she could survive. She works through the culture shock of her first years towards 'the timeless reality of a contained world of the imagination'.[10]

For Margaret Atwood, Susanna Moodie is a prime example of the Canadian national illness, 'paranoid schizophrenia':[11]

> The country is too big to inhabit completely, and in the parts unknown to us we move in fear, exiles and invaders. This country is something that must be chosen – it is so easy to leave – and if we do choose it we are still choosing a violent duality.

She develops this idea in a critical guide to Canadian literature, in which even the theme of survival, a theme so strong in Canadian writing, is strangely metamorphosed into non-survival: 'Pushed far enough, the obsession with surviving can become the will *not* to survive.'[12]

In her poems about Susanna Moodie, Margaret Atwood reconstructs the earlier writer in poems which mirror the Canadian dilemma of reconciling oneself with the terrifying landscape outside. In typical paradoxical fashion, once the attempt to break down the garrison walls in order to experience the outer continent is made, the real exploration takes place in the inner continent of the mind:

> We left behind one by one
> the cities rotting with cholera,
> one by one our civilized
> distinctions
>
> and entered a large darkness.
>
> It was our own
> ignorance we entered.
>
> 'Further Arrivals'

The preconceptions of the immigrant have to be sloughed, and in a sense it is only in the twentieth century that a real Canadian response to this new kind of nature has been possible in independent literary terms. But although the response is modern, the subject matter is often from the past. Margaret Atwood's use of the persona of Susanna Moodie has already been cited, F. R. Scott has mused on the long geologic history of the land in some of his poems, and Douglas LePan expresses his response to the country through the early *coureurs de bois*, as they voyaged to discover the secrets of the new continent. But LePan poses the question, when the country has been mapped, what remains to be discovered? Where can the voyager go?

> Unless
> Through the desperate wilderness behind your eyes
> So full of falls and glooms and desolations,
> Disasters I have glimpsed but few would dream of,
> You seek new Easts.
>
> 'Coureurs De Bois'

The poem closes with the tense Canadian balance:

> The voyage is perilous into the dark interior.
> But then your hands go to the thwarts. You smile. And so
> I watch you vanish in a wood of heroes,
> Wild Hamlet with the features of Horatio.

In E. J. Pratt's long narrative poem 'Brébeuf And His Brethren' (1940) the Jesuit priests enter the wilderness to convert the Indians to Christianity, but paradoxes proliferate. The priests are used as instruments of secular power to establish French rule in Canada so that the spiritual gives way to material dominance. The priests giving extreme unction as a means of salvation to dying Indians are regarded as instruments of death as they hover in their black robes over the death-beds. Finally Brébeuf because of his courage and steadfast faith is able to withstand the most excruciating tortures at the hands of the Indians, and this impassivity under the direst pain places Brébeuf in the ranks of the bravest Indians, for such obduracy under torture is their proudest boast. Priest resembles Indian, and Pratt emphasizes the paradox by describing the torture in terms of Christ's passion. This ambivalence within the poem has been the cause of debate among critics about Pratt's religious position. It is perhaps part of the Canadian split personality that one of the critical cruxes about Pratt is that question of his Christianity or his atheism. The epic heroism of the priests is repeated in other Pratt narratives and a similar epic vision is at the centre of the novels of F. P. Grove.

The dogged farmers in his novels have some epic stature, but unlike true epic heroes they do not fulfil their dreams. They work from humble beginnings and build an agrarian empire, but eventually their lives turn sour. Often their heroic stature dwindles to less than epic proportions because of personal crisis or overly passionate outbursts. The irony of Grove's vision of these prairie farmers is that the one epic structure that survives is the mill which overwhelms succeeding generations of one family in *The Master of the Mill* (1944).

At times the epic strain rises from seemingly unlikely places, for instance in the poetry of Al Purdy, the surface of which tends to be off-hand, colloquial, tough or prosaic by turns. Yet Purdy has hammered out for himself his own poetic method, intensely personal and yet also Canadian in its remarkable melding of disparate elements. It is almost as if Purdy wants to find an entirely new beginning for poetry to express the emergence of a new nation. The poet in fact did reject the first twenty years of his own poetic career as inadequate.

The epic strain comes out in his use of scrambled chronology and references to historic time in lightning juxtaposition:

Alexander turns from the gates of the Ganges
and moves with his generals and phalanx to bulldoze the Kremlin
while the eunuch priests conspire in Assyria
to defoliate the Vietnamese rice fields of bananas.

Purdy's is a haunted poetry, conjuring up a sense of the geologic age of Canada but setting it in a larger cosmic scale. Such a vision sounds romantic, and the poet is constantly on guard to prevent romanticism from taking over the poetry. He constantly injects realism into the poems in flat prosaic tones or in self-mockery. In 'The Cariboo Horses' he creates a tension between the ordinary horses and their displacement by the automobile, their immediate ancestry and the horse's long cosmic ancestry, and all this romantic and dangerously nostalgic piling up of detail is suddenly deflated in one undecorated picture of the horses at the end of the poem:

arriving here at chilly noon
in the gasoline smell of the
dust and waiting fifteen minutes
at the grocer's.

The largeness of Canada induces travel on a grand scale, and Purdy's poems partake of both the attraction and fear of travel. Travel for Purdy means encountering space, and space offers an opportunity to break out of bounds, to transcend even the limits of the human condition, so that for Purdy the national game of ice hockey, 'combination of ballet and murder', offers a chance to lift off from the realms of the ordinary:

thru the smoky end boards out
of sight and climbing up the appalachian highlands
and racing breast to breast across laurentian barrens
over hudson's diamond bay and down the treeless tundra where
stopping isn't feasible or possible or lawful.

And yet that vast space looms large over man in the poems, reducing him to insignificance, and this littleness of man in the face of an outer force almost beyond his comprehension results in some of Purdy's best poems, elegaic in tone, expressing the polarity of the transience and persistence of man. He finds a symbol of this in the miniature Arctic trees only eighteen inches tall, the roots of which constantly touch permafrost so that 'they use death to remain alive'. That is the kind of courage Purdy celebrates in his poetry, a kind of twentieth-century epic bravery. But the final paradox in the poetry is that Purdy is also a comic poet, often indulging in comic anecdote, raucous humour, even slapstick and wisecrack with more often than not the poet himself as the chief butt of the joke. So the poetry becomes a vehicle for the welding of poet, poetry and country into one whole:[13]

> after a while the eyes digest a country and
> the belly perceives a mapmaker's vision
> in dust and dirt on the face and hands here
> its smell drawn deep thru the nostrils down
> to the lungs and spurts thru bloodstream
> campaigns in the lower intestine.

Purdy has also attempted to express northern aspects of the country in his Arctic poems, *North of Summer* (1967). Northness is certainly a characteristic of Canadian literature, part of the stern, unbending quality of the landscape. The North represents a challenge, a new frontier as well as another polarity, for most of the settlement is along the southern border of the country, but the North remains an idea:[14]

> Canadian life to this day is marked
> by a northern quality, the strong seasonal
> rhythm . . . the wilderness venture now
> sublimated for most of us to the summer
> holiday or the autumn shoot; the
> greatest of joys, the return from the lonely
> savagery of the wilderness to the peace
> of the home; the puritanical restraint
> which masks the psychological tensions
> set up by the contrast of wilderness
> roughness and home discipline.

But Purdy's, however sympathetic and realistic, remains an outsider's response to Eskimo life. Strangely, the original inhabitants of our northern wilderness appear only marginally in the literary works concerned with the settlement of the land.

It is surprising that when nineteenth-century poetry in Canada came of age in the 1880s with the group referred to as the Confederation Poets (Sir Charles Roberts, Bliss Carman, Archibald Lampman and Duncan Campbell Scott), poets who showed a surer grasp of technique, even though it was derived from English Romantic and Victorian models, there emerged a voice with an individual vision based on a native mythology. Isabella Valancy Crawford, a young woman who lived for some years in the same area as Susanna Moodie, found a way to graft on to the Victorian form of the idyll her mythic vision of the country in a few lyrics and a melodramatic narrative, 'Malcolm's Katie'.

Crawford manages in the poems using imagery drawn in general terms from Indian materials to suggest the tension of love and violence that breaks away from the garrison mentality encountered in much nineteenth-century Canadian poetry. Her poems in this vein go out to encounter nature without drawing back from its mysterious force. It is something of a shock to encounter embedded in a volume that contains a great many rather ordinary genteel Victorian lyrics the almost erotic tone of the opening of the poem 'Said The Canoe'. In the poem Indians make camp, and their fire is both a light that reaches out into the dark forest and also a poor spark that has little effect on the outer darkness. The light from the flames is

> Sinuous, red as copper-snakes,
> Sharp-headed serpents, made of light,
> Glided and hid themselves in night.

The erotic note which begins the poem is then connected to the Indians' hunting. Love is equated with a slaughtered deer and a strange violent image of the fish, 'like swords / On saplings slender; like scimitars'.

The most expressive use of the ambivalent descriptions of nature occurs in 'Malcolm's Katie'. Although the story is standard Victorian fare – a love triangle with pretty virgin, stalwart hero and desperate villain, together with a heavy father – the plot does in fact contain elements to suggest the power of love to conquer violence and death, for Max, the hero, is crushed by a falling tree and left for dead by the villainous Alfred. However, he returns in the nick of time to rescue Katie, and love wins through. The poem also contains the contrasting views of Max and Alfred, the former believing in the transcending power of love, the latter believing only in the present and man's transience. All this, though of some interest, would not raise the poem above the level of other nine-teenth-century Canadian poems, were it not for the considerable framework of descriptive passages about the cycle of seasons written in forceful terms emphasizing an animate nature, the continual life of which surrounds the life of man. Nature passes through the Fall presaging winter ('the scouts of Winter ran / From the ice-belted north, and whistling shafts / Struck maple and struck sumach') through an Indian summer until Winter strikes Nature dead (the North Wind talks of binding 'sick rivers in cold thongs of death' and calls on the White Squaw, snow, to obliterate life). But just as Max is resurrected and his belief in eternal love is vindicated, so spring returns and the harvest comes to fruition. In a strange metamorphosis, Nature which has contained violence and death becomes at the end of the poem a paradise, a new Eden for the lovers.[15]

Such a bald summary of the poem tends to isolate the mawkish Victorian elements and reduce the descriptions of nature to mere exercises in the pathetic fallacy and personification. None the less, the poem is the first successful Canadian poem to reconcile elements of terror and passion, and to show the transcendence of that fear of the wilderness in the enclosed thoughts of the colonial, thoughts which are part and parcel of the garrison mentality.

Crawford's poetry cannot be considered to contain a unified vision, for the work deriving from native elements is only a small part of her collected poems. She is thus a poet divided between her original response to the country and her clinging to accepted literary forms; another case of a double vision.

A different kind of double vision can be seen in the work of an early humorist Thomas Haliburton, who lived before Canada existed as a nation. He has in fact been labelled as the father of American humour and yet he spent the last part of his life in England as a member of parliament. Earlier he lived in Nova Scotia and was very critical of what he considered the Nova Scotians' laziness and general lack of progressive vision. He puts much of his criticism into the mouth of an itinerant Yankee pedlar, Sam Slick, an example of American know-how, material advancement and patriotic fervour. Slick finds it easy to swindle the Nova Scotians by using his knowledge of 'soft sawder and human natur'. He flatters his customers to the point that he is able to foist off on them one of his clocks, 'a gaudy, highly varnished, trumpery looking affair'.

Haliburton is thus very satiric at the expense of the Nova Scotians, as he would like to see them imitate the industry of the Americans. But Haliburton's sincere belief in the British connection leads him to allow Sam Slick's own words to damn certain American traits, and there is something prophetic in what Sam repeats from his father in his criticism of the United States, as well as admonitory to Nova Scotia as a colony:[16]

> Our Revolution has made us grow faster and grow richer; but, Sam, when we were younger and poorer, we were more pious and more happy. We have nothing fixed, either in religion or politics ... If our country is to be darkened by infidelity, our government defiled by every State, and every State ruled by mobs – then, Sam, the blood we shed in our Revolution will be atoned for in the blood and suffering of our fellow citizens.

Haliburton, while he pokes fun at his fellow Nova Scotians, sees the hideous possibilities of revolution on the American model and every now and again is at pains to pull Sam Slick up short, even though paradoxically Sam is given the best of the language and allowed to do most of the talking.

Another humorist, Stephen Leacock, is true to the Canadian pattern of opposites, for in his best work he shows a dichotomy of viewpoint. The very title of Stephen Leacock's collection of anecdotes about the town of Mariposa, *Sunshine Sketches Of A Little Town* (1912), suggests that the tone will be benevolent and indulgent rather than virulently satiric. Yet critics have disagreed about the nature of Leacock's humour in this book; even Leacock himself at times seems uncertain, or at least seems to set up an ambiguous tone. The town which sees itself as a thriving hub of activity actually emerges as a ridiculously inflated settlement with closed mentality, short-sightedness and hypocrisy the main ingredients of the townspeople's characters. On the one hand, Leacock gives us simple humorous anecdotes about the inhabitants who appear perhaps foolish but generally unspoiled. On the other hand, Mariposa emerges in a different light:[17]

> A community in which the acknowledged leaders are windbags and self-serving clowns, and where the real leader is an illiterate saloon-keeper; a community that sees financial acuity

in a lucky little barber who makes a one-in-a-thousand killing in the stock-market; a community that will not support a church, but will swindle an insurance company with a fraudulent fire; a community in which an election is shamelessly rigged.

Leacock himself leaves the ambiguity unresolved, for his narrator continually shifts his point of view: a phrase such as 'to the eye of discernment' is set against 'to the careless eye', and the reader is constantly drawn into the stories with such phrases as 'you've seen him', 'you remember', as if all readers live within such communities and can accept the foibles of their fellow citizens. At times the narrator himself seems unreliable, for sometimes he appears as ignorant and illiterate as many of the Mariposans (he calls Goethe 'Gothey' and speaks very confusedly of some straightforward matters) and yet at other times he makes allusions to such things as the Papal Zouaves, the pastorals of Theocritus, Tennyson and Shelley as well as poking fun at some of the intellectual pretensions of others, as he repeats one of the characters' admission about his religious studies by claiming that he is an 'eggnostic'. It is possible, then, to see the book as a critique of small-town life which also includes the idyllic memories of such a life in nostalgic terms.

These paradoxical dualities surface in Canadian literature in a variety of ways. Leonard Cohen's Jewishness makes approaches to Christianity in the opening poem 'For Wilf And His House' in his very first volume, significantly titled *Let Us Compare Mythologies*. Cohen's obsession with violence often expresses itself in highly sensual terms, and the girl in the song 'Suzanne' partakes of the character of both saint and whore. Such extremes of pain and joy lie at the base of his novel, *Beautiful Losers*, where Catherine Tekakwitha's mortification of the flesh as religious martyrdom is balanced by Edith's utter sexual indulgence, and a further balancing of these extremes is achieved by the satiric implications of the novel, which at another level criticizes both Edith and Catherine as merely pursuing their own desires through extreme mechanical responses. In his latest volume of poetry *The Energy of Slaves* (1972) Cohen confesses his own predicament as both victor and victim in such a poem as 'Song For My Assassin':

> We were chosen, we were chosen
> miles and miles apart:
> I to love your kingdom
> you to love my heart . . .
> I work on your spirit
> you work on my sinews . . .
> the spider web you see me through
> is the view I've always taken.

Another Jewish poet, Irving Layton, builds his poetry on the dichotomy of Apollonian and Dionysian forces, the one symbolizing order, rationality and reality, the other symbolizing disorder, frenzy and imagination. The poet balances precariously between these two worlds, possessed as a prophet speaking of this division:

> In me, nature's divided things —
> tree, mould on tree —
> have their fruition;
> I am their core. Let them swap,
> bandy, like a flame swerve
> I am their mouth; as a mouth I serve.
> 'The Birth of Tragedy'

Layton sees the poet's mission as essentially tragic because he recognizes that there can be no permanent reconciliation of the divided things. He can write highly erotic poems as well as satiric jibes at human sexuality; he can see woman as creative force and destructive castrator. The poet for him lives uneasily between two worlds.

Early in his poetic career Layton attacked Canadian puritanism, stodginess and dullness in a series of ferocious squibs, loudly proclaiming the incompatibility of this country's mediocrity with the richly fulfilling life of poetry. For many people, this mediocrity was symbolized by the figure of MacKenzie King who, except for brief periods, remained in political power from the 1920s till after the end of the Second World War. King was a master of the balanced statement reduced to meaninglessness; one of his most quoted expressions was 'conscription if necessary but not necessarily conscription'. It was perhaps this apparent refusal to make a commitment that kept King in power, but F. R. Scott focused on this equivocation in his satiric poem about the prime minister; for him King is the epitome of mediocrity:

We had no shape
Because he never took sides,
And no sides
Because he never allowed them to take shape . . .

Let us raise up a temple
To the cult of mediocrity
Do nothing by halves
Which can be done by quarters.

'W.L.M.K.'

And yet MacKenzie King's prosaic dullness and refusal to be
definite had its obverse side. The blandness was balanced by an
exotic streak, as novelist Robertson Davies points out:[18]

Do you realize that man never calls an election without
getting a fortune-teller in Kingston to name a lucky day?
Do you realize that he goes in for automatic writing?
And decides important things – by opening his Bible and
stabbing at a verse with a paper-knife, while his eyes are
shut?

King is 'the embodiment of Canada – cold and cautious on the
outside, dowdy and pussy in every overt action, but inside a mass
of intuition and dark intimations'.[19] These irrational tendencies
manifest themselves in a curious way in Canadian literature: the
stark fact of the enormous land drives poets into the continent of
the mind, and even in the most realistic novels a strange irrational
element obtrudes, almost like a *deus ex machina*, to solve the
rational problems. Indeed, Davies's last two novels, *Fifth Business*
(1970) and *The Manticore* (1972), with their insistence on Jungian
archetypes and the interest in magic and sainthood set against the
background of Canadian small-town life and Canadian middle-class
conformity can be seen as representative of extremes that make up
the Canadian tension in polarities.

In his other novels Davies treats comically various aspects of
small-town life and, as in other literatures, the small town in
Canadian literature often stands as a symbol of puritanism, with
its rejection of pleasure as an end in itself, its insistence on work
as a duty, its distrust of beauty and sexuality which tends to cover
highly charged passions. Puritanism of this kind is at the centre of
Hugh MacLennan's novel, *Each Man's Son* (1951), set in Cape

Breton, a part of Nova Scotia settled by Scottish Highlanders. The inhabitants of the isolated village of Broughton live under the ancient curse of Calvinism. The men work in the mines and are crushed by them until they become as crippled physically as they are spiritually and mentally. They release their pent-up guilts in roistering drunken brawls on violent Saturday nights and slink repentant to church on Sundays. These two contrasting sides of puritanism are elaborated by the central conflicts in the novel. Archie MacNeil escapes the life in the mines by turning to the world of professional boxing, only to be beaten to near-blindness. After years away he returns home only to find his wife unfaithful and he can only resort to physical violence as an answer to his own guilt and that of his wife.

The doctor in Broughton is Daniel Ainslie, an intellectual who resorts to work as an answer to his fear of love and sexuality. He prides himself on having escaped the ancient religious curse but he in fact carries a burden of guilt. Ainslie has a granite exterior but is riddled by guilt on the inside, afraid of his genuine sexual attraction to his wife.

The novel is a splendid presentation of an enclosed community, feeding on its own narrow life, destroying itself through violent outbursts, half recognizing its own limitations, though few people are able to break away. Although the novel is rigorously realistic, MacLennan manages to suggest the seething unconscious desires of many of the people, catching that strange paradox of puritanism, its passionate nature beneath its confining surface.

Such outbursts of violence and feeling seem common in some realistic Canadian novels, mirroring that unconscious emotional life that commentators see underneath the placidity of Canadian life. Margaret Laurence's novels partake of religious feeling at an irrational level, especially her two novels set in the small prairie town of Manawaka, *A Jest of God* (1966) and *The Stone Angel* (1964). Both the protagonists in the novels come from the Scottish background of the town: Hagar Shipley is ninety, has rebelled against her dour and hard Scottish father but has grown to be just like him. Her last rebellious act is to run away to a deserted cannery by the sea to avoid being put in an old people's home. She journeys down into disorder, descending into herself, and she meets there a life insurance agent who by confessing his own guilt in his son's death which happened during his attendance at an apocalyptic evangelical service causes Hagar to reassess her life at this late stage.

A similar experience occurs to Rachel Cameron in *A Jest of God*. She is a thirty-four-year-old spinster, seething with unfulfilled sexuality but also timid and guilt-ridden. These pent-up feelings burst out of her when she attends an evangelical tabernacle (she normally attends the Anglican church). She has scoffed at the emotional atmosphere of the tabernacle but against her will she is caught up in it and loses herself so much that she 'speaks in tongues' during the service. This torrent of feelings is released in a summer love affair which, although finally unfulfilled in any real sense, does at least give her a new sense of acceptance of life.

These irrational outbursts in some realistic novels seem to be part of that strange mixture within the Canadian character. Morley Callaghan's novels present the reader with a world of moral ambiguity, where no rigid moral scheme or Christian virtue is propounded as offering a firm basis for life. *Such Is My Beloved* (1934) shows how a priest trying to help two prostitutes runs afoul of the church both in its social position and in the hypocritical conformism of its members. The priest is presented both as a Christ figure but also as an innocent idealist lacking in judgment. He finishes by withdrawing from the world to write a commentary, ironically enough, on the Song of Songs.

Callaghan presents us with another ambiguous figure in *The Loved And The Lost* (1951). Peggy Sanderson, a white girl, frequents the Negro districts of Montreal, but it is never clear in the novel whether she is promiscuous or simply another of Callaghan's innocent idealists. It may be that she is too innocent to exist in this world and so is destroyed, yet she seems to recognize that she lives in a kind of no-man's-land between innocence and violence, between spirituality and passion, these opposites symbolized by a scene in which she shows a fascination with the carving of a leopard: 'Maybe she could not turn from her contemplation of the leopard's jungle violence; she was rapt and still, waiting for the beast to spring at her.'[20] This is followed immediately by her visit to a church which in its architecture is 'light and simple in balance', and she is seen near the church covered in snow, a suggestion of innocence, although throughout the novel the snow is symbolic of both innocence and the way it is sullied in the city.

The man who becomes involved with Peggy, James McAlpine,

cannot make up his mind whether she is a serene innocent girl or a passionate uncaring woman. Each time he hears about her from different people, he changes his mind. His opinion of her vacillates through the novel until he allows his feelings to dictate to him and he is ready to commit himself to the girl. But it is too late; Peggy is destroyed, and the novel closes with McAlpine on a tireless search for the little church, but he is unable to find it. The equilibrium has been shattered by the very violence Peggy has tried to reconcile to an innocent vision.

Those underlying feelings of irrationality are coming to the surface more often in Canadian literature. It is apparent in the sudden swing away from realistic fiction to a more irrational and fantastic method in recent novels. Intense feelings of nationalism have come to the fore. These new disturbances of the even-balanced tenor of the Canadian way of life may develop new trends, although these feelings have been lying trapped within:[21]

> We are not a nation of talkers, as are our American neighbours. But we are a nation of feelers, and we . . . are ashamed of our feelings and bottle them up. If we could but recognize it, it is from this vast reservoir of pent-up feeling that our national individuality and our national literature might be drawn.

Douglas LePan, whose poem 'Coureurs de Bois' was quoted earlier, states in 'A Country Without A Mythology' that although the country has been travelled and mapped, the inner paradise at its heart remains undiscovered. The poem suggests that the undiscovered heart may never be revealed and that in fact what may reside within the landscape will not be a paradise but a much more horrifying and primitive core:

> And now the channel opens. But nothing alters.
> Mile after mile of tangled struggling roots,
> Wild-rice, stumps, weeds, that clutch at the canoe,
> Wild birds hysterical in tangled trees.
>
> And not a sign, no emblem in the sky
> Or boughs to friend him as he goes; for who
> Will stop where, clumsily constructed, daubed
> With war-paint, teeters some lust-red manitou?

Yet the voyage forward and outward may be also a continuing voyage back and inward to discover the real roots of our collective identity and individual voice. The voyage will be through both time and space in order to come to terms with our implacable wilderness, in order to find ourselves, as John Newlove maintains:

> we seize on
> what has happened before,
> one line only
> will be enough,
> a single line and
> then the sunlit brilliant image suddenly floods us
> with understanding, shocks our
> attentions, and all desire
> stops, stands alone;
>
> we stand alone,
> we are no longer lonely
> but have roots,
> and the rooted words
> recur in the mind.

'The Pride'

Our writers are perhaps all still *coureurs de bois*, but their wildness, their songs have been buried beneath our bourgeois settlements. Our authors are still on their voyages of discovery, puzzled in their minds about the marvels of the awe-inspiring landscape, searching for the deeper myths underlying it, yet somehow hanging on to a no-nonsense approach. There are more things than are yet dreamt of in our philosophy. Now we accept that reality, admitting the possibilities behind it, for the traveller in the heart of the country saw the animate spirit:

> But the moon carved unknown totems
> out of the lakeshore
> owls in the beardusky woods derided him
> moosehorned cedars circled his swamps and tossed
> their antlers up to the stars.

Earle Birney: 'Bushed'

But in the words of the same poet, 'It is not easy to free / myth from reality', so perhaps we will need to retain our sense of balance, look sharply at both the myth and the reality, continue to be Hamlet with the features of Horatio.

CHAPTER THREE

ENGLAND
William Walsh

To venture to speak about English literature in the space of some twenty pages would require a Confucian concision and a Thomistic inclusiveness, not to speak of courage – or rather nerve – beyond the ordinary. I shall not attempt even a long footnote on an unwritten literary history. For what, after all, is literary history? It is hardly history in the historian's sense, for that is always subject to the sprawling intervention of life. Literary history seems to exist in an enclosed, solipsistic world bounded by library shelves and filled with dusty air. It consists of the accumulation of influences, the confluence of sources, the marriage of books and the generation of papers. And since no human being could possibly be learned in the way of the specialist like Owst or Pollard over a thousand years of English literature, it forces upon the writer a special manner, that of the alert and confident lecturer. The literary historian on this scale cannot but affect to be blandly omniscient and imperturbably clever, a blend of Lord Buddha and Lord Keynes. Like the lecturer he has to set about briskly putting to rights the untidiness of a hundred years in fifty minutes: in the interests of history – literary history, that is – he can hardly even admit the existence of that large category of British authors who are merely boring. Tedium is taboo, even in Spenser or Sir Walter Scott.

I can only be savagely abstract and egotistically arbitrary, and suggest a few tips and themes which seem to me appropriate for the student to consider. The first, and most profound, is the English language itself. Literature in the end is only – only! – the most powerful, the most human, the subtlest and the most inclusive use of the language. English, which mitigates Latin rigour with British palpability, or which informs Saxon weight with continental lightness, is the supreme 'given' of English literature. It was only when the language itself had been organically nourished by the life of the people and brought to a point of readiness, early in Chaucer and mature in Shakespeare, that these two geniuses could appear. How true is the comment that Shakespeare did not invent Hamlet, but discovered him in the English language. It was the language which enabled the theocentric, hierarchical, sharply enclosed and contained medieval world, with its sum of certainties and its clarity of vision, to be vividly mediated in the folk poems and then more completely in Langland and Chaucer. It was the development of the language, in resource and range, which made Shakespeare possible, and it was its increase in sophistication and suppleness and in its capacity to manipulate ideas, which together with the social interests of new forms of communication made possible in the seventeenth century the appearance of English prose, at a moment of time, in fact, later than the beginnings of French prose. Compare the prose of the Elizabethan Florio's translations, still thick and sense-ridden, with the lightness and the intellectual grace of Montaigne's French.

English literature can be read as the self-illuming chronicle of the state of the language. Language is the means by which the setting of the human being is immensely enlarged and the context of his action made immeasurably more complex. Through language the biological individual becomes the historical person, and mere life turns into human experience. The sentence patterns we use, the idioms, the words and the images and the categories of thinking, feeling and valuing which they imply, come to us ripened by time, and both enriched by the insight, imagination and aspirations of many generations, and distorted by their errors, evasions and fatigues. Naturally, there is in language, which next to conduct gives the most intimate, most accurate testimony to the quality of feeling in a society and to its capacity for true relations, a natural tendency towards decline, as there is in every form of human vitality. But the life of language has been recurrently refreshed by the poets and by the people. And it has been recurrently refreshed by poets who turn from its literary and mandarin form to its use as a living tongue. New movements in literature are new uses of language, and this is as true of Chaucer, of Shakespeare, of Donne in the seventeenth century, of Pope in the eighteenth century, as it is of Wordsworth in the nineteenth and Lawrence in the twentieth.

The new mind requires the new voice, and the new voice is discovered by the poet's genius for intimately registering the idiom of his own time.

Language, then, is the substance of literature and its modification is the spring of literary development. There is a corresponding truth to be noted in the development of critical and discursive literature. The history of European culture, the philosopher Urban writes, 'is accordingly the story of two great opposing evaluations of the "word"'. One sees language as an obstacle to the experience of truth, a deceptive veil or a form of treachery betraying some original, spontaneous experience; the other regards language as a mode of access and illumination. In English literature, for example, alongside and opposed to the line of spokesmen for the low evaluation of the word, Hobbes and Locke in the seventeenth and eighteenth centuries, Bentham, James Mill and Horne Took in the nineteenth century, lies the line of the representatives of the high evaluation of language, the Cambridge Platonists, the third Earl of Shaftesbury and Blake in the seventeenth and eighteenth centuries, Coleridge and Matthew Arnold in the nineteenth. Language is the material of literature – a poem is composed of words and nothing else – its changes shape the development of literature, his attitude towards it the response of the reader. This is the intimate way of understanding the relationship between literature and society. In the medieval period, as we see beautifully and completely in Chaucer, there was for a short period an exquisite harmony between society and literature. One flowed without block or deviation into the other. But that dream or trance was broken in the Renaissance, when human consciousness saw itself as much more centrally placed in the scheme of the universe. Shakespeare came at the point in which there was still a vital tension between the brilliant but insulated certainties of the Middle Ages and the new and powerful expansion of human consciousness represented by the Renaissance. In the seventeenth century, in the passionate sensuality and the despairing intellectualism of Donne, we see the final dissolution of medieval certainty.

Even this generalization, though it does make a positive point, will hardly stand unqualified. Because there is a sense in which Chaucer, Ben Jonson, John Donne, Dryden and Pope belong to the same universe, one informed by the same medieval conceptions of God and order and meaning. This is a world utterly vanished for us, as it was for Coleridge, even though he believed in it and wanted to restore it. He was the first, I believe, in English literature consciously to register this new movement of the human mind. Our and Coleridge's world is the world in which the nervous individual consciousness works according to fluid and uncertain categories. Coleridge at the beginning of the nineteenth century was the first to speak the language of this world and the first to feel himself obliged to offer answers to questions which had hardly been formulated before. Coleridge's writings, so distorted and disorganized as works of art, are in fact in their very imperfections, especially in their lack of harmony and coherence, analogies of the modern mind.

English literature signals each step in the continuing modification of the English consciousness. It does this concretely, intuitively and immediately. Criticism, which is that part of literature which has to do with responding to and discriminating among works of literature, registers the changes in society mirrored in literature in a more conscious and discursive way. Criticism takes into account in reading literature the age, the place and the sensibility it embodies. Coleridge himself, for example, clearly saw the historical determinants of English literature. 'After the Revolution,' he remarks, 'the spirit of the nation became more commercial than it had been before; a learned body of clerisy, as such, gradually disappeared and literature began to be addressed to the common miscellaneous public.' In his view there were also revolutions of a different sort more disturbing in their effect than the openly political ones: 'There have been three silent revolutions in England: first when the professions fell off from the Church; secondly when literature fell off from the professions; and thirdly when the press fell off from literature.' In the *Biographia Literaria* he noted too the change in public taste illustrated by the gradual sinking in the pretensions of authors and the change in relationship between them and their readers. Francis Bacon, he notes, took it for granted that it was in the interests of posterity for it to be possessed of his dedications – dedications to popes and kings at least implied that 'the honour given was ... in equipoise to the patronage acknowledged'. But then

Poets and Philosophers, rendered diffident by their very number, addressed themselves to '*learned* readers'; then,

64

aimed to conciliate the graces of 'the *candid* reader'; till, the critic still rising as the author sunk, the amateurs of literature collectively were erected into a municipality of judges, and addressed as THE TOWN. And now finally, all men being supposed able to read and all readers able to judge, the multitudinous PUBLIC, shaped into personal unity by the magic of abstraction, sits nominal on the throne of criticism.

Let me take another example of the relationship of society and literature, literature and politics. The Renaissance mind, as a recent writer, Thomas R. Edwards, explains in a remarkable work, *Imagination and Power*,[1] had 'a primary, intense fascination with the possibilities of secular power'; and the contemporary air was thick with the glorification of great men, celebrations which, as *Tamburlaine* shows, by no means necessarily included elements of irony or moral scepticism in the attitude of the writer. In *Coriolanus* the cramped hero is diminished, in *Paradise Lost* he is turned into a subversive, and in *Hudibras* he is emasculated: three steps from arrogance to impotence. In *Colin Clout* the Court is where everything of any importance is and where one has to go in order to be a poet, whereas for the voice that speaks in the *Horatian Ode* 'the place of power is another place, which one may need to stay away from'.

Marvell's equivocal manner – dappling the metaphysical with the Augustan – is the fitting instrument of the ironic and pitying detachment with which he observed the private man raised to public office. But in Dryden and Pope, where we enter the realm of the bureaucratic and the functionary, the satirist speaks out of a grubby intimacy with the vices and stupidities of politicians, which makes his most urgent purpose one of exposure. Politicians, the successful manipulators, the oiled and tricky managers, now appear as the natural target, not only of criticism, but contempt. There is still a distinction between politics and private experience, preserved even in the next century in the solitary imagination of Wordsworth and the revolutionary imagination of Shelley.

In our world where the notion of a separate public life is harder to sustain, the distinction begins to crumple and inner and outer rush in on one another. In Yeats's 'Easter 1916' we see the poet make public experience tragically personal, whereas in Eliot's 'Coriolan' the poet flinches away not only from public but all secular life, and in Auden public life is reduced to a secret game for initiates.

If the treatment of politics is the outward sign of the relationship of literature to society, a more inward and inclusive one is the varying manner in which literature embodies the sensibility of the race. I use 'sensibility' here in the French sense, meaning that special combination of thought, feeling, value and assumption, that particular flavour of taste and sentiment, characteristic mode of action, which reveals the nuance and crystallizes the tone and temper of a period. I say, too, its varying embodiment because, of course, sensibility in this sense, the ethos and style of a given period, changes continuously, insensibly and profoundly. And yet in any given literature below these real and transient changes there is a steadiness of national tone, a continuing resonance of character and style. The particular quality of sensibility in English literature has been discerned more clearly by Henry James than by anybody else. He remembered the day, 1 March 1869, when there opened before him an opportunity that affected him then and there as 'the happiest, the most interesting, the most alluring and beguiling, that could ever have opened before a somewhat disabled young man who was about to complete his twenty-sixth year'.[2] 'Treasures of susceptibility' lay waiting to be enjoyed, and 'immediate intensities of appreciation' to be felt. His life, he saw, was to be henceforward simply a prolongation of the act of arriving in England, or of re-arriving after nine years' absence, 'in the gusty, cloudy, overwhelmingly English morning'. If I stress that it was England and not Europe which made possible 'the substantially continuous experience' and reunited 'life' and 'knowledge', this is not at all to suggest that there was involved in this any diminution of James's Americanness. There is no warrant in his account of his life or in his work as a novelist for supposing that he was ever anything else but thoroughly and fully American. England offered James the opaque surface on which his unencumbered American consciousness could work and in addition it faced him with the most attractively difficult tangle of implications to unravel.

During these first English days James's impression was of the palpable atmosphere pressing insistently upon him. A dense and richly loaded presence confronted him on all sides, and it is above all the solidity and weight of English life, both individual and social, that every turn of phrase evokes: 'he gorged on the general atmos-

66

pheric richness'; 'politics walked abroad in England, so that one might supremely bump against them';[3] 'condemned the human article over here was to *live*, on whatever terms, in thickness – instead of being free . . .'[4] This was a kind of weather worlds away from the clear, bright, empty air of America, and it had an overwhelming attraction for a sensibility which loved ambiguity, was susceptible only to the embodied and the illustrated, and looked for an order in which 'contrast flared and flourished and through which discrimination could unexhaustedly riot'.[5] 'The place, the places, bristled so for every glance with expressive particulars',[6] and not an item, an image, an aspect, was lost or missed.[7]

> I was again and again in the aftertime to win back the homeliest notes of the impression, the damp and darksome light washed in from the steep, black, bricky street, the crackle of the strong draught of the British 'sea-coal' fire, much more confident of its function, I thought, than the fires I had left, the rustle of the thick, stiff, loudly unfolded and refolded *Times*, the incomparable truth to type of the waiter, truth to history, to literature, to poetry, to Dickens, to Thackeray, positively to Smollett and to Hogarth, to every connection that could help me to appropriate him and his setting, an arrangement of things hanging together with a romantic rightness that had the force of a revelation.

I have chosen this passage from James not only because of the fineness and accuracy of the great American novelist's definition of the sensibility of English life realized in English literature, but also to illustrate – since it is an American reaction – the peculiar openness to external influences which is also characteristic of English literature. Not only does it recruit great writers from elsewhere, Conrad, James, Eliot, but it has always been susceptible to influences from without. In medieval times the formative influences of Europe were paramount, in the Renaissance immediately that of Italy and more remotely those of Greece and Rome, in the seventeenth and eighteenth centuries of France and Italy, and at the end of the nineteenth century, and increasingly in the twentieth century, of the United States and of Commonwealth literature. These influences have constantly helped to reconstitute and to give new directions to the sensibility of the literature itself.

I have referred, fleetingly, to language and to society as two of the great constitutive elements of the literary experience. But of course neither the medium nor the context would work without the intervention of individual, creative genius. Perhaps English literature is remarkable above all else for the astonishing, thronging frequency with which it has been able to produce the major writer. Between Marlowe, let us say, and the Second World War, a major writer has appeared in the English literary tradition every ten or fifteen years. Let me, then, in the second half of my essay, comment on a handful of these great masters, and take the opportunity offered by each name to stress a single theme of literary study. All English literature, and indeed all literature in English, flows from the one great fact of Shakespeare, all other writing being fragments of the universal whole collected in his genius. If I were to pick a single element from this world of creation, it would be the one that Coleridge pointed to in the famous passage of *Biographia Literaria* in which, it will be remembered, he undertook to elucidate 'the specific symptoms of poetic power . . . in a critical analysis of Shakespeare's *Venus and Adonis*, and *Lucrece*'.[8]

> In the 'Venus and Adonis', the first and most obvious excellence is the perfect sweetness of the versification; its adaptation to the subject; and the power displayed in varying the march of the words without passing into a loftier and more majestic rhythm than was demanded by the thoughts, or permitted by the propriety of preserving a sense of melody predominant. The delight in richness and sweetness of sound; even to a faulty excess, if it be evidently original, and not the result of an easily imitable mechanism, I regard as a highly favourable promise in the compositions of a young man. 'The man that hath not music in his soul' can indeed never be a genuine poet . . . But the sense of musical delight, with the power of reducing multitude into unity of effect, and modifying a series of thoughts by some one predominant thought or feeling, may be cultivated and improved, but can never be learned. It is in these that 'poeta nascitur not fit'.

Rhythm is the inmost quality of art and the first signal of life. Poetic rhythm has its biological origins and equivalents: it is the disposition of language which corresponds to man's unfolding,

68

serial existence, and to the profound rhythms, circulating, pulsing, breathing, which order his physical life. Rhythm is the one unfakeable organic thing: others may be worked for or affected, images, ideas, feelings, and even Coleridge claims 'their combination and intertexture' in a poem, but 'the sense of musical delight, with the power of producing it is a gift of imagination . . . [it] may be cultivated and improved, but can never be learned'. Rhythm is, as it were, the way poetry breathes, and one can no more get it up than one can learn to breathe by studying a textbook of physiology. Perhaps for the more acrid modern taste there is a touch too much molasses in Coleridge's terms for this original organic power – 'perfect sweetness of the versification', 'richness and sweetness of sound', 'music in the soul', 'the sense of musical delight'. Still, as used by Coleridge, the phrases were free of the accretions and confectionery with which they have been sugared over by so much minor verse and criticism. In any case, Coleridge's words certainly formulate the right impression of candid, youthful lyricism given by the verse in *Venus and Adonis*.

In this context, the terms are strictly relevant; and it is this, in fact, the relevance of rhythm in Shakespeare's poems, the fineness of its 'propriety' and 'adaptation', and not simply its buoyant presence, that Coleridge is pointing to as proof of Shakespeare's poetic promise. 'Propriety' in *Venus and Adonis* required a comparatively narrow range of effect, with 'a sense of melody predominant' and no 'passing into a loftier and more majestic rhythm than was demanded by the thoughts'. And yet even in this restricted span Shakespeare displays something of that power 'in varying the march of the words' that was to become an endless command of rhythm, a limitless subtlety of movement and stress; even here there are hints and miniature promises of the slipping and flowing, the gliding and tumult of the Shakespearean ocean. It is the natural power of producing variety and relevance of rhythm that Coleridge offers as the first symptom of a genuine poetic gift. But there is a rhythm of the whole as well as a rhythm of the parts, a rhythm which collects and concentrates the dispersed, fragmentary modulations of each phase into a total rhythm, of *King Lear* or *Hamlet* or *The Tempest*. And this is because rhythm, both local and general, is a constituent of meaning, of the inclusive theme of the play and all its particular manifestations. 'His rhythm is so perfect,' Coleridge says elsewhere, 'that you may be almost sure that you do not understand the real force of a line, if it does not run well as you read it.'[9] This is part of that power of 'reducing multitude into unity of effect and modifying a series of thoughts by some one predominant thought or feeling', which also 'may be cultivated and improved but can never be learned'.

The effect of much modern criticism of Milton, by tradition the second genius of English literature, is not very revolutionary after all, since what it does is to enforce the immeasurable superiority of Shakespeare. The impulse at the heart of *Paradise Lost* belongs to the century as well as to the man. There were many in the seventeenth century like Milton – Lord Herbert, Hobbes, Raleigh, Bacon – who had, as the seventeenth-century scholar J. B. Broadbent explains, this 'fierce desire to seek out the secrets of the universe, to control the world by linguistic comprehension. Upper, middle and nether regions, gods and men, science and history must all be visited.'[10] But *Paradise Lost* isn't completely embedded in the medieval half of the seventeenth century. It came out in the same year as Sprat's *History of the Royal Society*, and the movement of civilization represented by that book had its own curious, complicating influence on Milton. 'The steady movement, under Reformation, Humanist Renaissance and Enlightenment towards a rationalized religion, secularly sanctioned morality and constituted institutions bore Milton towards his poem and simultaneously carried away the value of its traditional materials.'[11] Above all, perhaps, its influence was to weaken the impassioned sense of sin which quickened Milton's earlier poetry into such vivid and disturbing life.

Perhaps this accounts for some of the structural distortion in the design of *Paradise Lost*. But the poem has also for many modern minds a strange deficiency in the ultimate coherence of the greatest works of art, which depends on things deeper and more personal than consistency in society or religion. What there is in Milton's life to explain this can be put without rolling the eyes too ecstatically towards a Viennese heaven. We should neither exaggerate nor underplay what is relevant in Milton's protected childhood, his over-ambitious father, his strained defence of virginity, the brutal shock of his marriage, 'the drudgery he used to cicatrise his wounds'. There are certainly many baffling faces lurking behind the gorgeous façade of *Paradise Lost*, the faces of looming and self-sufficient genius, maimed prophet, truculent fanatic, offended husband, sceptical mystic, devout believer, unconscious agnostic, spiritual logician, angelic gossip. Everybody has his own image of Milton: testimony to his enormous power. And, as Coleridge suggested, into this image the reader absorbs each detail of the gigantic, clangorously garrulous poem.

If the 'case' of Milton shows a writer in a deep way at odds with his time as well as the power of an overwhelming personality to dominate its contribution to literature, Pope, a comparable genius, exhibits on the other hand the rare instance in which an exquisite symmetry of assumption and tone and manner exists between the artist and his time. Pope's vision of civilization had a – just – sufficient ground in the reality of the Augustan period to orchestrate its ideal aspiration with solid good sense. His art was to use the spirit of the time as the medium and the material for a superb creative achievement which far transcends its time and place.

The name of Coleridge, paradisal spirit as well as 'damaged archangel', has recurred insistently in this account. But let me say one word about Wordsworth's severe, geological imagination and *The Prelude*. Wordsworth, in whom there was still a considerable weight of eighteenth-century good sense, was like Milton an example of an overpowering personality, an individual temperament of such force that it reshaped its experience in its own image. Any Wordsworthian subject had to have a triple quality. It had to fix the poet's eye upon himself, because when his self-scrutiny relaxed or his attention turned elsewhere, Wordsworth fell into gestures of large and unconfined significance. It had also to fix his eye upon himself as a child, since the further he moved from this primary source of his art, the less necessary, the more fabricated, his work became. In his own words his poetry ceased to flow from 'an inward impulse' and became cerebrally 'proposed and imposed'. And thirdly, Wordsworth found those experiences the most richly productive in which through 'familiar shapes', above all those of his childhood, he glimpsed the looming of 'huge and mighty forms'. It is the perfect conformity of their theme to every requirement of Wordsworth's creative power which gives the early books of *The Prelude* a vitality, an actual and present life, which deserves to be called dramatic.

And this in spite of Wordsworth's claim that in the circumstances of the nineteenth century the true voice of the poet was the narrative not the dramatic. In a letter to Coleridge, Wordsworth censured Lamb for failing to see that now the dramatist must give way to the narrative poet.[12]

> When it is considered what has already been executed in Poetry, strange that a man cannot perceive, particularly when the present tendencies of society, good and bad, are observed, that this is the time when a man of genius may honourably take a station upon different grounds. If he is to be a Dramatist, let him crowd his scene with gross and visible action; but if a narrative Poet, if the Poet is to be predominant over the Dramatist, then let him see if there are no victories in the world of spirit, no changes, no commotions, no revolutions there, no fluxes and refluxes of the thoughts, which may be made interesting. . . .

Wordsworth did not make the claim, which his best poetry would certainly have sanctioned, that a narrative conducted with his fidelity, with his devoted and undistracted attention, ceased to be merely a commemorative record and became a rendering of the events it describes. *The Prelude*, for all its air of meditative sobriety and its undramatic form, becomes by virtue of its unswerving allegiance to a subject inherently dramatic, a dramatic reconstruction of the growth of the human mind. The action of the poem is not dramatic in Wordsworth's sense of being 'gross and visible'; it is, in another phrase of Wordsworth's, 'fine-spun and inobtrusive'. But it has its conflicts – 'the changes and commotions of the mind', its crises – 'the revolutions, fluxes and refluxes of the thoughts', its resolutions – 'victories in the world of spirit'. For Wordsworth the growth of the mind is not a set process proceeding according to inescapable laws; and 'continents of moral sympathy' divide his recreation of it from an analysis based on any such presupposition. As I suggested in asserting that Wordsworth's subject was 'inherently dramatic', mental development is more than organic, and the growth of the mind is inseparable from the refinement of emotion and the maturing of a moral sense. Wordsworth is not dealing merely with the elaboration of a primitive into a sophisticated structure, but with the unfolding of human powers which make moral discernment and decision (and moral disaster) possible; he is concerned with the coming into being of those qualities which transform man from a physical object into a tragic person.

It may be objected that the subtitle of *The Prelude* is 'Growth of a Poet's Mind', not 'Growth of a Human Mind'. But the poet's mind is the most truly representative human mind. He is representative not as the norm of mediocrity, as the statistical average in which every living difference is obliterated, but representative in being genuinely and freely human. The poet is the standard of humanity, not the standard man. He is the standard of man as poetry is the standard of human discourse or – as Wordsworth said – as 'the true standard of poetry is as high as the soul of man has gone, or can go'.[13]

Wordsworth's career often seems to me a long decline from its splendid beginnings, at least from its first ten years. That of Keats, on the other hand, the other great poetic genius of the nineteenth century and the one with a peculiarly English sensibility, is the example of a very different sort of poetic development. In spite of his belief 'that if Poetry comes not as naturally as the Leaves to a tree it had better not come at all',[14] the truth was that Keats's best poetry did not come 'naturally' at all. It came only as the result of a sustained and deliberate effort of self-education. Indeed, an essential clue to the understanding of Keats's poetic life, that astonishing passage from cockney to classic, is an educational one, since Keats's career is the most brilliant example in literature of the education of a sensibility.

Keats had from the first, and kept throughout his life, a marvellous sense of the particular, and this sense fed and sustained his poetic power. In a letter to Thomas Keats which describes a scene in the Lake District and which vividly communicates Keats's sense of the peculiar character of the place, he voices this very sentiment. 'I shall learn poetry here . . .'[15] he says. In the same letter he uses an odd phrase, 'this countenance or intellectual tone', which is meant to convey the capacity of any thing or event to be differently and uniquely itself. The attraction that 'this countenance or intellectual tone' held for Keats meant that he had an acute susceptibility for forms, for the particular self and structure of a thing, even when it was 'smothered with accidents'. This is a habit of mind, or rather a specialization of insight often accompanied, as in many of the poems of Marvell or Hopkins, by an unusual intensity of feeling and a concomitant concentration of expression. Keats certainly

73

believed in the theory that the excellence of an art lay in its intensity. But the qualities of intensity and concentration showed themselves only in the best of his poems since there was another part of his nature which was infatuated by the drowsily vague and the languorously narcotic, which dimmed his clear eye for the object and betrayed him into the cult of 'silken phrases and silver sentences'. Indeed, Keats's career could be read as the history of the friction of these two elements in his nature.

Between *The Eve of St Agnes* and the great Odes Keats was, it is clear, astonishingly transformed, advancing from the status of a charming minor talent to that of a genius of the first order. As I see it, that development is in essence a brilliant, profound, and exemplary exercise in self-education. The complete maturity so earnestly laboured at in Keats's life, so lucidly and persuasively theorized about in his letters, is wholly realized in Keats's art in the *Ode to Autumn*. In this poem we see genius having at its disposal a perfected sensibility. Keats's meditations on maturity, his efforts to achieve it, here issue into a disciplined poetic act. The poem exhibits, like the best Romantic poems, a radically original, firsthand response to experience, and exhibits it, moreover, with the characteristic Keatsian virtues of density and definition, weight and pressure. Autumn in this poem is neither attenuated by customary perception nor conventional expectation, nor idealized away – as in other Romantic poetry – into a thin and misty abstraction. Keats's art shows us not an ideogram, not the pictured structure of the season, but its dimensions and complex savour. For it gives us not only the fullness and softness of autumn – the ripeness of it – but also its more masculine qualities, the acrid, the rough, and the vigorous. Or rather it embodies a more inclusive conception of ripeness. Not only does it offer mellow fruitfulness and clammy cells, the fume of poppies and the last oozings, but also the moss'd cottage trees, the granary floor, the brook, the cyder press, the stubble plains, the small gnats and the river sallows. By this point in his career it is clear that ripeness had come to be for Keats both a varied and ordered concept. It represented a rich fund of experience which had been examined and weighed by a scrupulously just and delicately balanced mind. It is no accident that the ripeness which is the theme of the poem should stand in so close an analogy to the maturity which is the theme of Keats's moral and intellectual life. In this poem maturity is both achieved and transcended.

Keats's poem gives us the right to use a dangerous and difficult word. It gives us a sanction for saying that here maturity is transformed into wisdom.

I have concentrated upon poetry, the soul of literature. But I must of course refer to the novel, the great creative form of the modern world, and to Dickens, the supreme novelist in the English tradition. How often we have thought of Dickens as some powerful gothic genius with a brilliant gift for melodrama and farce and for seeing the tip-tilted world of childhood.

Such an understanding of Dickens is absurdly limited and how indeed could such a Dickens have so powerful an influence on Tolstoy and Dostoevsky? Dickens had in fact, as the Leavises make clear,[16] an extraordinary intelligence, 'a potency of thought' and his work is a sustained, conscious and subtle study of the human spirit. He wasn't simply a social reformer, nor just a popular entertainer, but a master in the exploration of human feeling and a man with such a gift for words that it is not out of place to think of him in the context of Shakespeare. He was a great novelist because his ideas – perceptive, strong and subtle as they were – were dissolved into theme, character and dialogue. *Bleak House* and *Dombey and Son* are novels in which a mysterious poetic quality works in a way worthy of Blake or Wordsworth. Dickens was not only a writer of incomparable vitality in theme and situation, but also in image, language and poetic resource. The generosity of Dickens, his hold on human centrality, his social insight and his sense of moral value as well as his poetic power, made him, in the Leavises' words, 'the Shakespeare of the novel'. And as we can see the whole future of English poetry and drama present in its possibilities in Shakespeare, so in Dickens we observe the development of the English novel. In particular his work manifests that new movement in the modern world by which poetry became infused into the novel to make it the central creative instrument for embodying the human experience of the twentieth century.

If, as I draw to the end of this – impossible – undertaking, I ask myself how I can point to – what this series of essays is designed to illumine – something of what is purely distinctive about the tradition of English literature, and if I confine myself to the examples already called on, two or three things come to mind. I hope I will not be thought to be complacent in the British manner or arrogant in the English way, as some would put it, if I point out that it would not be very sensible, in my view, to take English literature just on the same basis as the others in this volume. I said that the whole of English literature proceeds from Shakespeare and that the universe of the English novel derives from Dickens. In the same way, all literatures in the English language, supremely because of that very fact, proceed from English literature in the narrower sense. Or to put it in another way, they too look back to and gather their force and identity from Shakespeare and Dickens. English literature is the ocean from which the others have evolved. But acknowledging this fact, one can still point to a set of characteristic lineaments. The language is a function of the society in a double way. Each creates and modifies the other, each is the subject of the other's influence. That society is notable, in spite of cataclysmic changes and revolutionary rhythms, for an unusual continuity of consciousness and manner. The great predilection of English writers – how clearly we see it in Shakespeare and Dickens – is to keep the past alive and influential; most great English writers, even when like Wordsworth or Lawrence they struggle for a new effort of awareness and a new structure of feeling, are also concerned with unblocking the conduits of history, and maintaining a continuous flow of consciousness. At the same time the manner of English prose and poetry has shown itself throughout its development as peculiarly hospitable to external influences – possibly because of the very confidence generated by its unbroken continuity. In the past these influences were supremely those of Europe; today they are both European and those of the new world, and increasingly of the Commonwealth world.

Corresponding to this openness to otherness, and in keeping with the clear desire for a lasting and unfractured 'mind', all great English writing shows the quality for which English critical terminology is constantly trying to find new terms. It is that of palpability, of an embodying or sculptured presence, a condition which is referred to by Leavis as enactment and which I referred to in speaking of Keats's density and definition, weight and pressure.

This firm, tactual quality in the writing goes with a sense of the thickness of texture, almost the marmalade quality, in English society, the condition that James's marvellously registering alien eye found so characteristic and enchanting in English life. It is a sense of the community, of its rich confusion, of its implicit orders, classes and kinds, of its fullness and differentiation. All great

English novels, with the possible exception of *Wuthering Heights*, the supreme version of the individual's quarrel with the world, are grounded in the complexities of English society. This heavy, some-times clammy quality of society can be riven by dissension, but it is a dissension of groups and classes rather than of ideas, of com-munities and castes rather than concepts. 'The truth is in the concrete', as Brecht said, and this is a view about life which English writers, and perhaps above all, English novelists, have grasped and worked on. The moral struggle in the English novel is itself a conflict of feeling, of style of life, of centres of power, of families, of town and country, and not an abstract moral ballet.

I conclude by reminding myself that the nature of the literary experience is to be inclusive, hospitable, enfolding. Music leaves its ideas wholly embedded in its own medium, science strives to expose the anatomy of existence, but literature, as Santayana explains,[17]

> takes a middle course and tries to subdue music which for its purposes would be futile and too abstract, into conformity with general experience, making music thereby significant.

The literary impulse aspires to digest, to classify, to become at every point pertinent to the facts of human existence. So that literature, as Leavis contends, is more than an array of distinct and independent works. It is an order expressive of and helping to form a common mind, imagination and sensibility. I must quote here a passage in which Leavis gives the most considered statement of his view. He is making the point that Ezra Pound's definition of literature, as 'simply language charged with meaning to the utmost possible degree', while it is positively right, is in-complete. He refers in the passage to Eliot, but it is clear that it isn't just Eliot's conception that he is advancing.[18]

> ... literature ... cannot be understood merely in terms of odd individual works illustrating 'processes' and 'modes'; it involves a literary tradition. And a given literary tradition is not merely, as it were by geographical accidents of birth, associated with a given language; the relation may be sug-gested by saying that the two are *of* each other. Not only is language an apt analogy for literary tradition; one might say that such a tradition is largely a development of the language

it belongs to if one did not want to say at the same time that the language is largely a product of the tradition. Perhaps the best analogy is that used by Mr Eliot in *Tradition and the Individual Talent* when he speaks of the 'mind of Europe'. 'Mind' implies both consciousness and memory, and a literary tradition is both: it is the consciousness and memory of the people or the cultural tradition in which it has developed.

The poets live in this consciousness and reproduce this memory; and the consciousness and memory live in them and fashion them. Less important poets illustrate the tradition; the more important ones significantly develop it. Literature so conceived takes in much more than writers and writing. It is the consciousness of the age and both the body and the soul of the experience of the nation.

CHAPTER FOUR

INDIA
B. Rajan

Indian literature in English has at least one distinguishing characteristic: its right to be a literature at all is insistently and acrimoniously questioned. Such questions would have been natural in the aftermath of India's independence and it might even have been disturbing if they had not been raised. But a quarter of a century has passed since India recovered her nationhood and the cumulative force of demonstration in fifteen authentically Indian languages ought to have persuaded English that it was time to die. That it has not died proves not only the stubbornness but the alienness of the patient; it becomes foreign by its inability to understand the justice of its own obituary. Thus, a recent article in the *Hindustan Times*[1] can observe that the notion that 'writing, thinking and speaking English is an un-Indian activity' is 'well on its way to becoming common currency. It finds expression in the daily press, in so-called literary criticism, in futile coterie discussions.' P. Lal's six-hundred-page anthology, *Modern Indian Poetry in English,*[2] devotes half its pages to maintaining that Indian poetry in English is indeed possible, instead of printing the poetry which in better circumstances should make the argument superfluous.

If we may put the case against English with a cogency not normally achieved by its proponents, it is that English is a language imposed upon India rather than nourished by its soil. It is not saturated by the Indian past. If anything, it is saturated by a political and eventually psychological relationship, a sense of the superiority of alien values, which make it incapable of conveying the inwardness of Indianness. Moreover, writers in English compound their removal from the source by giving their books to Western publishing houses. The fitful glimpses they may achieve of an Indian vision are thus fatally compromised by having to be merchandised. Even if this betrayal is avoided, it is not an Indian reader who is addressed. If the direction is wrong no act of discovery can be built upon it or shaped by its specifications.

A coherent rejoinder is entirely possible at the level of the assault. India has been conquered many times, yet the languages of conquest are upheld as Indian by those who question (usually in English) the pretensions of English. English has been present in India long enough to be part of the Indian landscape.[3] Day-to-day decisions are often negotiated in English. Bureaucracies function or fail to function in English. The twentieth century is known to have arrived in India and the language of its arrival is probably English.

At a deeper level we know that living in India is not necessarily Indian life. Some Indian writers in English mistake the first for the second; so do several writers in several Indian languages. If we are interested in literary nationality rather than in literary chauvinism we can all ask ourselves what it means to be Indian, not in a time of Vedic and mythic purity, but under the horizon of this particular day. That English is incapable of seeking the answer to such a question is an allegation that should only be made by those who have possessed the deeper life and returned to declare it in an act of literature.

The intelligent question is surely not whether an Indian literature in English is possible, but what range of literary possibilities is opened to a writer using English as his instrument. It is apparent at once that if the meeting of East and West is part of the Indian experience, then English is as capable as other languages of conveying the quality of such a meeting. But the meeting of East and West must be shaped within the meeting of past and present. English must learn to accommodate the weight and the penetrative power of a cultural tradition considerably older than English – a heroic tradition which includes a Mycenae, a dramatic tradition which includes an Athens and a metaphysical tradition that uniquely combines the precision of philosophy with the passion of literature. These structures of achievement must be brought to bear upon a time which is aware of their tyrannies as well as of their potencies. And they must further be brought into relationship with other 'Western' structures which challenge them but which are now seen to have erected their own tyrannies. We are unavoidably at a point where many roads cross and English is not the wrong language in which to understand what happens at this point. Though the writer in English is taunted with having chosen exile, there is a turbulence that all of us must move through in order to move anywhere. In that turbulence the representative experience may be that of not belonging or of being cast adrift. Those who have found it unnecessary to respond to this experience may be even less Indian than the writers they attack.

When we consider the possibilities open to the writer in English, we have to admit that literature in India has not fully risen to those possibilities. Few literatures do, and in a hostile climate there is a natural reluctance to take the larger risk. Even if the risk were taken, the conjunction of man and moment is not something which good intentions can legislate. Khushwant Singh (who has himself written a widely read novel of partition, *Mano Majra*) has recently remarked that 'Indian writers have not yet developed the stamina to pursue their characters and themes over the long distances that the novel demands, nor acquired techniques to paint on large canvases.'[4] It is an observation that is not uncharitable and Indian writing can be described less as a noble failure than as a cautiously limited success. The Indian returned from abroad, for example, is a standard figure in the meeting of East and West. But the encounter is held within its lesser implications – what are involved are collisions of behaviour rather than patterns of identity. Ruth Jhabvala is an expert in such collisions and her several novels on the clientele of Gaylord's Restaurant reveal a sharp ear as well as a keen eye. Possibly because she is not Indian by origin but the Polish wife of an Indian architect, she is dexterous at putting down the cadences of English spoken by Indians. Within their narrow compass her novels are skilful affairs. But the cast is limited, the tonal range restricted and the joint effect of her many books is unavoidably one of accumulation rather than growth. Even if we confine ourselves to the foreigner in India and those who have dealings with the foreigner, there are opportunities to move in deeper which Mrs Jhabvala avoids. She can use the *Gita* for the title of one of her novels (*Get Ready for Battle*) but the title merely indicates the distance between disinterested action and the courses of action the characters achieve. The characters never question themselves (or for that matter each other) on the meaning of disinterestedness. It would be a self-questioning called for if we were to take seriously the injunction 'Do not think of the fruit of action' in T. S. Eliot's 'The Dry Salvages' which for many readers brings the spirit of the *Gita* into a modern English poem. The agents in Mrs Jhabvala's book do not move towards understanding what the right action is or how to perform it only for its own sake. Instead they are placed and valued by the reader, in the tradition of this kind of novel, by the ironies of cross-talk and its interplay. But while the knowledge of an area outside the awareness of the participants helps to define how the participants are limited, it precludes anything being said about the nature of the area. Some of Mrs Jhabvala's novels stop short of even this degree of judgment. The 'clinical compassion' which one critic finds in her work is probably no more than amused acceptance.

Unlike Mrs Jhabvala, Kamala Markandaya is not a novelist of the lesser risk. *Nectar in a Sieve*, her first and best known book, is a celebration of the ferocious earth. Despite its merits, it left her future a question-mark. Peasant endurance can be movingly displayed in tried and true relationships but if this kind of book is to be fully liberated from its stereotypes, a subversive voice must at some time insistently ask the metaphysical as well as the socio-economic questions. After *Nectar in a Sieve* Markandaya has advanced through a succession of talented but not wholly successful novels with titles such as *Possession* and *A Silence of Desire* which bear witness a little too aptly to their contents. Her latest novel *The Coffer Dams* is a passage to India attempted under Point Four. Dams are not lacking in symbolic possibilities. Jawaharlal Nehru described them as the temples of the new India but worship in such temples calls for a repudiation or at least a drastic revaluation of the past. When the cost of progress stares us in the face – and a novel can arrange for some of the staring – we are made to inquire into the content of progress. The Indian sensibility of today is suspended between twin necessities which it is impossible to evade and nearly impossible to reconcile; and the stresses are compounded because the contention of the past against the present is also the contention of the organic against the alien. The discovery of how that sensibility interrogates and reconstitutes itself is what should be meant by 'clinical compassion'.

For all its strenuousness, Markandaya's ambitious novel does not succeed in taking up the further questions. Clinton, the master builder, is fully absorbed in what, if he were more imaginative, he would recognize as the mystique of building. Helen, his wife, tries to recover what technocrats demolish by increasingly frequent trips into the forest. Bashiam has advanced from the tribal state to an empathy with machinery that makes one wonder if he would not be like Clinton if he could. There are Indians who resent their dependence on the foreigner and white women who dislike the natives and the insects. A village headman can utter words of wisdom such as the following:[5]

> it is also necessary to guard the inner feeling. Because, you see, one is shaken to pieces if there is inaction without and a hurricane raging within.

The remark can serve to direct attention to a weightiness that is not always justified by what the characters are and do. Larger-than-life figures stride into confrontations and reflect with heavy internal eloquence on the not very extraordinary things they say to each other. Europeans are killed in an accident and their bodies are recovered at great risk. Indians are then killed in a counter-accident and the recovery of their bodies is demanded. Meanwhile Helen has given herself to Bashiam who undertakes the rescue operation, possibly as a restitution to Clinton which the latter implicitly accepts. He is trapped and crippled in the Avery Kent crane which he expertly and lovingly operates. The rains come and the dams hold. We have witnessed not a conflict of attitudes but a collision of group-egos. The author tries hard and writes with occasional distinction. Her habit of beginning every other sentence with a 'which' or a 'but' is sometimes effective in suggesting the rough-hewn nature of the landscape and possibly the muscular thinking of its characters. One is sufficiently aware of talent and earnestness to hope for the book in which it will all be put together.

Kamala Markandaya and Ruth Jhabvala made their reputations after India's independence. We need to consider others who helped to establish the Indian novel in English when independence was a dream and partition not yet a nightmare. Mulk Raj Anand is very much a figure of the thirties, of the Popular Front, the Spanish Civil War and of brave hopes given sustenance in English coffee houses. *Coolie* and *Untouchable*, published early in the Penguin paperback programme, were among the first Indian novels to gain a reputation abroad. Their content is adequately indicated by their titles. Less descriptive perhaps are *Two Leaves and a Bud* (1938) which deals with tea plantation labour in Assam or *The Road* (1961) which deals with untouchability after independence. *The Private Life of an Indian Prince* considers the failure of another and very different caste to come to terms with public realities. Among Anand's many other novels is a trilogy consisting of *The Village* (1954), *Across The Black Waters* (1955) and *The Sword and the Sickle* (1955). Lal Singh, the protagonist, the youngest son in a Punjabi agricultural family, exiles himself from the orthodox by his 'modernity', joins the army, fights in the First World War, is educated by the carnage into the understanding of injustice and the conspiracy of the rich against the poor, and returns to an India in which the world his family represented is dying and the world which should follow it seems powerless to be born. These and other works indicate that Anand's predominant if not his overwhelming interest is in the didactic novel of social content. It is a kind of novel distinctly out of fashion but it has roots in the Indian tradition and Anand writes it with a sense of life which has led to the expected comparisons with Dickens and Balzac and which makes the result more than a narrative with a message. With new names coming into prominence, Anand's accomplishment has receded into the background. Perhaps the reprinting of his works, now in progress, will cause interest in them to revive.

Indian novelists tend to write as if the development of the novel ended with Trollope, but in the forties G. V. Desani published an experimental novel of brilliance which nobody read and which is now a collector's item. *All About Mr Hatterr* is unfortunately the kind of performance that is possible only once. Joycean in its verbal exuberance, it reminds us that the English language, while not an enemy to the Indian novelist, is not usually found to be his ally. Desani uses words with panache but he has used them very little after Hatterr's definitive expounding of himself.

Raja Rao is another novelist concerned with language as a resource of the novel, a resource which is not simply used but remade in its usage. Indian English, in relation to which his work should be considered, is a cause with vociferous and unreflective advocates. After the original sin of writing in English, it is suggested, atonement can be made by concocting an English that is Indian. The word 'concocting' is used since some authors seek to write Indian English simply by importing into English an adequate number of italicized Indian words. The novel which results is the kind of novel in which the inevitable highlights are the wedding, the reception and the lesson in tying a sari. Mrs Jhabvala's reproducing of the speech patterns of Indians using English is an improvement on this and if an Indian had done what she has, the result might conceivably be certified as 'Indian'. But since Mrs Jhabvala has done it we can clearly see that it is not Indian at all. A novel can use dialect but it does not follow that the use of dialect is the proof of its national identity, or the condition of its validity as a novel.

Raja Rao himself speaks of the Indian writer in English using a dialect, but the word is put in its perspective when we realize that 'American' for him is a dialect of English. The point is that language is a way of saying which shapes the nature not only of the thing said, but eventually of the thing seen. Language gives access to an ultimate reality and it is the *kind* of access given which can legitimately have national characteristics and which can meaningfully be described as Indian or something else.

If language is to affirm a collective understanding, the understanding must be permitted to grow and to reconsider itself in its own way and at its own pace. The literary planners who call for national visions and national myths and for a language issuing from such a matrix will receive prefabricated structures which will answer their specifications but which will not be literature. It is well to reflect on how long it took American literature to establish an American grain and how many American authors of standing have either ignored the grain or written against it.

Raja Rao's own view of what constitutes Indian English displays some evolution over the years. In his foreword to *Kanthapura* published in 1938 he observes:[6]

> We, in India, think quickly, we talk quickly, and when we move we move quickly.
> There must be something in the sun of India that makes us rush and tumble and run on. And our paths are paths interminable . . . We have neither punctuation nor the treacherous 'ats' and 'ons' to bother us – we tell one interminable tale. Episode follows episode, and when our thoughts stop our breath stops, and we move on to another thought.

In the foreword to *The Serpent and the Rope* published twenty-two years later, we are warned that 'the Sanscrit language may not be read in a hurry, it must be sounded as well as seen; and its power depends upon its beat, upon rhythms the ear alone can detect.'[7] Elsewhere we are told that Sanscrit has 'a *gambhiryatha*, a nobility that seems rooted in primary sound' and that 'speech is sound, and sound is vibration, and vibration creation'.[8] A character in the novel can be described as 'the source of which words were made, Akshara-Lakshmi, divinity of the syllable; the night of which the day was the meaning, the knowledge of which the book was the token, the symbol – the prophecy'.[9]

It may be useful to look at the extent to which the realities of language in *Kanthapura* and *The Serpent and the Rope* achieve the theoretical metamorphosis. The following is an example of the earlier tempo:[10]

> The rains have come, the fine, first-footing rains that skip over the bronze mountains, tiptoe the grass, and leaping into the valleys, go splashing and wind-swung, a winnowed pour, and the cocoanuts and the betel-nuts and the cardamom plants choke with it and hiss back.

This is unusual language for a village woman, even one 'imbued with the legendary history of the region'. Perhaps the repeated 'ands' (there are eleven more in the following sentence) convey the excited volubility with which Indians are said to express themselves as they 'rush and tumble and run on'. A more important quality of the prose is its significant avoidance not of the treacherous 'ats' or 'ons' but of the even more treacherous 'ifs' and 'buts'. The language does not turn across itself or against itself. It is a stream without eddies. This characteristic, as we shall see, is not without a bearing on the understandings that the language affirms.

The later prose has a more deliberate movement, conveyed to some degree by the following sentence:[11]

> The whole of the Gangetic plane [sic] is one song of saintly sorrow, as though truth began where sorrow was accepted and India began where Truth was acknowledged.

Or to vary and yet not vary the mystique of rivers:[12]

> The river Rhone flows like the Ganges, she flows does Mother Rhone into the seven seas, and she built herself a chapel, that the gay gipsies might come and sing and worship Sarah in her

sanctuary. Ships go, rushing ships go now to India, to far India, to quick India.

These cadences are evocative but they are not the harmonies of Sanscrit as those harmonies present themselves for example on pages 331–2 of the novel.[13] In the first sentence the careful balances ('truth began' versus 'India began', 'accepted' versus 'acknowledged') and the enclosing of 'truth' and 'sorrow' within congruent sound patterns, point to the recognition that sorrow is one with truth. In the second passage the interwoven *g* and *s* sounds are picked up in 'ships go, rushing ships go now' and India, 'far' yet 'quick', becomes the urgent destination. It is a subtle music but not one characterized by an organ-like sonority 'rooted in primary sound'. The style in short is lyric and meditative, not heroic. It may be added that it is not particularly Indian in its vocabulary, in its syntax or even in its cadences.

Raja Rao says at one point that he shapes a sentence with 'word after word repeated back to silence, rediscovered through a backward movement'.[14] There is a resonance in his language, but is it best described as the resonance of sound against silence? The copia in which Raja Rao often indulges (in a sentence already quoted we have source and words, night and day, knowledge and token, symbol and prophecy) seem designed rather to suggest the convergence of relationships in the ultimate harmony. Perhaps they do so by lulling rather than sharpening the mind. Is the relationship between night and day analogous to the relationship between knowledge and its token?

In *Kanthapura* the voluble style with its animated, onward flow tells of the coming of Gandhiism to an Indian village, but it is Gandhiism felt as a mystical rather than as a political force. Truth finds its adherents who once they have woken to the call of the ultimate self within them remain steadfast in their loyalty to that self, both in its interior and its exterior consequences. A novelist could talk in these circumstances of the cause on more than one level, of the possible tension between the higher and lower allegiances, of divided minds which may or may not succeed in uniting themselves, of an ideal in both its fulfilments and its betrayal. What we have instead is a straightforward division between the transformed and the untouched. The book is a virtuoso performance, particularly when we remember that it was written at the age of twenty-one; but it avoids several of the explorations which one takes to be the natural business of the novel. In this sense, the absence of treacherous 'ifs' and 'buts' indicates the nature of the work we are considering.

The title Raja Rao has chosen for his next novel is significant. What seems a serpent at night is found to be a rope by day. The contrasts are between appearance and reality, darkness and light, ignorance and knowledge, death and life, enmeshment in becoming and deliverance into being. Sankara, from whom the thought is taken, did not rule out the possibility that both serpent and rope may be forms of limitation and that reality is neither of these forms. For Raja Rao 'the world is either unreal or real – the serpent or the rope'. At the same time 'the real has no name' and 'the rope is no rope to itself'.[15] The metaphysical agility exhibited here may bewilder some but initially it is sufficient to recognize that the mirror-scaled serpent is multiplicity and that the struggle with it is not creative as it is for Yeats.

The cosmopolitan cast of the novel includes a Spaniard, a White Russian, a Frenchwoman and an Indian. The *locale* shifts between India, France and England at the time of the Coronation. The Seine, the Thames and the Ganges are the same river. In fact, Heraclitus's statement that we can never step twice into the same stream seems metamorphosed into the proposition that we can never step into anything else.

Not everyone is a pilgrim of the absolute and even among those who are, some can be uncertain of the point of the pilgrimage and some can wonder if they have chosen the wrong road. It is possible to feel that the purpose of the gift or even the delusion of life is that we should experience life fully in its ordinary humanities. The mind does not simply search for and find itself. It questions itself, accuses itself, torments itself and may not even know when it knows itself. Yet that the novel should situate itself at the centre of 'that subtle knot which makes us man' is, we can argue, a basically Western convention. Those unprepared to commit themselves to such a convention might suggest that we should concern ourselves with what is found rather than with how it is found. Yet paradoxically, we do not begin the search by asking what we are searching for. We begin when the sound of what we are searching for is heard commandingly within the self. To proceed further is simply to strip away the layers of distraction that separate us from the ultimate in ourselves. Art is not life precisely because art seeks to render the purified presence of the real in life. It is concerned in the end not with the human situation but with that situation's metaphysical envelope.

These rejoinders are plausible and it can be added that tragedy is not one of the Indian literary genres because the essence of things is known to be beyond tragedy and because literature should reveal and not obscure the essence. Development is not one of the characteristics of Indian music because form is manifold rather than progressive, declaring the one in its infinite variations. The danger in pressing these arguments too far is that the novel can emerge as a fundamentally Western genre, unsuitable for singing the song of the self. Raja Rao's determination to see people and events as notes in the everlasting melody results for example in the death of Rama's newly-born son being virtually lost in the metaphysical envelope:[16]

> I was neither in pain, nor was I relieved, I felt above both, like a child looking at a kite in the sky . . . I laughed as a child laughs, playing with the subtleties of the breeze. I was happy.

Other consequences include strange interpretations of political movements, notably Stalinism, and a treatment of the Coronation that can only be described as awkwardly transcendental:[17]

> The world gave parties to itself, and everybody felt every-where . . . No one was another's adversary, for there was no other and all was simplified. . . . There was about London a restrained effervescence, as though princes, Zulus, soldiers and politicians; theatrical actors, workers on the arches, policemen on horses; the very manipulations of electric lights on houses and towers, were, so to say, interchangeable enti-ties, as though man were discovering himself. . . . The very aeroplanes seemed sure of themselves like storks when they go a-mating.

The Serpent and the Rope is a novel of richness and distinction but there are times when in reading it one longs for the un-convinced voice, the counter-pull of existence and its impurities, the fury and the mire of human veins. Is the longing no more than a Western malady?

Raja Rao and Kamala Markandaya are both novelists from Mysore, notable in their lack of resemblance to each other. R. K. Narayan, the third and most important of the Mysore novelists, differs even more strikingly from the other two. Both Narayan and Raja Rao display a strong sense of South India in their novels, but this may be the only connection that is possible between them. Narayan writes of the situation rather than the envelope, though the situation when adequately and repeatedly characterized can be made to suggest a certain envelopment. His interest is the man and not the melody. Language is not one of his primary resources. His Indian English represents the way in which Indians talk and think but it is not used to style an Indian vision or to sound the depths of an Indian sensibility.

Narayan has been more prolific than any other Indian writer of our time. His novels are cumulative and do not merely accumulate. Each of his stories (and he is fundamentally a story-teller) is about the town of Malgudi and its people. Narayan is singularly successful in implying a world that is fully established behind his novels and out of which his novels seem to issue. The aesthetic distancing which his works effect is expertly chosen and consistently held. It is sufficiently close to maintain verisimilitude and yet sufficiently removed for the comic exaggeration to be arranged.

The comparison of R. K. Narayan to Chekhov is nearly as frequent as the comparison of every Indian woman novelist to Jane Austen. Both comparisons are less than instructive. The Indian female sensibility is not in the least Jane Austenish and neither its strength nor its serenity is reflected in those novels of chit-chat to which the comparison with Jane Austen is applied. To compare Narayan to Chekhov is not to put the finger on Narayan's inventiveness and his sense of the comic contrivance. Narayan's surface is that of the actual. The slightly bizarre incidents into which the surface gives entry are designed to suggest that we do not know our neighbours and that the extraordinary lies an inch below the everyday.

Narayan's characters move forward within trains of events which they do not create and are in the end unable to control. *The Financial Expert*, widely held to be his best novel, underlines this characteristic even in the irony of its title. The manipulator is manipulated. He makes his fortune not by financial wizardry, but by publishing a pornographic book. And the book is not acquired as a result of native acumen. It is given to and virtually forced upon the 'expert' in return for all the money he happens to have at that moment. Destiny accosts a man and he yields to the opportunity without necessarily recognizing it as such. The wheel rises and falls. The fortune which Dr Pal makes available through a single gift is taken away by a single rumour which he instigates. Meanwhile he has fully corrupted an already spoilt son who is doted on by his parents. The expert ends as he begins under the banyan tree with an empty cash box and another infant to succeed or fail with.

The Guide offers us guidance on more than one level. Railway Raju graduates from tourism *via* a jail sentence to leading the uninstructed in the country of the spirit. The two roles (Raju is a self-confessed role-player) are juxtaposed through a series of flash-backs. Like his predecessors in Narayan's work, Raju rises and falls, flourishes when failure seems most imminent, survives many lawsuits and is finally brought low by a forgery which injures no one and is actually designed to be helpful. Emerging from prison he takes refuge in a deserted temple and is mistaken for a holy man. He offers oracular advice which is ambiguous enough to seem infallible. He becomes what he is thought to be. The rains fail and the crops die. Raju embarks on a fast through a misunder-standing and continues with it because he is too identified with his role to be able to desist. He tells his story to one of his followers but it makes no difference. He is the symbol that events have made him. He becomes a national, indeed an international celebrity and dies as the first of the rain is heard in the hills. Even more than in *The Financial Expert* events not of the man's making surround the man and interpret what he is.

In the *Man-Eater of Malgudi* the force of events is incarnated in a strong man turned taxidermist, a conservationist whose passion is to preserve life by stuffing it. Moving uninvited into a spare room above the press of Malgudi's printer, he proceeds to interfere with and then to dominate his host's life. Efforts to put him in his place merely result, as might be expected, in stronger assertions of the will to stuff. From being the ruin of his host he becomes the curse of the neighbourhood. Proceeding steadily to bigger game, his climactic enterprise is the attempted killing of a processional elephant. Evil with a comic *e* cannot be dealt with – it vanishes as arbitrarily as it comes into being. In demolishing with a karate blow an annoying insect on his forehead, the man-eater is so successful that he also demolishes himself.

Ask an Indian student of English to name his favourite novelist and the answer is likely to be Hardy. Probe deeper and as often as not the reason for the preference will be the place of accident in Hardy's scheme of things. The accident is the turning point in Narayan's novels and typically it lies outside the control of the man whose road it can make, reverse, or ruin. If the view offered is not tragic it is mainly because the scale of events is held securely within the decorum of comedy, because life can begin again under the banyan tree, because no anguished voice is heard demanding the 'wherefore'. The result is an art that is highly skilled but unavoidably limited. Growth is precluded because growth would move us into an area of investigation rather than affectionate acceptance. Yet Narayan's work is characteristically Indian, even possibly in its implicit boundaries. For many of the less fortunate, life in India can be bitter and brief and if it is not a long disease it can seem a continuing penance. Both in the cruelty and benediction of the elements and in the often crushing routine of achieving a livelihood, the pressures of the given seem too heavy to be turned aside by the individual effort. Endurance becomes the principal weapon and the accident the main means of deliverance. The tragic is too close to need aesthetic underlining. It is the comic frustration which provides the welcome catharsis.

There are many voices in the Indian novel and their variety makes it less than useful to point to an Indianness which is common to all of them or, as hostile critics would prefer it, to point to an Indianness which all of them conspicuously lack. The absence of a subversive element is common to all the writers we have discussed but one hesitates to conclude that development through conflict is foreign to the Indian imagination. If it is, it cannot remain foreign much longer. It is part of the cost of living in this century.

Several Indian novelists are read with respect abroad and more than one can be said to be internationally established. Poetry presents a less encouraging picture; that it presents a picture at all is largely the work of a single individual. For fourteen years P. Lal has operated the Writers' Workshop in Calcutta. During that time the press which supports the Workshop has put into print over two hundred titles. A recent book by Krishna Vaid, *Silence and Other Stories*, testifies to a standard of production which is fast becoming impossible to achieve in the affluent West. Vaid, it might be added, teaches English at an American university and has published a good first novel, *Steps in Darkness*, as well as a critical study of Henry James. The Workshop is not entirely free of the vices of the coterie, but nine-tenths of Indian poetry in English after 1958 has been printed under its auspices and nine-tenths of the remaining tenth should never have been printed. To have done this much in the most turbulent city in the world after Detroit is an accomplishment that indicates more than persistence.

It would be pleasant to conclude that the Workshop is India's answer to the Hogarth Press, or that, in the style of Tambimuttu's management of *Poetry* in the forties, its less than fastidious criteria have brought forth among much debris, poets of the status of Dylan Thomas and David Gascoyne. But the sixties is not the decade of the urgent individual voice, of a poetic world which the writer creates, entered into and sustained by his individual poems. One might say that much of the poetry Lal prints is derivative, that his practitioners imitate each other as well as the old masters, that voguishness looks less persuasive when it is five years behind the times. But these failings are natural in an enclosed literary situation in which restrictions on travel and on the flow of books cut the writer off from the other streams of literature. One must remember too that after fourteen years and over two hundred books, it is still necessary for the Workshop to insist that English has a creative role to play in Indian literature. If literary chauvinism has any distinguishing capability it is resistance to the facts of literary life.

Nevertheless, poetry is an act of language, of significance found through language, through its particularity and its creative interplay. If an Indian English is to be meaningful it is surely in the accomplishment of poetry that the meaning can be most fully and accurately defined. Here more than anywhere else, we should be able to enter the immediacies of being born under a particular sky or even of being trapped within a specific horizon. It is therefore significant (the fact is simply registered, not criticized) that Indian poets in English show no particular yearning for Indianness, or interest in achieving an idiom which unlike that of their predecessors will be more than scenically Indian, which will be able to penetrate and recover an Indian experience. 'i am not an Indian poet', one writer protests 'but *a poet* writing a universal language of poetry, of feeling, of love, and hate and sex'.[18] Rather more may be said than is intended here by the lower-case ego and its restricted range of concerns. Another voice, that of Kamala Das, can tell us[19]

> The language I speak
> Becomes mine, its distortions its queernesses
> All mine, mine alone. It is half English, half
> Indian funny perhaps but it is honest.

When the choice is between the authentic and the national, between the *Akademi* specification and the personally felt reality, it is obvious what decision must be made. But the more moderate case for nationality in literature is that identity is found, not suppressed, within its boundaries. It is also not clear that sex and hate are the primary ingredients of an international language, and to the extent that they are they seem likely to find expression in forms more decisive than those of poetry.

What remains persuasive is that the concerns of poetry grow out of immediate relationships, those that still lie within the perimeters of honesty. These are the corners left in the West by the inroads of an impersonal technology, the residues of what cannot be charted or polled. The authentic is the little that is kept apart from the standardized enactments of our lives. In India the erosions of technology may be less deadly but the country can offer as a substitute, a comprehensive and Olympian bureaucracy as well as life-rituals within a hierarchic structure which the individual can feel himself doomed to perform. In these circumstances, exhortations to assist in forging a national image or to contribute to a national myth can be rightly distrusted as calling not for honesty but for an aesthetic masquerade. Moreover, the Indian poet in English is a double dissenter, both by virtue of his profession and his language. It is unlikely that his divided and to some degree defiant understanding can be accommodated within cultural communiqués.

It was T. E. Hulme who advised us that beauty was to be found in small dry things. The soft-sell, low-risk poetry into which this principle can be pursued, successfully avoids the verbal tantrum but also bypasses verbal excitement. Such excitement is occasionally approached by Adil Jussawalla but it is not characteristic of Nissim Ezekiel, the leading Indian poet writing in English. 'I ride my elephant of thought / A Cézanne slung around my neck'[20] is probably the maximum of exuberance that Ezekiel allows himself. More characteristic are the later Audenesque effects of 'Enterprise' or the following from 'Marriage':[21]

> I went through this, believing all,
> Our love denied the Primal Fall
> Wordless, we walked among the trees,
> And felt immortal as the breeze.

Ezekiel has maintained these spare, staid rhythms through five volumes, displaying a muted awareness not only of what the sum of things is but of how it is computed. The irony of the last lines is appropriate; but the 'neutral tone' which Donald Davie described (two decades ago) as 'nowadays preferred' invites us to remember and to apply the rest of Davie's celebrated poem on the Thirties. P. Lal has suggested that Ezekiel's work represents 'the bare bones of poetry, life stripped and stripped, till the translucence emerges not through feeling but intellect.'[22] It is a comment which recalls the question in *Ash Wednesday* – 'Shall these bones live?' The answer probably is that they will, but that the estate of poetry cannot flourish on such lean articulations. Translucence, one might add, is not in itself an objective of poetry any more than complexity, or even a condition of the poetry of thought. Such poetry can define itself through intense verbal energy as well as through verbal deprivation. Ezekiel is a more than competent craftsman whose work can be read with appreciation; but it does not grow or gather force as it proceeds. His accomplishment would be more reassuring if there were someone else to stand beside or beyond him.

At one time it seemed likely that Dom Moraes would be the someone else, but after a widely-hailed first volume which won him the Hawthornden Prize, he has put down little to fulfil the promise. Stamina, the cohesive, forward-thrusting sense of something felt and grasped by the mind, that opens out as it moves on, taking over language and shaping it to the mind's signature, is something Yeats taught us to look for and which we can only find rarely. But at a lesser level, the style that is the man that is the poem is something we should see and do not see often enough. Among the newer poets, A. K. Ramanujam, whose first volume *The Striders* won the prize of the Poetry Society, may succeed in developing a recognizable and significant poetic identity.

'The best of Indian English verse' Buddhadeva Bose observes 'belongs to the nineteenth century.'[23] This is a statement surprisingly insensitive to the cosmic declamation and mellifluous sentimentality that has marred so much of the poetry of that period. In moving away from what T. E. Hulme called the spilling over of the infinite, Indian poetry has followed lines which are familiar elsewhere. Thus when we are told that the best of Sri Aurobindo's poetry belongs to the twentieth century (this is a rejoinder to Norman Jeffares' view that Sri Aurobindo is the leading nineteenth-century Commonwealth poet),[24] we think of those drastic changes of style and stance which enabled Yeats to achieve his citizenship of both periods and even to lay down the criteria for membership of the time in which we write. No such transformation occurs in Sri Aurobindo's writing. It may well be that obsolescence is valid as well as dignified, the only means left of reasserting nobility. And it may also be true that ears untuned by *vers libre* are insufficiently sensitive to Sri Aurobindo's prosodic and other innovations, carefully described by V. K. Gokak in an anthology that is alarmingly entitled *The Golden Treasury of Indo-Anglian Poetry*.[25] Lal, who once saw Sri Aurobindo as a purveyor of 'Soul-Stuff', now considers his long poem, 'Savitri', the failure of a Titan.[26] Ezekiel, on the other hand, straightforwardly says that 'anyone who thinks highly of Sri Aurobindo as a poet has no feeling for the English language.'[27] Defenders of Sri Aurobindo are not lacking in numbers or in ardour and his works can sometimes be made a touchstone of taste. A scintillation from the touchstone is quoted without comment.[28]

> Beauty shall walk celestial on the earth,
> Delight shall sleep in the cloud net of her hair
> And in her body as on his homing tree
> Immortal love shall beat his glorious wings.
> A music of griefless things shall weave her charm;
> The harps of the perfect shall attune her voice,
> The streams of Heaven shall murmur in her laugh,
> Her lips shall be the honeycombs of God,
> Her limbs his golden jars of ecstacy,
> Her breasts the rapture flowers of Paradise.

Some remarks on criticism in India are called for, because criticism is part of the tradition of literature and not simply an element of the literary climate. It can be said at once that scholarship is alive among Indians, notwithstanding the great difficulties of access to primary sources. A. N. Kaul's *The American Vision* and his book on comedy, Vaid on Henry James, Shiv Kumar on Bergson and the stream of consciousness in modern writing, Chari on Walt Whitman and Indian philosophy and R. W. Desai's *Yeats's Shakespeare* should be sufficient to bear out this statement. Yet with talent available, the standard of reviewing in the national dailies is best passed over in silence. If we look at periodicals with a specifically cultural orientation, *Quest* and *Thought*, despite their titles, do not convey the sense of an intellectual adventure. The Writers' Workshop preaches to the converted in tones with which the converted are familiar. *The Literary Criterion* flies the Leavis standard but is out of its depth when the master has made no judgment. *The Literary Half-Yearly* tries creditably to be wide-ranging and openminded and to sustain an interest in Commonwealth literature; but some of the established writers whom it prints do not seem to have given it their best work. Much criticism of contemporary Indian writing skill consists of the ill-concealed airing of private feuds. A minority literature, if it is to flourish, must show a greater capacity for agreement within itself. It is not necessary for a writer to prove that he can write by demonstrating that everyone else is incapable of writing. The economics of publishing in India permit the survival of little reviews, unlike the situation in the Western world where rising costs act in destructive unison with a shrinking public for the literature of intelligence. The need is for a review that can speak with conviction and understanding for Indian writing in English as a whole.

If we assess the situation twenty-five years after independence, we find novelists with more than national reputations, poetry that often bears the impress of talent, and, most important of all, a continuing and vigorous interest in the creative possibilities of a language, the obituary of which has repeatedly been written. In an environment less than sympathetic to writing in English, this is an achievement which connotes commitment and vitality. Perhaps writers in the main Indian languages will come to recognize that writers in English are not unequal to them and that their own failure to carry off Nobel prizes is not entirely due to the misdeeds of their translators!

CHAPTER FIVE

IRELAND
A. Norman Jeffares

Anglo-Irish literature is notoriously hard to define. It is the product of the differences between two islands: cultural, political,
racial and religious. It spans them, sometimes seeming entirely the
product of one island, sometimes of the other, in its expression of
thought and feeling. It generally straddles the differences and benefits from the tensions of opposing extremes: at its best, to be considered as literature of the world, as the plays of Sophocles, the
poetry of Virgil, the prose of Cicero, shall we say, are not primarily
thought of in terms of the racial origin of their creators. Anglo-
Irish literature was defined by Daniel Corkery as the literature
written in English by Irishmen, and this provides a good working
definition.[1] So, if we adopt his terms, it begins when Irishmen
wrote English, and would continue to this day. There is, however,
a case for regarding the establishment of the Irish Free State in
1922 as a suitable date for terminating the category, and calling
the writing of Irishmen Irish literature after that (or perhaps the
writing of those *born* after 1922?). But then there arises the com-
plication of Gaelic or Irish literature. Corkery suggested that by
Irish literature we mean the literature written in the Irish or Gaelic
language and that alone. Inevitably this problem of definition exists
and it will be solved in different ways.[2] It often revolves around the
apparently easy question of who is or is not an Irishman; but it is
not always an easy question to answer. Do we, for instance, instinctively think of Steele or of Sterne, both born in Ireland, as Irishmen? The expression or term Anglo-Irish which was used a great
deal in the nineteenth century for historical purposes by Froude
(but notably not by Lecky who was himself an Anglo-Irishman)
is a relatively new one when applied, in Corkery's terms, to litera-

ture. According to Terence de Vere White it has been used thus[3]

> since the establishment of independence in Southern Ireland, where most of these writers came from. Until then the English treated Irish writers as part of their general stock. Since the distinction has been made critics have fancied that this Anglo-Irish writing has a special character of wit and feyness. This is an illusion. Nowadays, instead of blandly accepting the Irish contribution without separate recognition, every effort is made in Britain to identify what is Anglo-Irish. Miss Iris Murdoch, for example, is now so described. Her name is Scots, but she was born and spent some of her childhood in Dublin. The bizarre character of her writing sought definition; and some critics categorised it as Anglo-Irish. Nobody in Ireland has ever written in her manner.

The identity of an Irishman can indeed be a difficult problem.

Swift is an obvious example of the complex nature of an Anglo-Irishman. He was born of English parents in Ireland, had hoped to become a Bishop or at least a Dean in England. He had happened to be 'dropt in Ireland', he commented, and since he did not regard Ireland as his *patria*, his position was hardly that of an expatriate in England; indeed his return to Dublin, even as Dean of St Patrick's, must have seemed depressing after his experience of the power and wealth of England, and the relatively more important position of the Anglican Church there. On his return to Ireland he determined to have nothing to do with Irish politics, but he could not keep out of them once he realized what colonial status meant. After being silent for several years he began to urge self-help on the Irish, while flaying the measures of the English government. His indignation and his biting irony animate his political writings. *The Story of the Injured Lady*, the powerful and effective *Drapier Letters*, the devastating *A Modest Proposal*, the virtually nationalistic *A Proposal for the Universal Use of Irish Manufactures, A Short View of the Present State of Ireland* and his fierce sermon *On the Causes of the Wretched Conditions of Ireland* all argue for independence and self-reliance. Swift's own desire 'to be used like a lord' animated his work and made him demand freedom.

The freedom conceived by the members of the Protestant

ascendancy did not extend beyond their own immediate concerns. Swift, when Dean of St Patrick's, was revered by the weavers in the Dublin slums, but earlier in his career he had suffered humiliations in his first incumbency in the north of Ireland where he was surrounded by Presbyterians (and he had a strong resentment of what his grandfather, the rector of Goodrich in Herefordshire, had suffered at the hands of 'Cromwell's hellish crew' for his loyalty to Charles I). Equally his parishes in the south of Ireland were largely populated by Catholics. Swift apparently attacked the Protestant dissenters with more violence than he did the Catholics (it is often difficult to sift out his personal position because of the irony in his political writings, or of the expediency he employed in argument) who seemed to him to be no longer dangerous.[4] He regarded himself as 'appointed by Providence',[5] to defend his post as a clergyman of the Protestant Church of Ireland. He had an awareness, no doubt, of the existence of the old Gaelic civilization even in its lowly state in the eighteenth century, but his library contained 'hardly ten books of Irish interest'[6] and apparently he did not know more than a few words of Irish.[7] Oral tradition, however, suggests he may have been aware of Irish legends.[8]

Swift's mythology, apart from what he himself created and passed on to us in his major satiric works, especially *Gulliver's Travels*, was classical. In this he was a typical product of the Trinity College of his day and of future years. The question of his identity arises. Was he an Irishman or an Englishman? The answer must be that he was Anglo-Irish: not so much dropped in Ireland as born on the isthmus of a middle state.

Other writers of the eighteenth century (Yeats listed some of them proudly along with Swift – 'Goldsmith and the Dean, Berkeley and Burke') shared this capacity to look both ways. Berkeley thought all that was best in Ireland came from England, yet wanted Ireland to be independent. Burke regarded the Penal Laws which were enacted by the Dublin Parliament after William's victories as designed for the oppression, impoverishment and degradation of a people – but he himself sat in the Westminster rather than the Dublin Parliament and preached conciliation from there.[9] Like Burke, Goldsmith lived in England, yet he looked back on his Irish youth with nostalgia and had a hope of returning to 'die at home at last' as he put it in that classical poem 'The Deserted Village' through whose eighteenth-century couplets his personal emotion beats so insistently.

Goldsmith lived by his pen, and *She Stoops to Conquer* will probably remain his best known and liked work. But he followed a very different set of dramatists. The point about Trinity's classicism is brought out in the work of Congreve, who, although he was born in England, had the same education as Swift – at Kilkenny College, followed by Trinity. Congreve's case may well explain some of the Irish dramatists' successes. He had experienced an Anglo-Irish education when he fled to England at the time James II was in control in Ireland. In London he had subject matter enough in the fine world for *The Way of the World*, that classic play of Restoration comedy. We can only guess how much of Congreve's comedy was delighted observation of fops and beaus and the cynical world of London society. But his somewhat ruthless wit was superseded by the gentler humour of Farquhar, who shifted comedy out of the conventions of Restoration comedy, out of the London world, and instead depicted life in the provinces with *The Beaux' Stratagem* and *The Recruiting Officer*. Goldsmith substituted fun for wit in *She Stoops to Conquer* and Sheridan added polish and sparkle to his view of Bath's social life in *The Rivals* and *The School for Scandal*. Many other Irish dramatists found their audience in London: Charles Macklin, Authur Murphy, Hugh Kelly and Isaac Bickerstaff, to name but a few of these dramatists. Trinity College had provided many of them with an urbane detachment, a Latin capacity for satire.

Where did the Irish element enter obviously into Anglo-Irish writing? In the novel there is an obvious starting point, Maria Edgeworth's *Castle Rackrent* of 1800. This dealt with the 'manners of the Irish squires before the year 1782' and traced, through the account of Thady Quirk, one of the family's retainers, the decline and fall of four generations of the Rackrent family. This novel was the first regional novel written in English, and it stimulated Sir Walter Scott into writing the Waverley novels. Maria Edgeworth followed it with *Ennui*, *The Absentee* and *Ormond*. *The Absentee* showed what happened to Ireland after the Act of Union (1800): a country without a parliament has no capital, and Dublin became dingy and dull. This novel also analysed the evils of absentee landlordism and was the precursor of many nineteenth-century novels on the same theme. It gave a larger vista of Irish life than her earlier concentration on the history of one family. *Ormond* deserves to be better known: it shows us, in Fieldingesque manner, the development of Harry Ormond who, true Anglo-Irishman, is influenced by several styles of living, that of Sir Ulick O'Shane, an Irishman who works for the government, that of King Corny of the Black Isles who lives an Irish-style life and that of the Annalys, who are model English-style landlords.

These novels present a lively view of Ireland, intended to show the English reader something of the different style of living in Ireland. They capture the differences between landlord and tenant, gentry and peasantry; despite Maria Edgeworth's position as the daughter of a 'big house', unusually well aware of socio-economic-political problems because of her father's unusual, liberal character, she was able to capture the nuances and richnesses of the English spoken in Ireland (some of her manuscripts which survive show us her recording examples of this graphic speech)[10] and she was able to convey some of what must have seemed the mercurial temperament of Irish people to English readers.

Sydney Owenson, later to become Lady Morgan, wrote *The Wild Irish Girl* (1806), a sentimental tale of an ancient Irish chieftain and his romantic harpist daughter Glorvina, which showed the decaying ruins of the virtually vanished Gaelic civilization in Connaught. This was Ossianic: it explained the past and offered, somewhat vaguely, hope for the future. Lady Morgan's writing grew out of the interest in history and antiquarianism which developed in the last three decades of the Irish eighteenth century: this arose, no doubt, out of the existence of more settled conditions in the country and echoed English interest in medieval material, ballads, etc. Such books as Joseph Cooper Walker's *Historical Memoirs of the Irish Bards* and Charlotte Brooke's *Reliques of Irish Poetry* bear witness to the re-discovery of Irish customs, language and traditions. The interest became patriotic in Lady Morgan's novels. She followed *The Wild Irish Girl* with *O'Donnel, a national tale, Florence McCarthy,* and *The O'Briens and the O'Flahertys*, the last an admirable interpretation of the complexities of Irish life which faced a young man torn between the attractions of secret revolutionary activity or open parliamentary work for his country.

Irish sensibility and scenery were handled with a certain excitement by the early novelists, who knew they had a new subject to offer especially to their overseas readers. Maturin, for instance, was an impressive innovator in *The Women* as well as the creator of that Gothic novel to end all Gothic novels, *Melmoth the Wanderer*. But the quality of Irish verbal artistry did not fully emerge until poetry carried Gaelic subtleties into the English language. Thomas Moore (1779–1852) brought the plangent note of Irish poetry into London drawing-rooms, but he also gave Ireland a means of expressing nostalgia for a golden past in songs which echoed a little of the intricacy of Irish rhyming. The dangers of lapsing into rhetoric were there: but against them we can set the achievement of his cadences. He was over-fluent, over-facile, often over-sentimental, but his *Irish Melodies* do capture and interpret the spirit of one country in the language of the other. He was influenced at first by the revolutionary mood of Lord Edward Fitzgerald and Thomas Emmet, though, like Maria Edgeworth and Lady Morgan, he came to distrust the new style of Irish politician who emerged in the period of Daniel O'Connell. In fact both Lady Morgan and Moore had idealized the Irish past and found past reality as unpleasant as that of the present: they left politics aside once Catholic emancipation was achieved in 1829.

Moore was soon surpassed by James Clarence Mangan (1803–49), who, often working from prose versions, brought the dragging rhythms of Irish poetry into English, with a superb awareness of the subtleties of assonance and consonance in such poems as 'O'Hussey's Ode to the Maguire' or, especially, 'The Dark Rosaleen'. Morgan's adaptations and translations from other languages had equally haunting power, and many of his pseudonymous or anonymous contributions to journals are only now being identified.

If Catholic emancipation preoccupied much attention in the early part of the nineteenth century, the great water-shed of the century was the disastrous potato famine of 1846, the result of which was a drop in the population of Ireland through death and emigration from approximately eight to five million. We can measure some of its effects if we read the novels dealing with Irish life before the famine. Here William Carleton (1794–1869) emerges as a bilingual observer well qualified to write of the earlier and lively, teeming, unpuritanical population with its often difficult existence, in the period of the penal laws, which 'The Poor Scholar', for instance, portrays well. This was included in the second volume of his *Traits and Stories of the Irish Peasantry* (1833; the first was published in 1830). There was ample material for novelists in this poor, overcrowded, and lawless population. It was a time of faction fighting, a period when emotions were given their head in vigorous language, for despite all the poverty and insecurity, an overwhelming energy surged through Irish life in pre-famine days. Carleton lacked the skill and artistry necessary for pruning his prose (he wrote some potentially fine poems which also could have benefited from cutting), but he does convey a sense of the vitality of the period. As do the Banim brothers and Gerald Griffin, whose novel *The Collegians* has a rugged force and vigour.

Charles Lever has been denigrated by Irish critics for his rollicking, apparently stage-Irish novels of the *Harry Lorrequer* variety. His novels from *Jack Hinton* (1842) – with its Englishman who has to lose his naïve view of Ireland – on through the novels of his middle period, *Tom Burke* (1843), *The O'Donoghue* (1845), *St Patrick's Eve* (1845), *Roland Cashel* (1848) and *Sir Jasper Carew* (1852), provided a much deeper view of Irish society and history. *Tom Burke* is set in the ascendancy period but contains serious thought on Irish political conditions. *The O'Donoghue* seized on land tenure as the crux of the Irish problem, *Roland Cashel* criticized English rule in Ireland – Dublin Castle's officialdom and the society around it – *Con Cregan* showed the vast differences between rich and poor, and *Sir Jasper* demonstrated Lever's awareness of Irish history. *The Martins of Cro-Martin* (1854) explored the need for mutual tolerance and the actuality of selfish self-interest. In this novel Lever seized on the decline of the Anglo-Irish aristocracy and the rise of the new politically conscious Catholic middle-class. Lever's sense that change was coming about was altered to its having happened in *Barrington* (1862), a daringly ironic view of the ascendancy's decay – the house where the great squire had held his revels had now fallen to 'the resort of the traveller by canal-boat, the celtic salesman, or the priest'. *Sir Brooke Fossbrooke* (1865) continues this theme, while *Lord Kilgobbin* (1870) moves into the period of rural and political unrest with a clear but gloomy picture of a potentially explosive situation.

Earlier in the nineteenth century, after Catholic emancipation, literature had become political. Thomas Davis edited the *Nation* (founded in 1830) which was an organ for nationalist propaganda. John Mitchel, a revolutionary of 1848, wrote his *Jail Journal*, an impressive account of his spell in the hulks in the West Indies and in the convict settlement of Tasmania.

After the famine and the revolution of 1848 Sir Samuel Ferguson was the most impressive writer in a period when creativity was at a low ebb. His work has lasting qualities. He lacked sensuousness in his translations of the Irish legends and in his poems, which possessed a masculine strength in their portrayal of the Gaelic mythology and legends. Ferguson certainly knew his material well and his *Lays of the Western Gael* (1865), *Congal* (1872), his epic poem, and the *Lays of the Red Branch* (1897) are true to their sources. Some of his original poems, notably his 'Lament for Thomas Davis', exhibit a striking power and flexibility of language: he had a Hopkins-like capacity for creating new combinations of words, and his technical skill in metrics was excellent. In 1898 Yeats, writing his first critical article, thought Ferguson's 'Conary' the 'best Irish poem', and Ferguson certainly showed writers of the later renaissance the riches of Gaelic legend and its potential as poetic material.

In the lull in politics which occurred after the split in the Irish party caused by Parnell's liaison with Mrs O'Shea and his subsequent death in 1891 Yeats launched the Irish literary renaissance. He was himself a good example of a new kind of Anglo-Irish literary sensibility. He realized Ireland needed a mythology of her own – he had found the English one unattractive as a schoolboy in England – and he realized, once John O'Leary, the old Fenian, had turned his attention to translations of Gaelic literature, that the material was there, needing but to be treated in fresh ways. Dignity had to be sought. To achieve it, the stage Irish element, the role of acting as humorist or butt for an English public, provincialism and the crude patriotic vulgarity of the Young Irelanders, overblown rhetoric and the sentimental melodrama of earlier nineteenth-century Irish writing, all had to be shed. Irish writing in English had not only to learn from and match English writing but to fuse Christian and Irish pagan ideas in a new kind of literature. Yeats's aims developed from his earlier wish to write about Irish places and local folk traditions as he came to realize the extent and attractions of Gaelic mythology. His work took on extra dimensions as his interest in the supernatural was reinforced by his studies in the occult and his increasing interest in symbolism.

He wrote criticism in which he ceaselessly poured out his ideas, his concern to create and shape a literary movement in Ireland. His earliest prose article on Sir Samuel Ferguson shows his delight in finding the heroic Gaelic subject matter with its 'barbarous truth'.[11] Yeats had also been deeply influenced by Standish James O'Grady's *Bardic History* (1880), though he thought O'Grady's work was not free of the faults that marred the Young Irelanders' writing for him. George Russell (AE), Yeats's friend from their days in the School of Art in Dublin, was also affected by O'Grady's writing which included the evocative stories in his *Bog of Stars* (1893) and the atmospheric historical detail of *The Flight of the Eagle* (1897), a novel of Red Hugh O'Donnell's captivity and escape. Russell wrote that in O'Grady's work 'the submerged river of national culture rose up again, a shining torrent', while Yeats saw in Ferguson the re-discovery of a fountain overgrown with weeds and grass 'so that the very way to it was forgotten of the poets', and proclaimed that the living waters of this fountain were needed to heal the nation. One of the problems facing Yeats in the early stages of forming his literary movement was that he needed allies of a strength and potential equal to his own: he created the audience for them busily in the nineties, founding literary societies in Dublin and London, and writing his own Celtic twilight poetry which, while it emasculated its Gaelic sources, did allow Yeats to impose his own kind of order on his material, to display the techniques he had learned among contemporary English poets, and to show that Ireland's rich mythological heritage could be revived. The work of the earlier nineteenth-century scholars and translators, such men as John O'Donovan (1806–61), and Eugene O'Currie (1794–1862) who worked for George Petrie (1789–1866), was followed by Standish Hayes O'Grady's *Silva Gadelica* (1892), a collection of Irish texts. O'Grady wrote in a vigorous often off-putting English; he was partially responsible for the founding of the Ossianic Society which published many Gaelic texts.

The stage was set for the establishment of the Gaelic League in 1893 and the Irish Texts Society in 1898. The moving spirit behind the Gaelic League was Douglas Hyde, the son of a rector who grew up in an Irish-speaking area, collecting, editing and translating folk tales and then the love songs of Connaught. Hyde was concerned for the future of the Irish language; he wrote plays in Irish himself, and he stimulated others to use the language: his *History of Irish Literature* (1899) did much to show those who knew no Irish themselves the resources of Irish literature, and to provide sources for many of the expressions used in the English spoken by country people. One of the problems of many of those who were helping Yeats to bring the renaissance into being was their ignorance of Irish – Yeats never knew more than a few words himself.

He, however, had other rich resources through which he interpreted the Gaelic stories and legends he found in the translators' often dull prose. These led him into a dreamy verse, his unrequited love for Maud Gonne giving it a defeated air, and he delighted in mystery, combined with an air of *fin de siècle* weariness. Out of this had come the mood of the 'Celtic twilight' which infected many of the younger writers whom Yeats's example was stimulating into creativity. When he persuaded Lady Gregory to join him in his plans for an Irish theatre, and when he suggested to John Millington Synge (1871–1909) in 1896 that he should find his material in the Aran Islands, he had discovered the two allies who were not only to influence the more realistic, tougher treatment he gave to Gaelic mythology and other material in his middle and later periods but were to be most important in the creation of an Irish theatre, as were two other members of the landlord class, Edward Martyn, Lady Gregory's neighbour at Tulira, Co. Galway, and George Moore, of Moore Hall in Co. Mayo. The latter two dropped out of the movement fairly soon, but Lady Gregory and Synge became directors of the Abbey Theatre with Yeats when it was established in 1904. Lady Gregory, the widow of a landlord, an ex-colonial governor, lived at Coole near Gort in Galway: Yeats first met her in 1896 and from then until his marriage in 1917 he spent part of every summer at Coole, where Lady Gregory invited other writers and artists to stay. She had good organizational powers, and she took to literature with great success, writing very successful short comedies for the Abbey such as *Hyacinth Halvey, The Workhouse Ward* and the patriotic *Rising of the Moon*. She learned Irish and collected folk lore, bringing Yeats with her on her visits to cottagers, which had the effect of reviving his youthful interest in country legend and speech; she wrote two excellent books which are versions of the two major Gaelic cycles of legends, *Cuchulain of Muirthemne*, based on the Red Branch Cycle and *Gods and Fighting Men*, based on the Fenian Cycle. These books echoed various Gaelic idioms and terms of English speech employed in Galway in their 'Kiltartan' English, which is rich and graphic.

Synge originally intended to be a musician, to his widowed mother's intense anxiety (his lack of religious belief deeply disturbed her evangelical Protestant conscience), but, when he wanted to write, Yeats's suggestion that he would find his material in the life of the Aran Islands (which Yeats had visited with Arthur Symons in 1896) bore a rich and strange fruit. Synge knew Irish, and out of his stay in Aran came *Riders to the Sea* (1904), his tribute to the bravery and fatalism of the isolated islanders whose simple, heroic and wild lives were dominated by the Atlantic: his delight in their wildness was given its head in *The Playboy of the Western World* (1907), based on an Aran story. His sardonic humour had appeared in his first play *In the Shadow of the Glen* (1903), a play with a Wicklow background. Synge was a melancholy, somewhat withdrawn man, but his engagement to an Abbey actress Maire O'Neill when he was thirty-five and she twenty-one gave rise to some intense and beautiful poems written before he died in 1909.

Sparkle, dash and mischief overflowed in George Moore (1852–1933). He had gone to Paris to be an art student and had turned to literature, regarding himself as 'Zola's ricochet' in England when he wrote his naturalistic novels *A Mummer's Wife* (1885) and *Esther Waters* (1894). It is *Esther Waters* which gets set occasionally on the curriculum of English courses in universities, not the Turgenev-like stories of *The Untilled Field* (1903), genuinely realistic accounts of Irish country life, written by someone who knew about it. Moore's experimental novel *The Lake* (1905) with its beautiful melodic line, and the entrancing malice of his trilogy *Hail and Farewell* (1911–14), his account of life in Dublin during the period of the literary renaissance, are not now read widely. Yet both are literary landmarks. *Hail and Farewell* gives us as much of a picture of the life of Dublin as Joyce's *Dubliners* or his *Ulysses*. Moore left Dublin in 1911 for London, and there, in Ebury Street, he continued to write, experimenting further in the evocative prose of *Heloise and Abelard* (1921) and the simple sentences of his prose epic *The Brook Kerith* (1916), a strange conception – of a Jesus who did not die on the cross but was rescued by Joseph of Arimathaea and lived among the Essenes where Paul discovered him: all of it freshly, simply and warmly told, and less strange since the discovery of the Dead Sea Scrolls.

Yeats was the central figure in the renaissance: this often self-conscious burgeoning of literature was largely his creation. His own verse plays, however, were not popular with the Abbey audiences, and Synge's *Playboy* caused rioting because it presented a picture of Irish life to which Irish nationalists objected strongly. Yeats continued to work as manager despite his dislike of the plays which did appeal: the realistic 'cottage comedies'. As he changed his style at the turn of the century and moved towards a tougher disillusioned poetry, dropping the belief that poetry should only concentrate on the beautiful – so clearly exemplified in his *The Wanderings of Oisin* (1889) and in his increasingly difficult 'rose' symbolism of the 1890s, where he was blending Gaelic mythology with some occult ideas and writing sad, defeated, weary adjectival poetry – he began to dislike those who had taken up his early 'Celtic twilight' style, largely the poets who were encouraged by his friend (AE) George Russell.

The variety of Irish literary talent in the early part of the century was impressive. In Dublin there was a tradition of wit and good conversation. Mahaffy, the famous classical scholar at Trinity College, had allegedly advised his pupil Oscar Wilde to go to Oxford with the words 'You're not clever enough for us here in Dublin, Oscar' and Wilde had left, to take his place in the procession of Irish dramatists who found their audience in England and made London their own stage. George Bernard Shaw (1856–1950) left Dublin too, and explained later why Dublin was not for him: every Irishman who felt that his business in life was on the higher planes of the cultural professions felt also that he must have a metropolitan domicile and an international culture; that is, he felt that his first business was to get out of Ireland. Shaw knew his Ireland, and *John Bull's Other Island* (1904) is not only a wise series of observations on national character but a brilliant linguistic *tour de force* in its use of Anglo-Irish idiom. Dublin, however, was not a city in which to make a reputation. The competition was strong, the openings few. 'Great hatred, little room' wrote Yeats in words that might be applied to some of Dublin's more savage repartee. And the literary movement has been defined as a number of writers living in one town and cordially disliking each other.

Yet Dublin was to provide the material for yet another exile, James Joyce (1882–1941). Joyce left Dublin in 1904, living in Trieste, Rome and Zurich before settling in Paris in 1920. His poems *Chamber Music* appeared in 1907, but the short stories of *Dubliners*, though written by about 1905, were not published until 1914, on the grounds that they were too sordid, too realistic in their portrayal of low life. In these stories Joyce portrayed the city he knew in all its stasis, futility and hopelessness, as well as indicating his view of the artist's need for detachment. *A Portrait of the Artist as a Young Man* (1917) carried this picture of the artist further in its basically autobiographical account of Joyce reaching for his own style, creating his own aesthetic attitudes to life to replace the Catholicism he rejected as a student. The interior monologue appeared in all its force in *Ulysses* (1922) and in it Joyce recreated one day in Dublin, displaying his genius for parody, for punning, for portmanteau language in the style of Lewis Carroll, and for the artistic association of ideas in a large structure modelled on the episodes of the *Odyssey*, its irony deriving from the modern characters Joyce set to play the original roles of Telemachus, Odysseus and Penelope. This is the Dublin of pubs and politics, of medical students' parties, of the busy Edwardian streets with their trams and cabs. *Finnegans Wake* (1939) is very different with its dream sequence, its parable history of the universe, its cyclic nature, its dependence upon concentrated linguistic punning, its serio-comic associations, its composite characters, its continuous river-like flow between domestic and cosmic.

Joyce's Dublin differed from George Moore's: one saw the city through the eyes of an ambitious, penniless, proud student, the other from a position of success; Joyce's family was on the way down, Moore was a landlord. Both men came from Catholic families and found their church oppressive; they moved away from it; they moved through realism to more fluid prose, the change from *The Untilled Field* to *The Lake* perfecting Moore's melodic line; the change from the facts of *Stephen Hero* to the aesthetic thought of *A Portrait of the Artist as a Young Man* giving Joyce's imagination its freedom. Each author improved his style, Moore's early stage-Irish dialogue of *A Drama in Muslin*, his account of the Land Wars, gradually becoming convincing in *The Untilled Field*, just as Joyce moved from the occasionally hieratic prose of *Dubliners* to a flexible, convincing speech which could operate on several levels in *A Portrait of the Artist as a Young Man*. Both moved to their own view of this particular city, and after to their own particular kind of imaginative creation, in *The Brook Kerith* and *Finnegans Wake*.

Moore's *A Drama in Muslin* (1896) had mingled the unease of the Irish countryside with the tinsel and glitter of Dublin Castle society, the 'marriage market' of young girls in the social season. A finer study of social manners attaining tragic stature was *The Real Charlotte* (1898) written by Edith Somerville (1858–1949) and 'Martin Ross' (1862–1915; she was Violet Martin in real life), two cousins coming from big houses in Cork and Galway. They are rightly known for their easy humour and dashing narrative in *Some Experiences of an R.M.* (1899), but *The Real Charlotte* with its grim portrayal of Charlotte Mullins full of scheming ambition, her silly suburban niece, and, between them, Roddy Lambert, moving in a world of delicate social relationships, is a novel which portrays its Ireland faithfully and powerfully. *The Big House at Inver* (1925) carries on Maria Edgeworth's awareness that the degradation of a family can make a superb subject. Martin Ross envisaged the book in 1912 after visiting an old derelict family house[12]

> perfectly empty ... on a long promontory by the sea, and there rioted three or four generations of X's, living with the countrywomen, occasionally marrying them, all illegitimate four times over. ... About one hundred and fifty years ago, a very grand Lady ... married the head of the family and lived there, and was so corroded with pride that she would not allow her two daughters to associate with the neighbours of their own class. She lived to see them marry two of the men in the yard.

Flann O'Brien (1912–66; his real name was Briain O'Nualain) followed Joyce's example in his prodigious learning, capacity for parody, and sense of humour. He was a considerable scholar in Gaelic and drew upon techniques of Gaelic poetry – notably in his exaggeration, overstatement and his listing attributes of his characters. His sense of humour burst out in *At Swim Two Birds* (1939) and was followed up in a daily column in the *Irish Times* which he wrote under the pseudonym 'Myles na gCopaleen'. Later novels, *The Dalkey Archive* (1965) and *The Third Policeman* (1967), carried his inventive exuberance further. The Dublin of Flann O'Brien has some affinity with that of Joyce in its impecunious student drinking, its public-house nuances; but times had changed, and the kind of Dubliner whom both George Moore and Joyce knew is best recognized in the personality of Oliver St John Gogarty (1878–1957), surgeon, wit, poet and playwright, friend of AE, of Moore, of Yeats and, for a short time, of Joyce, who wrote of him as Buck Mulligan in *Ulysses*. Gogarty's lyrics are very impressive minor poetry, and his exuberance appeared in *As I Was Going Down Sackville Street* (1937) the title of which autobiographical extravaganza was taken from the opening line of a ballad Joyce had picked up in a bawdy house. Gogarty's wit echoed that of Mahaffy ('an Irish bull, Madam, is a male animal which is always pregnant') and his part in the literary life of the city is typical of a delight in words which was the oral Gaelic civilization's gift to Irishmen writing and, of course, talking in English.

There were other echoes in two writers born in 1896. Austin Clarke, now the doyen of Irish poets, whose *Collected Poems* were published in 1936, has incorporated in his verse plays and his satiric poems the subtleties of Gaelic metrics. He began writing on subjects of Gaelic mythology: his latest work, notably in *Mnemosyne Lay in Dust* (1966), *Old Fashioned Pilgrimage* (1967) and *The Echo at Coole* (1968), has an intensity and superb control. F. R. Higgins (1896–1941), another director of the Abbey Theatre, brought ballad techniques into his lyrics and owed some of his vigorous masculinity to the pagan power of Gaelic poetry.

The flagging fortunes of the Abbey Theatre were revived in the 1920s by Sean O'Casey's plays, *The Shadow of a Gunman* (1923), *Juno and the Paycock* (1924) and *The Plough and the Stars* (1926). The directors decided not to produce his play *The Silver Tassie* which he submitted to them in 1928: this was one of the factors which led to O'Casey's decision to live in England where he wrote many other plays, among them *Red Roses for Me* (1946). But though he experimented in new forms of more poetical drama he never matched the dramatic effectiveness of his early plays, which were largely about the contrast between dream and reality, which demonstrated the effect of revolution and war on women. His tragi-comedies universalize the experiences of Dublin slum-dwellers while capturing their lively language. O'Casey's (1884–1964) later work is best seen in his series of autobiographical volumes, *Knock at my Door* (1939), *Pictures in the Hallway* (1942)

and *Drums under the Window* (1945), which have a Joycean freedom
about their use of English: they are colourful, vivid, and evocative.

One of the most curious things in the history of Irish drama is
the neglect of George Fitzmaurice (1877–1963). *The Country
Dressmaker* (1907) was his only successful play, yet his *Five Plays*
(1913) contained *The Dandy Dolls* and *The Moonlighter*, both
possessing dramatic force and imagination. Eight of Fitzmaurice's
plays were published in the *Dublin Magazine* between 1924 and
1957, including *The Enchanted Land*, an excellent satire on Celtic
romance. Fitzmaurice had a genius for fantasy and farce, an
awareness of the irony of life; but he was ignored by the Abbey
Theatre – though Austin Clarke and Liam Miller have produced
one-act plays of his.

Brendan Behan (1923–64), whose brief legendary life resembled
that of Dylan Thomas, wrote *The Quare Fellow* (1954) in Irish in
its first one-act version, then re-wrote it in English in a three-act
version. Behan's comic gifts resemble Shaw's in his ability to
invert the audience's attitudes; his capacity to blend comedy and
tragedy is reminiscent of O'Casey's writings. *The Hostage* (1959)
shared the language Behan put into *The Quare Fellow*: lively,
idiosyncratic, and funny. His ability to write as well as live farcic-
ally is shown in *Brendan Behan's Island* (1962) and *Hold your
Hour and have Another* (1963).

Liam O'Flaherty (b. 1897) drew on the life of the Aran Islands,
where he was born, for some of the material of his stories and novels,
later moving to the slums for *The Informer* (1925). His *Mr Gilhooley*
(1926) is a powerful novel filled with the strength he could combine
with tension, especially in his stories, the best collections of which
are probably *Spring Sowing* (1924) and *Two Lovely Beasts* (1948).
O'Flaherty's strength derived from his desire to show the facts of
Irish life in all honesty. Brinsley McNamara had done this in 1918
with his first novel *The Valley of the Squinting Windows*. This
caused a controversy which matched the reaction to *The Playboy
of the Western World* in bitterness. The creation of censorship in
the Irish Free State in 1927 caused many problems for writers
since most of the distinguished Irish writers were banned. The
nadir of intellectual nullity was reached, according to Frank
O'Connor, in 1943, when the banning of *The Tailor and Ansty*
(1942), a collection of folk tales and country anecdotes, was questioned in the Senate in a debate that lasted four days and was like

'a long slow swim through a sewage bed' because of the pre-
posterous nature of the arguments used against the book.[13] O'Connor was one of the wave of writers who owed much to the teaching
of Daniel Corkery (1878–1964), whose work included a novel,
The Threshold of Quiet (1917) and various plays and short stories,
as well as *The Hidden Ireland* (1925), an account of the Irish
eighteenth century, and *Synge and Anglo-Irish Literature* (1931).
Corkery was Professor at University College, Cork, and he had a
particular influence on Sean O'Faolain (b. 1900), a short-story-
writer of distinction, whose work is best read in *The Stories of
Sean O'Faolain* (1958). His novel *Bird Alone* (1936) is written with
the craftsman-like skill which marks all his work. Frank O'Connor
(1903–66), largely through Corkery's advice, concentrated on writing about his own background and experience. Out of this came his
first macabre story, 'Guests of the Nation', an account of the
murder of two hostages. He continued to write stories, collected
in many volumes: they are to be equated with the best of de Mau-
passant in their artistry. O'Connor (his real name was Michael
O'Donovan) wrote novels, plays (he was a director of the Abbey
Theatre from 1936 to 1939), essays and superb translations of
Gaelic poetry, notably of Brian Merriman's *The Midnight Court*
(his *Kings, Lords and Commons* contains some of his characteristically simple yet effective translations of early Irish poetry). He also
wrote excellent, stimulating criticism.

Samuel Beckett's (b. 1906) novels *Murphy* (1938), *Watt* (1953),
Molloy (1951, 1958) and *Malone Dies* (1958) establish his reputation among discerning critics. His plays, however, have marked
him as one of the most effective and in many ways influential
playwriters of an age. *Waiting for Godot* (1952), *Endgame* (1957)
and *Krapp's Last Tape* (1958) all share an apparently bleak attitude
to life: in part this is a form of comedy but a basic pessimism
allows Beckett to strip illusions – and dialogue – to a bare mini-
mum. And so his plays deal with distress; but ultimately they
reflect his humanity and compassion, as well as his ironic Dublin
style of mocking humour.

What are the main elements, then, to be discerned in Irish
writing in English? Generalizations on such themes are dangerous,
but it is perhaps worth regarding Irish humour as comprehending
many of the most easily distinguished characteristics. This humour
goes back to the Gaelic. Vivian Mercier in his admirable and

discerning study *The Irish Comic Tradition* (1962) separates off the stage Irish qualities (drunkenness, pugnacity, hyperbole, malapropisms, boasting and exaggeration) because he regards them as a naïve view of Gaelic culture, adopted by writers who did not understand it, observing from the outside and from a different cultural outlook. What is left? His answer is a capacity for fantasy, the grotesque and the macabre. These lead to an intense interest in word play and wit, to parody and, of course, to satire, where powerful feelings overflow into a brimming reservoir of words. Even writers like Yeats, generally regarded as solemn and serious, allow sardonic humour to escape upon occasion. This occurred mainly in their conversation, but often in letters, and, in Yeats's case, in the strange and fantastic comedy of *The Player Queen*. Scholars can ignore Joyce's vast Rabelaisian humours only at the cost of their own credibility. The humour is often a basic element in Irish writing.

The exuberance of those medieval monks – who not only illuminated the vellum pages of their copies of the gospels with exquisite calligraphy but filled the spaces between, within and around the letters with a delicious mixture of designs and drawings – notably of strange beasts – has continually found echoes in the vitality and energetic inventiveness of the Irish writer.

CHAPTER SIX

KENYA
Douglas Killam

At the time of the Conference of African Writers of English Expression which was held in Makerere, Kampala, Uganda, in 1962, Bernard Fonlon, in an article summarizing that conference, noted that '[creative] literature is still in its early stages in East Africa'.[1] Of the fifteen African writers who contributed to the conference nine were West African. (Prominent among these were Chinua Achebe, J. P. Clark, Christopher Okigbo, Gabriel Okara and Wole Soyinka, whose literary reputations were already more or less established among those who knew and cared about modern African writing.) Only three East African writers attended – Grace Ogot, John Nagenda and Rebecca Njau. Two years later, in his essay on literary barrenness in East Africa, Taban Lo Liyong is able to add only one other name to Fonlon's list, that of James Ngugi who had attended the Makerere Conference as an excited and somewhat awestruck observer, who had since published *Weep Not Child* and *The River Between*, and has since come to be regarded as the major East African writer in English.

I want to go on a bit further with Taban's 1965 essay (which was republished in *The Last Word* in 1969) because its content – the account it offers of 'the reason for this barrenness' and the answers it suggests to two important questions 'why do we need writers' and 'what could be done to spark interest in literary production' – is relevant today and the debate it initiated not only proceeds but continues to be elaborated.

Why this barrenness, this dearth of imaginative writings? 'I blame the British', says Taban:

> the education they came to offer was aimed at recruiting candidates for a Christian Heaven and eliminating others for

a Christian Hell; they sought to teach clerks, teachers, servants and administrators. Culturally, they stood aloof ... The two cultures were kept apart. ... Because the British are a practical-minded people, we became practical-minded too. ... Poetry writing and the art of fiction were not taught us though we debated and reasoned. This led directly to early writings which were of a quarrelsome nature; political grievances (about land, mostly) and answering back the white racist charges through pamphlets, and biographies and anthropological works.

He goes on to list titles by Kenyan and Ugandan writers to support his statements. The list is impressive and includes works by Kenyatta, Koinange, Kariuki, Mboya, Gatheru, Ngugi and Grace Ogot from Kenya and Sir Apolo Kogwa, Ham Mukasa, Nyabonga, Kalibala and David Rubadiri. Of these, only Ngugi, Grace Ogot and Rubadiri produced works which are strictly imaginative:[2]

This short survey shows that after reading the fables, biographies, and political works, we do not have much else to read for relaxation and enjoyment. Our intellectual leadership has been left to the politicians.

The product of British intervention, then, so far as the writer is concerned, is the alienation of the East African from his culture. It is for writers to achieve a new balance.[3]

Our political leaders have done their best to liberate us. We now need writers to liberate us culturally and through ideas. They will be the ones to revive, maintain and found our cultures for us. The clashes between Western, African and Asian cultures which are taking place in East Africa are some of the finest subjects for writing. They are as suitable for the fictional writer as for the social scientist.

Since 1966 the literary landscape of East Africa has changed quite decisively. Ngugi has published *A Grain of Wheat* which establishes him as a major fiction writer and Okot p'Bitek published *Song of Lawino* in 1966 which inspired a number of imitations and critical debate on the uses and purposes of literature, Whereas Taban could list three or four promising writers and a

handful of titles of imaginative works in 1965, Hans Zell and
Helene Silver, in *A Reader's Guide to African Literature*, are able
to list thirty-four authors and forty-four published volumes in
1972. Of these, twenty writers (and twenty-three books) come
from Kenya, eleven authors (and eighteen books) from Uganda
and three authors (with one book each) from Tanzania. And this
list is incomplete: to it must be added the abundant miscellaneous
publication of stories, poems and plays (and segments of plays and
novels) in university publications – *Darlite* (now called *Uuma*),
Penpoint, Busara and *Ghala*; in *East African Journal*, the old and
new series of *Transition*. Moreover, the announcements of East
Africa Publishing House and the various literature bureaux offer
impressive lists of works scheduled for publication.

Many of the themes of Kenyan literature are part and parcel of
African writing in general and are familiar to its readers – such
themes as the political, social, cultural and economic impact of
the West on Africa through the agency of colonialism. A spectrum
of themes appears from the results of cultural conflict. We find the
presentation and dramatization of conflict worked out in terms of
the recognition of the richness of the African past juxtaposed with
the attraction of modernity; the emergence of a westernized élite;
the theme of the 'child of two worlds' and the reaction of parents
to such children; the examination of traditional African customs
and responsibilities, and the position of the individual in the traditional context – his duties and responsibilities to the family, the
clan and the tribe, and the measure of personal autonomy he can
achieve within this context. These themes are consolidated in
Okot's *Song of Lawino*[4] (and in the rejoinder to Lawino found in
Song of Ocol[5]) and in the works, cast in the same poetic/lyric form,
of Joseph Buruga (*The Abandoned Hut*[6]) and Okello Oculi
(*Orphan*[7]) who says in defence of his emulation of Okot:[8]

> *Song of Lawino* is written to touch the African nerve. There's
> really no other work that has succeeded in touching the
> African nerve as has *Song of Lawino*. A lot of these authors,
> like Joseph Buruga, a botanist here at Makerere who has
> written *The Abandoned Hut*, have been accused of being
> followers of Okot. I don't think this is a bad thing. All that
> Joseph Buruga seems to be saying is that Okot hit exactly
> on the kind of nerve, at the tissue, of the system. I don't

think people should blame him for being what Okot was telling people.

Okot was accused of crying for the simple, routine, boring, unsophisticated, primitive, savage culture of yesterday. If not yesterday, of the village, the life of the people. And Okot was depicted as somebody completely ungrateful to all the civilizing energies – the missionary, the gold mining prospector, the copper mining prospector, the business man and so on and so forth – had put into Okot's environment . . . the accusation was that ultimately what Okot was saying is that the African mind is so simple, so underdeveloped, that . . . all these intrusions into his environment, all this effort . . . were never able to break through into his mind, into his brain, for him to be able to move away from the crying for the simplicity of the village. And they said, 'Well Okot is not writing poetry. It's too simple. Look at the rhythm. It's too simple.' They almost said it was too lyrical but then that would have embarrassed them because in the history of European literature there is a tradition that's lyrical. So they just said it was too simple. So me, I said 'all right'. There may be a point in being a disciple of Okot . . . So that in that sense I think we were responding to various factors. We were responding to intrusions into our environment. We were responding to the needs of our people – their political and social aspirations. We were responding to their cultural outrage.

The theme of the conflict between traditional and modern, between African and European values, and the complexity of motivations economic, political and cultural forming this conflict is worked out in the three novels (cast in a familiar western form) of Ngugi, *The River Between, Weep Not Child* and *A Grain of Wheat*. In Ngugi's novels the theme of the struggle for Kenya's independence receives its fullest treatment. In *Weep Not Child* the emergency period is evoked through the eyes of a schoolboy. *A Grain of Wheat* is set in a present which is the eve of independence in Kenya in 1963 but moves backwards to the emergency period in the mid 1950s. The action is then moved forward through these critical years by recreating the experiences of five or six principal characters and a host of minor ones. Ngugi introduces comment on the racial, moral and social issues which formed

Kenyan life from the time of the coming of the white missionaries (i.e. when political questions were introduced into Kenya) at the period evoked in *The River Between.*

The symbolic structure of *The River Between* and the central place of the ridges and the river are stated in the opening pages of the novel:[9]

> The two ridges lay side by side. One was Kameno, the other was Makuyu. Between them was a valley. It was called the valley of life. Behind Kameno and Makuyu were many more valleys and ridges, lying without any discernible plan. They were like many sleeping lions which never woke. They just slept, the big deep sleep of their Creator.
>
> A river flowed through the valley of life. If there had been no bush and no forest trees covering the slopes, you could have seen the river when you stood on top of either Kameno or Makuyu. Now you had to come down. Even then you could not see the whole extent of the river as it gracefully, and without any apparent haste, wound its way down the valley, like a snake. The river was called Honia, which meant cure, or bring-back-to-life. Honia river never dried: it seemed to possess a strong will to live, scorning droughts and weather changes. And it went on in the same way, never hurrying, never hesitating. People saw this and were happy.
>
> Honia was the soul of Kameno and Makuyu. It joined them. And men, cattle, wild beasts and trees, were all united by this life-stream.
>
> When you stood in the valley, the two ridges ceased to be sleeping lions united by their common source of life. They became antagonists. You could tell this, not by anything tangible but by the way they faced each other, like two rivals ready to come to blows in a life and death struggle for the leadership of this isolated region.

From a distance what the ridges have in common is clear; but for the people of the ridges it is the differences between them which matter. Makuyu is the village of Joshua, the leader of Christian converts, and Kameno is the village of Chege, a descendant of Mugo wa Kibiro (a prophet who foretold the coming of the white man and the building of a railroad, and who was spurned by his people). The river which should unite the villages because it gives life, in fact divides them: the people of Kameno use the waters during the rites of circumcision whilst for the Christians the water is the agent of purification through baptism.

Waiyaki, the hero of *The River Between* (a descendant of Mugo wa Kibiro), sees education as essential to the progress of his people and as the agent for reconciling opposing factions. His love for Nyambura, the daughter of Joshua and an uncircumcised Christian, is a measure of his will towards reconciliation, since he is a 'Teacher', a member of the Kiama, a society dedicated to the preservation of Gikuyu religion. Opposed to Waiyaki is Joshua, whose unflinching devotion to the Christian religion makes it a divisive force. He casts out his daughter Muthoni when she decides, though a Christian, to be circumcised (an act which shows her will to reconciliation). Also opposed to Waiyaki is Kamau, a rival for Nyambura. Ultimately, Kamau betrays Waiyaki to the Kiama, partly out of spite and partly because his father, Kabonyi, has become jealous of Waiyaki's success and influence as a teacher. Waiyaki's own people, whose children have benefited most from his concern for their education, turn on him because they construe his love for Nyambura as a betrayal of their standards. Waiyaki, like many well-intentioned people in such circumstances, is partly responsible for his fate since he makes errors in judgment at critical times. For example, he gets caught up in the fervour of a public meeting and forgets to preach the reconciliation which is his cause. As Eustace Palmer points out he 'neglects the fact that the educational thirst and enthusiasm he himself has stirred up will have to be given expression and fulfilment at a political level'.[10] Waiyaki intended to lead the people in a 'political movement that would shake the whole country, that would tell the white man, "Go!"'[11] But this intention (indicating a structural weakness in the novel) is not made clear until near the end of the book. Ultimately Waiyaki is outmanoeuvred by Kibonyi and Kamau, more militantly anti-European than himself, who discredit him and denounce him as a traitor because of his love for Nyambura. The Kiama at the end destroy Waiyaki and in his martyrdom there is perhaps the suggestion that his pain has not been in vain and that the ridges have achieved some sort of harmony:[12]

The land was now silent. The two ridges lay side by side, hidden in the darkness. And Honia river went on flowing between them, down through the valley of life, its beat rising above the dark stillness, reaching into the heart of the people of Makuyu and Kameno.

The novel reveals several themes which preoccupy Ngugi and which, despite the diversity of his subject matter, he elaborates in all his fiction, and these are: tribalism as a divisive force in Kenyan societies, the role of Europeans in Kenya and their contribution to social, cultural and political disintegration, the religious significance of the land, the role of education, the necessity of tempering one's hopes and shaping conduct by living vividly in the present.

Weep Not Child reveals these themes although it belongs in subject matter to the period shortly after the Second World War when nationalist sentiments came to the boiling point in Kenya. The events these sentiments provoked, culminating in the Mau Mau emergency, are seen as they influence the lives of three families, Ngotho's, Jacobo's and Howlands's, particularly the first of these since the action and events of the novel are seen mostly through the eyes of Njoroge, Ngotho's youngest son. The three families have much in common and can therefore be taken as typical of the Kenyan scene at the time. Both Ngotho and How-lands (for whom Ngotho works) love the land and feel that it is theirs by right; each interprets the right differently and fails to understand the sentiments of the other. This failure to understand each other on the question of the land when transmuted to the national level accounts for the emergency. Further similarities are revealed by the fact that both Howlands and Ngotho have lost sons in the Second World War and each has a son in the same school. Howlands's daughter is a mission teacher as is Jacobo's eldest daughter, and another, Mwihaki – with whom Njoroge falls in love – is also at school. Ngotho eventually dies because he has been tortured by Howlands; Jacobo and Howlands are both killed by Ngotho's son, Boro (who is in turn killed). It is left to the youngest children of these three – Njoroge, Mwihaki and Stephen – to build a united Kenya.

Weep Not Child is not an allegory – the situations and characters are much too concretely presented to allow this claim. Nevertheless, there is a symbolic quality and the characters and situations, though unmistakably real, can be seen as representing something more. The small village of Ngotho is a microcosm of Kenya at the time of the emergency, and the principal characters – Ngotho, Howlands, Jacobo, Boro and Njoroge – represent the various points of view which obtain within it. Certain scenes, as well, can have a symbolic reference, the most notable of which is when the white man Howlands threatens to castrate Njoroge, an action suggestive of the desire of the European to deprive the African of his rights and his manhood.

A love for and faith in education, bound together with a passionate religious feeling – in Ngotho, revealed in his love for the land and in Njoroge in a love of God – is as central a concern in this novel as it is in *The River Between*. *Weep Not Child* begins with Njoroge's mother asking him 'would you like to go to school?' and the boy gasping because he 'half-feared that [she] might withdraw her words'.[13]

> Njoroge always thought that schooling was the very best that a boy could have. It was the end of all living. And he wanted everyone to go to school. . . .
>
> 'Education is everything,' Ngotho said. Yet he doubted this because he knew deep inside his heart that land was everything. Education was good only because it would lead to the recovery of lost lands.

As Ngugi comments, Njoroge's belief in education is symptomatic of a general belief among the Gikuyu:[14]

> Somehow the Gikuyu people always saw their deliverance as embodied in education. When the time for Njoroge to leave came near, many people contributed money so that he could go. He was no longer the son of Ngotho, but the son of the land.

Njoroge and Ngotho are disillusioned at the novel's end. Education does not (yet) lead to the recovery of the land. The impotence of Njoroge's belief is systematically revealed as the emergency develops – by the death of his teacher (who had education and a strong faith in God), by the failure of his headmaster to protect him, a mere boy, from the torture of Howlands, by the death of his father and brother. His optimism at the beginning of the novel is replaced at its end by shame and despair (symbolized by his attempt at suicide) which proceeds from his recognition that the hopes of his people will not be fulfilled through education.

Ngugi's consideration of the independence movement is in a sense suspended at the close of *Weep Not Child*. The novel ends with the despair of Njoroge, but with the emergency still in progress. *A Grain of Wheat* takes up the subject again and through the use of a complicated system of flashback scenes alternating with events in present time – which take place on the four days leading up to Independence Day celebrations in Kenya – moves the action of the novel forward until the flashback scenes and present time merge. In this novel, Ngugi introduces a larger number of characters than in the other novels and explores their motivations, experiences and sensibilities at much greater depth. Point of view shifts persistently in *A Grain of Wheat* so that Ngugi is able to present and explore the complicated pattern of guilt and responsibility which obtains among the principal characters in order to reveal that there is more than one side to any question. The novel's success rests in large part on Ngugi's ability to convince his reader that all of his various witnesses are trustworthy.

A Grain of Wheat, in the working out of its themes, displays a major irony supported by a series of minor ones. Before the emergency period Mugo, Karanja, Gikonyo, Mumbi and Kihika had imagined and discussed the means by which Kenya might achieve her independence and what benefits this achievement would yield. As they prepare for the Uhuru Day celebrations we learn how far their lives have diverged as a result of the ways in which they have pursued the dream. Kihika became a great forest freedom fighter and achieved martyrdom by being betrayed to the British. Karanja, believing in the invincibility of the British, becomes their servant against his own people. Gikonyo, placed in a detention camp because of his activities with the freedom fighters but unable to bear separation from Mumbi, his wife, forsakes his oath so that he may return to her. When he does he finds she has had a child by Karanja and in his bitterness repudiates her love. Mugo, the greatest friend of Kihika, who sought to be and is regarded as the leader of his village, is asked to lead the Uhuru Day celebrations only to reveal that it is he who has betrayed Kihika. All these characters have been tested and found wanting; all must live with the remorse of their knowledge and recognition. The ironies of the lives of the various characters – the differences between their hopes and their ability to realize them, between their public appearances and their private knowledge of themselves – reveal the major irony of the novel, that the country has its independence but that the cost of achieving it has been terrifying in terms of the suffering it has occasioned. A note of hope is sounded at the close: Mugo's confession gives him the peace he has sought to find for ten long years and allows Gikonyo to come to terms with himself and gain some understanding of what Mumbi suffered when he was in detention. The novel ends with Gikonyo carving a wedding gift for Mumbi – 'I shall carve a woman – big with child.' Nevertheless, the road to Uhuru has not been travelled its full length: as Gikonyo learns through his dealings with a cabinet minister, incipient political betrayal is already apparent in the country.

All of Ngugi's novels are about disillusionment, of a people and of individuals who are typical. All of his major characters have their expectations thwarted because they are caught up in situations where self-deception and betrayal become paralysing.

The struggle for independence and the effect of the emergency on the sensibilities of young (at the time) Kenyans is also the subject of most of the short stories in *Potent Ash*[15] by Leonard Kibera and Samuel Kahiga, in two novels, *Ordeal in the Forest*[16] by Godwin Wachira and *Daughter of Mumbi*[17] by Charity Waciuma. These themes are also prominent in Leonard Kibera's experimental novel, *Voices in the Dark*,[18] of which R. C. Ntiru writes:[19]

> Leonard Kibera, in his magnificent and incisive novel *Voices in the Dark* . . . [presents] us with former freedom fighters in the Mau Mau nationalist movement whose mobility is now dependent on the crutch if the Government hospitals can deign to allow them that indulgence. Yet these are the same personalities, as in Soyinka's *A Dance of the Forests*, whose names are invoked at independence celebrations, at high state parties and such august national occasions. Yet those who drink to their (ill) health at cocktail parties are not prepared to dole them a ten-cent coin when they meet them on the streets!

This novel in content and tone, though not in treatment, resembles Ngugi's third book in many ways. It extends, however, well beyond the independence period, and in its treatment of the dislocated and disillusioned men of the modern city represents both a departure in subject material and a breakthrough in East African writing in the implied judgments about the quality of Kenyan life it offers.

Mrs Ogot's writing deals mostly with aspects of traditional African society. Her novel *The Promised Land*[20] (the title is ironic!) tells the story of the Western Kenyan Luo pioneer family which seeks a more satisfactory life in Tanzania where conditions are better. The family is defeated when a curse is placed upon the hero of the novel, Nyapol, by an envious and vindictive neighbour. The novel is subtitled *A True Fantasy* not so much because the events of the novel are offered as historically accurate, but because the fantastic physical manifestations which result from the curse placed on Nyapol (his flesh breaks out in festering, painful, thorn-like growths which drive him mad) are meant to show the force, the truth of the belief in indigenous religion. The novel fails to convince because there is too sharp a break between its two halves. The realistic and matter-of-fact evocation of domestic conditions of the first part gives way to passages describing Nyapol's hallucinations in his pain. There is as well a rather contrived eighth chapter interpolated into the text to show the utter inability of Western medicine (as practised in a mission hospital) in coping with African medicine used by a pagan practitioner for nefarious purposes. The reader's credibility is too much strained. Nevertheless, the novel occasioned one enthusiastic review (which claims too much for it), part of which is worth reproducing here:[21]

> [Grace Ogot's] novel emphasizes again the universal nature of human experience while being in every sense unmistakably African in approach and spirit . . . It is an African *Book of Job*, which I am sure the author intended it to be. More important still, it is a powerful indictment against materialism and a too rapid shedding of traditional values. . . . The author's use of myth, the most effective way of conveying truth – as the Bible, Plato and countless writers have shown – has been done in such a manner as to free her of any reckless charge of contriving or manipulating the story.

The stories in her *Land Without Thunder*,[22] which offer themes dealing with traditional village occasions, events in mission hospitals in colonial days, the tragedy of young girls in contemporary Nairobi, and the problems of sophisticated Africans at an Egyptian airport, have an authenticity which is quite convincing and reveal a fine command and inventive use of the short story form.

So far as drama is concerned there has been relatively little produced in published form in Kenya. Taban urged in 1965 that drama festivals should be held in secondary schools throughout East Africa, that these should comprise a play from outside Africa, a second from a part of Africa other than East Africa and a third written and produced by the local school where the festival is held, and that prizes be offered to local plays according to their originality of composition or production. This would foster playwriting, he argues, and this is important because plays command a larger potential audience than novels, poems and essays. Nevertheless, all that is available in published form to date appears to be Ngugi's *The Black Hermit* and *Three Plays*,[23] James Gatanyu's *The Battlefield*[24] and Robert Serumaga's *A Play*.[25]

Very few volumes of poetry, either that of a single author or those of poets in anthology, have been published in East Africa, although there is a persistent publication of individual poems in university magazines (*Uuma, Penpoint, Ghala*) and in such as *East Africa Journal, Transition, Nexus*, etc. Of single volumes John S. Mbiti's *Poems of Nature and Faith* (1969)[26] and R. C. Ntiru's *Tensions* (1971)[27] are the most impressive because of the seriousness of the concern they reveal about the shifting values and quality in East African society. The most impressive anthology is *Drum Beat*, edited by Lennard Okola, published in 1967 and offering sixty-two poems by twenty-one poets, who come from all parts of East Africa, with the exception of four who are expatriates. Okola's introduction is interesting for the comment it makes on the status of English as a language of international literary exchange, for the comparisons it offers between East and West African literature, and particularly for the comment it offers (which in another place might well bear sustained scrutiny) on the way in which East African literature, though later in its development than that of West Africa, has been the beneficiary of the latter in an important way. Okola makes the point that West African poetry and fiction have dealt largely with 'two aspects of one major theme: the impact of colonialism and the clash between the old and the new'. Preoccupation with these themes was understandable and necessary. West African writers did 'a splendid job in reasserting the real "majesty of Africa" and protesting against colonialism'. In contrast with West African literature, Okola claims, East African writing has not been concerned with 'negritude enthusiasm'. West African writers have explained away the colonial situation:[28]

> It may also be that the protest will come later [in East African writing] when the dust of some of the protest-worthy events has settled down and things have quietened down well enough for more 'objective' protest. This is unlikely, since it is more usual to protest in the heat of the moment, and 'emotions recollected in tranquillity' have rarely produced what can be termed protest literature.

Okola is, I think, quite right in suggesting that protest against external forces – specifically the colonial situation – is very much a thing of the past and not any longer a feature of East African writing. But there is little 'tranquillity' in this scene. The question of 'what is African literature', such a prominent debate in the early and mid-1960s, has been largely settled by the fact of there being a great deal of African literature. The questions now are 'what purposes should this literature serve?' and 'by what criteria shall we judge it?' The first steps towards supplying an answer to these questions were taken by Ngugi and his colleagues when they initiated the debate over the literature syllabus at the University of Nairobi. The formulation of the terms of the debate and of the component parts of a new syllabus presupposes the purposes which the study and practice of literature will serve and, less directly and over a longer period of time, probably, the criteria which will evolve for judging the worth of that literature. Ngugi, Taban and Owuor-Anyumba took the debate out of the abstract in demanding that the literature syllabus be made relevant to local needs and aspirations.

For Ngugi, the study of literature is broadly interpreted in educational and social terms as assisting the creation of general literacy in the country – it also assists, might even be in the vanguard of creating[29]

> . . . a revolutionary culture which is not narrowly confined by the limitations of tribal traditions or national boundaries but is outward looking to Pan-Africa and the Third World and the needs of man. The national, the Pan-African, and the Third World awareness must be transformed into a socialist programme, or be doomed to sterility and death. . . .

> Any true national culture . . . that nurtures a society based on co-operation and not ruthless exploitation, ruthless grab-and-take, a culture that is born of a people's collective labour, such a culture will be best placed to contribute something truly positive and original to the modern world.

Ngugi's conception of the function of literacy is not, I think, typical of criteria generally applied or adopted in Kenya (the editors of the journal in which the article is published note that 'the views expressed are personal and do not necessarily reflect those of the sponsors'); they are very like those which have become almost a national pedagogical policy in Tanzania. The production of literature and its teaching serve, first, local, social and political needs. How far the debate about 'what is African literature' has progressed since 1966! It is seen to exist and can be pressed into service.

The second part of the debate, the question of the criteria or internal norms by which individual and general literary achievement is judged (implying the development of a critical system centred in African writing but as heterogeneous as all such systems) still goes on, and it is worth while considering the arguments and judgments recently published by R. C. Ntiru. A graduate of Makerere, a poet and member of the editorial board of *East Africa Journal*, Ntiru has the advantage of time and the production of a sizeable canon of literary works when he addresses himself to a discussion of 'The notion of modernity in African creative writing'. Thus he is able both to summarize African literature over the past fifteen years, and also to offer certain judgments about the uniqueness of African literature in terms of its relation to the societies which have produced it, and to admit to the danger that in deriving criteria from the local scene one opens that literature to the charge of parochialism. Also important, he is able to comment on (without any hope for the time of resolving) the dichotomy which exists between the notion that literature should perform a 'universalizing' function and the possibility (or impossibility) of it doing so in East Africa. Ntiru concludes his article in this way:[30]

> The burden of this inquiry has been to try and indicate aspects of African writing which evince signs of modernity. The word 'modern' itself, we have admitted, is capable of analytical treachery and indeed some of this inquiry must

exhibit effects of this. Sometimes, and necessarily, the appellation has operated on a partial, local and internal level. For instance, some of the thematic evidence for modernity, like the status of the individual in society, would not be valid if this inquiry was exposed to a 'universal' literary tradition because this is what the development of the European novel was all about in the nineteenth century.

What are the terms of Ntiru's inquiry? His article, once he summarizes the achievement of African literature production over the past fifteen years, becomes a plea for the production of a sustained criticism. There is, he says, a 'glaring lack of critical writing which has traditionally given impetus to creative writers' and he cites Iconoclastes writing in *Ghala* (in July 1971) who puts the case in this way:[31]

> We would like to suggest that the time has now come for the establishment of a local critical tradition, to develop alongside our creative literature. This tradition must be based on the conviction that literature has an important place in our culture, that honest and intelligent criticism of locally produced works is essential, and that the critic's job is not to destroy, or to create reputations out of a vacuum, but rather to collaborate with the creative writer in forming literary sensibility. Ideally, the serious critic should be familiar with the writer's cultural milieu, even if he is not of it, and he should interpret his role very largely in terms of nurturing both the literature he is criticising and the reading public.

Ntiru centres his discussion in his conviction that[32]

> The key-word in the consideration of the modern trends in African writing is disenchantment, or disillusionment. In this respect, there are very few African writers of whom we can say: this one is modern, this one is conventional or unmodern. I have already indicated that more or less the same creative minds still hold sway. Any attempt, therefore, to delineate what is modern in African writing must be prepared to bear in mind certain phases in the development of the same writer. Thus Soyinka, Achebe, Lo Liyong, p'Bitek, and others simultaneously exhibit conventional and modern aspects in their writings. Their modern confluence covers a number of areas.

Soyinka, Taban, Okot, Achebe, Rubadiri, Serumaga and Kibera have all written books which by various ways and treatments, describe or dramatize the hopes experienced by Africans at the time when an independent policy and possibility is achieved and their disillusionment when these hopes are lost. The process by which these writers arrive at their contemporary disenchantment is summarized thus by Ntiru (note how he identifies the writer as the spokesman for the *individual* in African and one may safely specify East African society):[33]

> The progression towards the modern status of the individual can be apprehended in five phases. Before the colonial period, the social order may be unjust, but it is stable and guarantees human dignity as it was understood and defined. With the advent of dominating foreigners, the attitude, 'collaborators' notwithstanding, is to hang together in the face of a common enemy who threatens their common interests, values and rights, including life. At the dawn of independence and the period roughly coeval with the first legally constituted generation of leaders, the feeling is one of the blinding euphoria followed by a desire not to 'wash our dirty linen in public'. All these three phases we have lived through. The contemporary phase is the one I described earlier as the phase of disenchantment as the emissaries to whom we entrusted our fate fail to deliver the goods. The last phase – the phase that signals social cataclysm – is one in which the individual does not see society as any more capable of guaranteeing his basic rights than himself on his own.

Recognition of the developing general social situation has caused writers to react in a variety of ways and produce works of different approaches and tones. Ntiru calls this body of writers anti-nostalgic or anti-romantic. Soyinka and Okot, for example, write books which satirize or bring into contempt 'the automatic and uncritical aping of foreign ways by Africans'. Ntiru lists other writers – Taban, Achebe, Rubadiri – who reject *via* their work what Dr Ras Makonnen has identified in modern African society as 'bourgeois form without bourgeois content'. The confused form of modern African society, the paradoxes it contains, is nowhere better summarized (nor the form more precisely and suitably evoked) than in the passage Ntiru cites from Kibera's *Voices in the Dark*, which can usefully be reproduced here. (He notes the subtle and effective way in which the form of the passage reflects the situation it describes.)[34]

> Little ethnic groups with big minds and big ethnic groups with small minds professing, individually, to hang together for security so that they might not swim separately when the rains at last fell. Little institutions with big clauses and big institutions with little constitutions all of which contributed vigorously to charity. Little groups of white women with uncertain histories who still walked their masculine puppies on Public Streets and gave freely to the poor. Little groups of black toffs who played cricket with white men on Sunday mornings and gave large tips to the attendants. Little groups of everybody who was nobody and big sister groups of nobodies who were everybody's important nobody son all sticking out their necks for promotion and stone houses. . . . Little groups of advisers who sought big advice on how to give little advice that the ultimate advice output, to speak business, was no more or less than the initial input, only contradictory. Big people who fooled everybody. Everybody who hated Catholics. Protestants who contradicted Catholics. Catholics who contradicted both Protestants and Methodists alike but all of whom vigorously misunderstood Moslems. . . . Misdirectors who directed. Directors who did not even misdirect. Everybody who loved everybody and everybody who hated nobody and all the little nobodies who so righteously hated nobody except everybody's dirty fingernails and smell of pepper. Clergymen and other fishermen. Makers of history. Small hats and big hats. Sub-editors who edited and editors who subtracted. Large groups of goldfish in the affluent family pool which refused to bite. . . . Them enemies. Them enemies. Them enemies.
>
> And so it came to pass that from their little wood beyond the little bridge no group was spared.

Ntiru contends that African society has not decayed into the fifth stage described above, and thus the African

> creative model, with respect to the individual, has been different from the European model . . . to the extent that the

African writer still believes in the organic unity of a society of mutual social obligations.

Modern African writing reveals elements of revolt and of surrender where the literature encompasses 'reaction to, or revolt against, stagant or repugnant moral and political miasma', but the recognition of collective obligation is reflected in the writing and offers future hope.

I have cited Ntiru's article at length here because it seems to me to be one of the most impressive commentaries yet to be published both in its summary of the themes and patterns of modern African writing (with the focus mostly on writing from East Africa), and for the judgments it offers on artistic achievement in relation to thematic material.[35]

> ... African writers will do well to re-examine their conception of literature. The poets will need to accept the realistic present in order to outgrow their divided loyalties so they can move from the pastoral, pseudo-epic dramatic monologue. The novelists will need to modify their pastoral vision and redirect their sensibility to accommodate the city which affects the whole of the national life directly or indirectly to a considerable degree. The short story writers will need to move from sketches of bad picaresque novels in order to master the art of the significant emotional moment. And the dramatists – in many ways the most effective of writers with the greatest potential audience – will need to modify many of the traditional myths and legends that form the sounding board of their plays to give dramatic expression.

The subject of this chapter is Kenyan literature as one of ten English literatures, and, as is obvious from what has been put down here, there is a difficulty in distinguishing distinctly Kenyan literature within the broader context of East African writing, unless we construe Kenyan literature more narrowly than the situation really admits. The body of literature which emanates from East Africa is referred to by its practitioners as East African literature and this means literature produced by citizens of Uganda and Kenya with a few examples from Tanzania. Moreover and more importantly, this is a body of writers which is concerned with East African sensibility. Some of the historical reasons for this way of regarding things are – the fact that from colonial times the three countries were called, and treated as, East Africa; the fact that there has been a close correlation between literary training and production and the universities and that this referred (until very recently) to Makerere University College; the fact that because writers of each of these countries move freely across borders, it matters little, at least as yet, what the nationality of a writer is.

More relevant than these other things is the fact that this literature reveals a series of concerns and considerations which relate to East Africa and not to one or another country. My guess is that this is likely to change. A literature of revolt against conditions emanating from the colonial period has been written, and while it is not clear in what direction writers will choose to travel, it may be – though one would be both foolish and unqualified to risk more than a tentative guess – that a more distinctly national literature will emerge from each of the three East African countries as a result of the break-up of the East African identity (consolidated, politically and economically, in the fact of the East African Community) currently under way, a break-up brought about by political ideologies and practices radically different from each other. So far this break-up has not been reflected in the writing. And while, doubtless, writers in East Africa will continue to be concerned with the realities of the day-to-day social and political circumstance of their countries (two recently published novels – Charles Mangua's *Son of Woman*[36] and Eneriko Seruma's *The Heart Seller*[37] – make this plain enough), if there is a thrust into a new dimension or the emergence of a new literary ideology it may be found in the 'cultural synthesism' of Taban who writes:[38]

Let the black blood flow into your blood, let it flow uncontrolled. A racially and culturally mixed person is the universal man; all is in him; he identifies with all; he is kith and kin to all other Homo sapiens. This leads us to a super-Brazil . . . He will have slant eyes, kinky hair, Roman nose, Red Indian knighterrantry, democratic folly, dictatorial changeability, Maori tattoos, use English as a tool for rebuilding Babel Tower. All these (and more) will make him the hundred per cent African – the descendant of Zinjanthropus, the culturally and racially mixed man of the future.

As Ntiru observes

This is still in its formative, amorphous years, and still suffers from contradictions ... [it] is thorough going romance replete with robust optimism, but there is a recognizably positive element of modernity about it.

To this might be added that, as Taban's passage suggests, 'cultural synthesism' is outward-looking and away from narrow and local definitions.

CHAPTER SEVEN

NIGERIA

D. S. Izevbaye

What is most often emphasized about the role of a colonial language like English is its ability to promote communication between separate peoples and reduce what Joseph Jones has described in *Terranglia* as 'an incessant Babel of clamorous nationalisms'.[1] Nationalism is of course a legitimate political means of discovering one's personality, as it is a means of giving literary expression to one's identity. This identity need not find expression only in local vernaculars. In a multilingual society a foreign language has an initial advantage over the vernaculars since it is not merely a medium for international communication but also a means of achieving cohesion within the nation. In a similar manner a common language like English can help to develop the national character of a literature. In spite of being part of an international community, writers from a country which shares in the common wealth of the English language can retain their national individuality because of the nature of their relationship to the language. The attempt to describe the local landscape in a foreign tongue will itself create a sufficient need for modifying the language. But the more important pressures from the living vernaculars will affect the use of a second language either by causing linguistic interferences in the work of the less sophisticated writers or by providing a source of linguistic experiments for the more sophisticated ones. Thus English provides a basis for a national literature by creating a meeting point for the country's cultural diversity. Because this diversity finds expression in a multiplicity of local languages it appears at first to be a mixed blessing. This is implied in 'Were I to Choose', a 1957 poem by Gabriel Okara. At thirty-one, the poet takes stock of his world and sees in his growth from childhood to adulthood not a growth in understanding through a common language but the confusion of Babel:[2]

> And now the close of one
> and thirty turns, the world
> of bones is Babel, and
> the different tongues within
> are flames the head
> continually burning.

Okara's expression of frustration either here or in his better known 1959 poem, 'Piano and Drums',[3] is not a typical reaction. But it dramatizes the need for a common national language by using an image which anticipates that of Joseph Jones, and which finds its closest parallel in an identical image used for a different purpose by another poet, J. P. Clark. Clark sees English as a means of taking 'a positive step back from Babel's house of many tongues'.[4]

But the advantage of English does not lie merely in its ability to perform this unifying function, for it is an historical accident that gave it this advantage over any of the local vernaculars that could have performed the function as effectively. Its second function has been to gain for Nigerian literature a much wider audience than is available to the older vernacular literatures in, for example, Hausa and Yoruba. Fagunwa's *Ogboju Ode Ninu Igbo Irunmale*, the earliest work by the first important Yoruba fiction writer, was published in 1938, and *Gandoki*, a Hausa tale by Bello Kagara, was published in 1934.[5] The earliest works in English to be known to the outside world are Tutuola's *The Palm-Wine Drinkard*, published in 1952, and Achebe's *Things Fall Apart*, published in 1958. Although both came about two decades after the vernacular works, they have received much greater attention because they were written in English. Such attention from an audience whose taste has been influenced by its familiarity with the tradition of English literature has had the effect of emphasizing the indebtedness to English literature more than anything else, especially since some of these debts are explicit enough.

Many of the literary devices and forms are familiar enough even when they do not derive directly from a particular English writer or school. This is true of the novel, a form stimulated by contact with Europe. With the occasional exception of a novel like Okara's

The Voice (1964) which is closer to the allegory or morality tale than to realistic fiction, many Nigerian novels operate within the well-tried convention of developing an ordinary story chronologically and telling it in the third person. But even the experiments can be related to contemporary practice elsewhere. Achebe's *A Man of the People* (1966) has a more sophisticated technique than *Things Fall Apart*, being an ironic first-person story of how a young man is forced to operate double moral standards in the tough political environment in which he finds himself. In *The Interpreters* (1965), Wole Soyinka tells the story of a group of characters in search of identity in a corrupt and changing society. The technique of using rapid, sometimes baffling, time shifts to reveal the influence of past events on the present action of characters belongs to a tradition that has developed under the influence of Joyce and Faulkner. The method of blending two incidents from the past and the present by making one fade into the other at a point of association derives from the use of montage in cinematography.

Apart from such general experiments within a well-known tradition, there are explicit instances of borrowings from specific works. The best known of these are the phrases from Yeats and Eliot which Achebe uses for the titles of his first two novels. Such features make the literature at first seem an extension of the literary province of English, although the English influence is only one of at least two factors that have influenced the literature. The second factor, the background of vernacular cultures, has helped to give Nigerian literature its character, and can provide a touchstone for understanding and identifying the peculiar characteristics of the literature. A common feature is the reference to products of modern technology in a setting of ancestral Nigerian cultures where traditions die hard. The combination is sometimes an uneasy one, but it often shows not a rejection, but a struggle to understand and assimilate some of the foreign items. The expression of this struggle accounts for the experimental approach to English by Nigerian writers, and may be seen in phrases like Achebe's 'iron horse' for bicycle and Nkem Nwankwo's 'landboat' for motor car. The composure with which Amos Tutuola offers us the cultural mixture in *The Palm-Wine Drinkard* is matched only by the resourcefulness of his hero who sees magic and technology as equally acceptable means of getting out of trouble, and therefore employs them indiscriminately. At a threat from beasts in a spirit-infested jungle, he takes over control of the situation by commanding:[6]

> I told my wife to jump on my back with our loads, at the same time, I commanded my juju. . . . So I became a big bird like an aeroplane and flew away with my wife, I flew for 5 hours before I came down, after I had left the dangerous area.

Achebe's description of the problems and the possibilities in the use of English by an African writer makes allowance for Tutuola, whose solution he does not accept in principle:[7]

> Those who can do the work of extending the frontiers of English so as to accommodate African thought-patterns must do it through their mastery of English and not out of innocence. Of course, there is the obvious exception of Amos Tutuola. But even there it is possible that he has said something unique and interesting in a way that is not susceptible to further development.

In spite of their differences both writers experiment in a manner which suggests a confident acceptance of English. It is a confidence that assumes the relevance of the local vernaculars. This assumption expresses itself in various literary styles, and can be seen working consciously or spontaneously in the work of various writers. It exists as an enactment of a people's way of life and modes of thought in the novels of Achebe where the style is itself a demonstration of the Ibo saying that 'proverbs are the palm-oil with which words are eaten'. An important part of Achebe's achievement is the way in which he successfully creates a feeling of authenticity in the speech and thought of his characters by a sufficiently accurate transcription of the modes of expression of a non-English people. Without tampering with the normal patterns of English as Tutuola does, he convincingly creates the awareness that English is merely the telegraphic line across which the vernacular speech is being simultaneously transmitted and translated to the reader. The exuberance and sheer verbal joy of Soyinka's writings similarly has its source in the vernacular; for the Yoruba, like many other Nigerian groups, delight in making sense out of mere sound. The influence of the vernacular can be seen at its most conscious and most extreme in *The Voice*, a novel in which

Gabriel Okara tries to handle English not just as a new language, but almost as an extension of his own vernacular.

Apart from the more obvious influence of English literature, there are two important antecedents to the literature. First, there is the oral tradition of folktales, folksongs and traditional festivals. The oral tradition is an important background to the literature because it is the first experience of literature for most Nigerians. Although the oral form of transmitting literature exists in all cultures it is more alive and more strongly felt in a country like Nigeria than in countries with longer histories of literacy. It is therefore more often treated by writers as the primary, though not necessarily more accessible, literary tradition. The other, but not so influential, antecedent to the literature in English is the vernacular literature. Each of the two vernacular examples referred to earlier is within a tradition of creative writing dating back to early in the century. The oral tradition is antecedent to both the English and vernacular traditions, while the written vernacular traditions are antecedent to the English, as is now becoming evident in the use being made of Yoruba material.

The presence of the oral tradition is best felt in Tutuola's *The Palm-Wine Drinkard*, a work that is often treated as the missing link of Nigerian literature. This work, like the five others which have followed it so far,[8] belongs a little outside the normal experience of written fiction. The medium is alien to the matter and manner. Each of the romances repeats the same basic story – a human venture into the fearful world of ghosts, spirits and Deads. Because of the ink and paper medium the stories come in a more extended form. There is therefore a repetition in the use of certain types of incident, and this has produced the mythical pattern which Gerald Moore first analysed ten years later.[9] Within this extended pattern which developed as a result of the more leisurely control afforded by writing, Tutuola exhibits the typical qualities of the traditional teller of tales, the most obvious of which is the raconteur's freedom to innovate as he goes on. The elusive 'allegorical' manner comes from a tradition of personification in which the characters in a tale, be they animal, vegetable or mineral, are seen as having a soul or essence, and are therefore given a corresponding proper name. Similarly, Tutuola's synthesis of traditional Yoruba and modern scientific ideas belongs to the vernacular tradition, for it is part of that tradition to be innovative by assimilating all new elements in order to reflect the changing nature of the society. This is what has happened to the Yoruba myths of Sango and Ogun. Developing originally from an age when real technological power was only a dream, the myths of Sango, god of thunder and lightning, and Ogun, god of iron and war, have now become the very real myths of electricity and metal technology.

Even more typical of such a tradition is Tutuola's cosmography. In his map of the universe the boundary between fact and fantasy, if it exists at all, is very tenuous:[10]

> I could not blame the lady for following the Skull as a complete gentleman to his house at all. Because if I were a lady, no doubt I would follow him to wherever he would go, and still as I was a man I would jealous him more than that, because if this gentleman went to the battle field, surely, enemy would not kill him or capture him and if bombers saw him in a town which was to be bombed, they would not throw bombs on his presence, and if they did throw it, the bomb itself would not explode until this gentleman would leave that town, because of his beauty.

The triumph of beauty over scientific power is a magical triumph. As there are no limits to magic, there is no boundary between living and dead, between Man and Spirit. If there is, it is merely slightly physical, being no more than that which separates town and bush in Tutuola's works, or Town Dwellers and Forest Dwellers in Soyinka's play, *A Dance of the Forests* (1962). The adventurous may cross into either realm. The view of the world which occurs in these two works is valid socially as well as artistically, and occurs in works from different areas of Nigeria. It is used in a novel like Elechi Amadi's *The Concubine* (1966), a story about an attractive and good-natured but unfortunate woman, who the villagers insist is the wife of a sea god.

While the growth of a Nigerian literature is being strongly influenced by the combination of these three traditions in various degrees, the literary tradition is also developing, mainly in response to social changes. Social change is a common theme in Nigerian fiction, and writers are often concerned with the relationship between the city and the rural areas. Cyprian Ekwensi brings to the Nigerian novel his Ibo sympathy for rural life; from his urban upbringing he brings a reporter's gift for evoking city life. *Jagua*

Nana (1961), his most successful novel so far, is an impressive chronicle of Nigerian city life. It is concerned with the fortunes of a Lagos prostitute. But apart from being an effective character study of a prostitute, Ekwensi's portrayal of Jagua becomes an appropriate opportunity for a fairly comprehensive picture of the city. Because Jagua's 'profession' enables her to move at all social levels we get a picture of what 'Lagos life' is like at the British Council meetings where young men improve their minds, or at night clubs where young women sell their loves to swell their purses. The story also takes the reader into the den of thugs, and Ekwensi develops it to include the search for leisure by politicians, rich traders and lonely executives. The social realism of the novel is enriched by the almost literally transcribed pidgin speech of the characters, for pidgin belongs to urban Nigeria.

Like most Nigerian novels, *Jagua Nana* is not as experimental in form as *The Interpreters*. Although it has a similarly functional disorder in its ordering of incidents, it is not the same kind of novel and one does not expect the artistry and the power of organization which one often finds in Soyinka. But its episodic form and journalistic style are appropriate for its theme. The closest that it gets to a symmetry of form is in its use of the contrast between the city and rural areas, a common contrast in the Nigerian novel. Jagua's return home in this novel is not so much an invitation to the virtues of pastoral life, as a device for emphasizing the sterility of city life in spite of its seductiveness. The savagery of the city merely drives Jagua to the outskirts of the city, not out of it. It takes the death of her father and her brother's insistence to make her leave it. The temporary fertility with which the author consoles his heroine, and the oddly self-conscious treatment of sex in the last chapter of the book, together suggest that the rejection of the city is the author's, rather than the character's.

It is not only among novels about urban life that the picaresque novel is found. It is appropriate for the purely comic purpose of Nkem Nwankwo's *Danda* (1964), a novel which derives its humour from its irreverence for all established values, whether these are traditional or recent. The loose form enables the author to make the best of his hero's nonconformity. The hero's irreverence, which provides the comedy, is possibly the product of a society experiencing great change, for it also fortifies the comedy of Soyinka the satirist, who charges head down at all establishments, especially where these provide a refuge for the unworthy and the hypocritical. A typical *Danda* incident is that of the boorish relation from the backwoods enjoying the good fortune of his better educated 'brother' from the city. As the herdsman in his dirty clothes climbs into the shiny car of his kinsman, he appeals to a maxim that is traditionally accepted but is wholly irrelevant in the present situation as far as the kinsman is concerned: 'What belongs to one belongs to one's kindred.'

It is a slightly similar inadequacy of ancestral wisdom that gives Achebe's work its sometimes wry humour. In *Things Fall Apart* the men of Umuofia hear news of men with white skins and no toes, but they treat it with levity, dismissing it with flippant allusions to lepers. It is no laughing matter when the white man turns up with his guns. Such inadequacy is present when the men tie the 'iron horse' of a murdered white man to a tree to prevent it from running away to call other white men. The incident is not really comic because its uncomfortable humour rests on our knowledge that the villagers' action is not completely foolish. Since it arises from ignorance rather than naïvety, it does not permit us to feel superior to the victims of this self-betrayal. The more serious purpose in Achebe's novels often reins in the comedy.

It is the awareness of the historical significance of local events which dictates the form of the village novels of Achebe. The form is not merely episodic, but is made sufficiently loose and flexible to incorporate the details of social life. That is why Achebe can evoke a society whose complexity and self-sufficiency are realized within two hundred pages. Achebe's works are an important interpretation of his people's history. Just as Ekwensi is concerned with survival at the urban level, so is Achebe concerned with survival at the historical level. His first three novels are studies in defeat. The two so-called village novels examine in turn the inadequacy of unyielding strength and then of a fine intelligence stubbornly applied, in coping with the problems of social change. Both novels show the inevitability of change and consequently the necessity for adaptation.

In *Things Fall Apart*, Okonkwo's strength of will is shown to be an extreme reaction to his experience of a weak father. The author shows his disapproval of such inflexible strength by making it operate against socially approved codes, as when Okonkwo beats his wife during the Week of Peace, or his killing of his ward.

Ezeulu, the hero of *Arrow of God* (1964), is defeated for a similar inflexibility of will. From the start he is shown to possess the fine perception that is necessary for survival in his kind of situation. His intelligence is at its finest when he proposes to enrol his children in the white man's school, a mode of adaptation which the author evidently approves of:[11]

> The world is changing. I do not like it. But I am like the bird Eneke-nti-oba. When his friends asked him why he was always on the wing he replied: 'Men of today have learnt to shoot without missing and so I have learnt to fly without perching'. I want one of my sons to join these people and be my eye there. If there is nothing in it you will come back . . . My spirit tells me that those who do not befriend the white man today will be saying *had we known* tomorrow.

Ezeulu is ruined because either he is unable to sustain this perception or he refuses to let it guide his actions. His determination to avenge his wronged god blinds him to the established adaptive processes of his society. The people of Umuaro can cite 'numerous examples of customs that had been changed in the past when they began to work hardship on the people'. Ezeulu's hubris is his refusal to eat the new yam in spite of these precedents.

In spite of the heroic tone and the elegiac mood, these novels are not nostalgic. The elegiac mood comes from the author's original intention to show that the African past 'with all its imperfections was not one long night of savagery',[12] and is artistically necessary for creating a society that will become familiar without footnotes or explanatory asides within the text. If the tragic mood indicates an affirmation of the validity of the past, the movement of the plot indicates an acceptance of the present as it is. At the end of both novels the fate of the hero is played in counterpoint against the general social adjustment which takes place. In *Things Fall Apart* the sympathy is weighted in favour of the hero because of the patent cowardice of the crowd.[13]

> The men of Umuofia were merged into the mute backcloth of trees and giant creepers, waiting. . . . Okonkwo's matchet descended twice and the man's head lay beside his uniformed body.
> The waiting backcloth jumped into tumultuous life and the

meeting stopped. Okonkwo stood looking at the dead man.
He knew that Umuofia would not go to war.

And yet, in spite of this faint-heartedness, the inexorable character
of the people's experience shows that there is wisdom in their
action. The guide to behaviour is provided, ironically, in the
proverb of Eneke the bird who, when asked why he was always
on the wing replied: 'Men have learnt to shoot without missing
their mark and I have learnt to fly without perching on a twig.'[14]
True foolishness is exposed when a particular interpretation turns
the meaning of this proverb against the interpreter. This is clear
even if we need to look for the relevance of the use of Yeats's
phrase for the title of the novel. Yeats's theory of historical change
in 'The Second Coming' does not stop with the mere statement
that things fall apart, but also implies that because all important
social and historical change is drastic and tragic, it is necessary to
adapt or be destroyed. No one knows better than the people of
Umuaro in *Arrow of God* that 'these are not the times we used to
know and we must meet them as they come or be rolled in the
dust'.[15]

As a novelist, Achebe is not, however, obsessed with adaptation
at all costs. In the village novels the historical processes which
made adaptation a condition for survival also destroyed the heroic
last stand for tradition and prepared the ground for the moral
decline of the present. This is the link between Achebe's novels of
the past and the two novels about contemporary life. The anti-
heroes of his urban novels are willing to roll in moral dirt if it will
enable them to survive. In his examination of this other side of the
coin of survival, he does not give artistic approval to the kind of
adaptation which demands not only a renunciation of idealism but
also of social morality. It is partly because of the ability to move
comfortably in the corrupt society that Odili survives in *A Man of
the People*. And even though Odili is not as deeply involved in filth
as other characters, Obi the hero of *No Longer at Ease* is really a
finer, if feebler, man in spite of his dirtier hands. Achebe's emphasis
on the necessity for constant personal adjustments to changes in
social situations as well as the need for a sustaining moral code is
also strongly felt in the post civil war stories. It is responsible for
the buoyant spirits of 'Civil Peace', and the redeeming act of
sacrifice by Gladys in 'Girls at War'.[16]

In contrast to Achebe we do not find a moral position giving direction to Soyinka's plot in *The Interpreters*. Its more exploratory form is dictated by the need to dramatize the psychological problems of a group of individuals who are kept together mainly by their common reaction against a corrupt society in which actions and events seem meaningless. The characters are constantly seeking to create meaningful patterns by piecing together fragments of their experience both from the past and in the present. The problem is explored in an appropriately episodic manner. Certain recurrent motifs provide a meaningful link between episodes, just as the images of bridge and water indicate the search for continuity and meaningful relationships. Water is in fact a complex, often ambiguous symbol, sometimes representing both continuity and flux, and sometimes being used in association with sex to show how one of the key characters is repeatedly seduced and made too impotent to move from a disabled position to a more active and meaningful life.

If the formal characteristics of the Nigerian novel, a literary genre that has developed mainly under European influence, have been influenced to an important extent by the need to portray the problems of the Nigerian society, Nigerian drama is able to draw nourishment from roots that extend even more deeply. West of the Niger there has been a steady development of dramatic performance, so that it is now usual to link the dramatic activities in town halls and university theatres with church plays and the traditional rituals and festivals which are still performed today.[17] The frequency of song and dance which make the works of Hubert Ogunde and Duro Ladipo 'operatic' has been adapted by Soyinka in *Kongi's Harvest*.

The European influence is still strongly felt, of course, especially in the continued use of the 'picture-frame'. But playwrights are conscious of the need for a creative breakaway from the constricting limits of the proscenium arch, and of the advantages of a courtyard performance. The call for such theatrical freedom had been made by Soyinka as early as 1963.[18] Within dramatic texts, European influences range from the deliberate Shakespearean echoes of J. P. Clark's *The Masquerade* (1964), an adaptation of a folktale, to the transplantation of the Greek theme of Oedipus on African soil in Ola Rotimi's *The Gods Are Not to Blame* (1971). The fact that dramatists writing their first plays are more strongly attracted by the possibilities of tending such foreign material on local soil when there is an existing tradition of popular drama suggests, not just the vitality and prestige of Greek plays, but the fact that the home soil is congenial to such themes and may give them growth. The pathetic involvement of the human and the divine is natural to Clark's *Song of a Goat* in spite of the Greek suggestion of its title. The problem is not with the literary resonances but with the development of a theme whose power to communicate its dramatic idea is largely restricted to the immediate cultural environment from which it is evolved. Later Clark turns to the more substantial qualities of the local environment for the material of *The Raft* and adapts a local saga for *Ozidi*.

If Clark takes his cue directly from oral sources after a brief flirtation with European drama, Ola Rotimi turns to the use of historical material in the tradition of the popular drama. History as a source of dramatic themes was popularized by Duro Ladipo and taken up by Ola Rotimi who has now written two historical plays after his Greek adaptation. *Kurunmi* (1972), the first of these plays, is a swiftly-paced tragedy based on a historical reconstruction of nineteenth-century Yoruba wars. This type of material has had an ambiguous value for Nigerian drama. While it provides an opportunity for evoking the heroism and glories that must have existed in a country's history, it also carries the temptation of exaggerating the heroism and failing to qualify the rhetoric used to justify carnage.

Soyinka wrote *A Dance of the Forests* to commemorate Nigeria's independence. The play shows how a playwright may interpret traditional material and contemporary political events for his own artistic purpose. Forest Head, Soyinka's version of *Olu igbo*, the Yoruba supreme forest god, takes the opportunity of a tribal celebration to expose the presence of envious murder, murderous incompetence and murderous passion within the human community. He leads the central characters on a spiritual journey deep into the forest in order to make men discover their own regeneration through a series of confrontations which would uncover hidden guilt. Probably the most striking thing about the play is the cynicism underlying the playwright's adaptations of traditional gods and religious institutions. Forest Head, traditionally a god that can be appealed to as giver of health or wealth, is made a limited, almost ineffectual god, because he is unable to change the course of events which he himself originally ordained for mankind by fixing a neutral pattern of cause and consequence. The best he can do is to help men see the dangers in the vicious option they have chosen:[19]

> My secret is my eternal burden – to pierce the encrustations of soul-deadening habit, and bare the mirror of original nakedness – knowing full well, it is all futility. Yet I must do this alone, and no more, since to intervene is to be guilty of contradiction, and yet to remain altogether unfelt is to make my long-rumoured ineffectuality complete; hoping that when I have tortured awareness from their souls, that perhaps, only perhaps, is new beginnings.

These words help to bring out the Town Dwellers' blindness. They place soothsayers and dirgemen at the centre of their communication with gods, relying on the mere power of the Word and on the efficacy of sacrifice to alter events which are the consequences of their own original sins. But though an individual may occasionally interfere with the vicious pattern by a humane act, as the artist unconsciously does in the play, the odds against mankind are really too strong, because the active principle of evil among the gods will insist on interfering with human affairs. This is the function of Eshuoro in the play. *Oro* is the traditional cult of justice through retribution. Soyinka, however, sees retribution as another aspect of vengeance, as he combines *Eshu*, the spirit of mischief, with *Oro*, the punitive principle. The new creature, Eshuoro, is meant to represent the unpredictable and wayward aspect of retribution which continues the malignant cycle by seeking links with wronged human beings.

The play has not proved a producer's favourite because the meaning – a complex combination of the political theme with the more personal theme of individual regeneration – is locked up in the use of traditional gods and the symbolism of acrobatic dances, and it does not have the clarity and friskiness of an earlier play like *The Lion and the Jewel.*

Soyinka blends traditional material more easily into two later plays, *The Road* (1965) and *Kongi's Harvest* (1967). The latter play draws on traditional festivals with the singing and dancing, and uses the harvest idea as a central image for its political comment. The play is topical, being a satire on contemporary dictatorship.

But it is rescued from excessive topicality by the element of myth which Soyinka employs in his criticism. The monster yam which is harvested during Kongi's reign is Soyinka's way of showing that one man's tyranny over others is a crime against the earth. The yam is described as being 'Like a giant wrestler with legs / And forearms missing'. The 'wrestler' yam represents mother earth's protest at the tyrant who has wrestled and thrown her other sons. *The Road* is less topical, although as in all Soyinka's major writings the artist casts a satiric eye at specific national problems. The 'road' refers literally to the country's death-traps, incompetently maintained and recklessly used at great risk to life and limb. But it very quickly becomes mythical, as with most images in Soyinka. It is simultaneously the hungry god whom we encounter in his poem 'Death in the Dawn' and the Professor's path to the meaning of death. The presence of thugs and politician suggests the political road to destruction. Again in Soyinka, the spiritual or religious meanings become more important than the political ones.

In a recent play, *Madmen and Specialists* (1972), written about the time of the Nigerian civil war, a humane attitude can be glimpsed beneath the enveloping cynicism. Old Man in the play says 'a part of me identifies with every human being'.[20] *Madmen and Specialists* is the drama of a doctor who loses his medical vocation in the wars. As usual, Soyinka examines the spiritual significance of a political action. When Dr Bero, the specialist, tells his sister how he sat down to a communion of human flesh his description of the dehumanizing experience of war becomes a definition of the driving force behind war-mongering:[21]

> Aftrewards I said why not? What is one flesh from another?
> So I tried it again, just to be sure of myself. It was the first
> step to power you understand. Power in its purest sense. The
> end of inhibitions. The conquest of the weakness of your too
> human flesh with all its sentiments. So again, all to myself I
> said Amen to his grace.

The grace that was said before this 'meal' shows how impossible it has been for man to resist the temptation to war. The historian in *A Dance of the Forests* found war the only consistency in human history. The grace pronounced by Dr Bero's father translates this view of war into a religious statement. We still have Soyinka's playfulness, but the usual exuberance has been disciplined to produce the grim utility of the 'grace': 'As Was the Beginning, As is, Now, As Ever shall be . . . world without. . . .'[22] The playwright perverts the usual meaning by merely applying a new punctuation and elevating a mere adverb, 'as', into the substantive divinity, 'As'. Even the elision of the final 'end' has the effect of suggesting that the god 'As' will eventually do without the world.

This sheer delight in wit is reminiscent of Elizabethan practice. In the following example, it almost erases the mood of gloom which has been created in our minds, except that the playwright manages a political denunciation even while tossing his puns around:[23]

> you splint in the arrow of arrogance,
> the dog in dogma, tick of a heretic,
> the tick in politics, the mock of democracy,
> the mar of marxism, a tic of the fanatic. . . .

Such punning is in the vernacular tradition in which the syllabic sounds of names and titles are manipulated to yield a desired meaning for the purpose of praise or blame. In this passage Soyinka suits his sounds to his meaning, and the passage is as earnest as it is playful.

Writers who can rely on a background of such a vernacular tradition would naturally carry over its literary practices into their poetry. The *double entendre*, a device found in proverbs and riddles, can be particularly effective for political mockery because usually the sexual innuendo reinforces the more direct political mockery. Thus in 'Cuba Confrontation', one of Clark's lighter poems, the sudden shift from the lizard exemplar to the far-fetched simile of the courtesan is meant to point out that the braggart male can turn out to be a woman after all:[24]

> With my hammer head
> I'll smash up the earth,
> Said
> The lizard:
> And up reared
> The aroused crown,
> And then down
> The blow
> Came – like a courtesan's head,
> Deep in her pillow.

The conceit can also be used for a serious purpose without any humorous effect, as in the title of Soyinka's second collection of poems, *A Shuttle in the Crypt* (1972). This refers to the incarceration of creative energy, for the shuttle is a 'unique species of the caged animal, a restless bolt of energy, a trapped weaver-bird yet charged in repose with unspoken forms and designs'.[25] Soyinka's poetic art does not, however, derive from the oral tradition. The sources of his techniques are mainly *literary*, and except for 'Idanre' where he adapts a few Yoruba incantations for his Ogun epic, the poetry remains largely individual in form. What Soyinka adapts from the vernacular tradition is the religious system rather than the literary technique. This provides him with a useful parallel for his synoptic view of history. In 'Idanre' he adopts the Ifa divination technique in which an understanding of contemporary problems is arrived at by interpreting the problems of a mythical, usually non-human protagonist. 'Idanre' is a re-telling of the Yoruba myth of Ogun, god of war, in order to predict the bloody climax of the Nigerian experience. The hero of the poem is a god who becomes drunk and gets out of control when invited to a feast.

In contrast, J. P. Clark and the late Christopher Okigbo, two of the other major Nigerian poets, have shown greater interest in utilizing the literary properties of Nigerian oral poetry, as distinct from the use of landscape, religious systems and images from their environment. Whereas Soyinka's work has remained mainly consistent in style almost from the first, the works of Okigbo and Clark have increasingly shown an experimental interest in the devices of the oral tradition. This increasing interest may best be described as a homecoming for both poets, since both began by using English poets as models until they found their feet and later attempted to develop certain verse techniques found in vernacular poetry.

Okigbo began his experiment with traditional poetic forms by emphasizing that instrumental music and the performing arts of singing and dancing are important to his poetry. Not only are his poems mainly 'songs', 'laments' and 'dances', they are also dedicated to instruments for artistic performance like flutes, drums and masks. Although the models for the early poems were Pound and Eliot, some of the later poems have the structure of traditional Nigerian poetry. 'Lament of the Masks', a poem dedicated to W. B. Yeats, adopts the structure and phrasing of Yoruba praise poetry.

Okigbo's borrowing of phrases from other writers recalls *The Waste Land*. But this same quality makes his verse akin to older poetic forms which are similar in their use of fixed formulas. The made-up phrase is common property, and the originality depends on each poet's use of well-known phrases, as poets used epithets in epics and kennings in Old English poetry. The structure of Okigbo's poems also has this ancient quality. Each poem is a sequence which can be lengthened, shortened, or re-arranged by the poet. The formal range of such poetry is limited. Each new poem is often a structural repetition of an earlier poem and the poet's career is an almost unending spiral of a single thematic development.

The repetitive structure is organic to Okigbo's theme, that of spiritual rebirth. Because the group of sequences called *Labyrinths* deals mainly with the exploration of a personal experience, it deals almost exclusively with a central protagonist and uses obscurity as a deliberate device to keep the poems personal. But in a sequence called 'Distances' the poet ends his artistic and spiritual quest to enter a public career as a mantic poet.

Although J. P. Clark is a very different kind of poet from Okigbo, his career may also be mapped very roughly as a movement from the use of European models towards a creative adaptation of the devices of vernacular poetry, as well as a progress from personal experience to a poetic involvement in the political crisis which hit the country as from the mid-sixties. The poems in *A Reed in the Tide* (1964) bear the stamp of poets like Hopkins and Dylan Thomas whose work Clark obviously admired. Some of the best-known lines in the volume come from an early poem, 'Night Rain', where the poet tells how[26]

> like some fish
> Doped out of the deep
> I have bobbed up bellywise
> From stream of sleep
> And no cocks crow.

However, the strongest impression on the poems is not the shadow of poets like Hopkins and Thomas but the poet's eye for the Nigerian landscape. Moreover, Clark attempts, even under the constricting influence of other poets, to make the lines of his poems follow the development of his subject. It is, however, in a later volume, *Casualties* (1970), that the poet breaks completely free from the formal restrictions of his early work to experiment with a more prosaic freedom of expression. In this latter volume it is tempting to see the later Yeats displacing Hopkins and Thomas as the poet's idol, in his search for the bare, hard expression. But even a slight familiarity with the true models for this volume would direct one to folksong and folktale as the groundwork for the poems.

Casualties, like Okigbo's last poems and Soyinka's 'Idanre', has the Nigerian crisis as its main subject, because no serious poet can ignore the important issues of his time. So for the first time, all the major Nigerian writers are united in writing about a common subject. This is significant for the development of Nigerian literature. A national literature requires more than local images, landscapes and belief systems for the formation of a character that is distinct from that of neighbouring countries with similar vernacular cultures, a common historical association with colonizing Europe, and a common European lingua franca.

The presence of English in Nigeria has done more than provide an opportunity for communication with a wider world. It has offered a new medium for literary expression and the challenge of a new imaginative activity in which the experiences of various cultures may find a common channel. Molly Mahood once drew attention to the signs of a dramatic renaissance in Africa.[27] There is also an opportunity for a kind of renaissance in the other literary forms. A renaissance is after all an awakening of creative energies caused by the turbulence at a confluence of cultures.

CHAPTER EIGHT

SOUTH AFRICA
John Povey

Present political circumstances have made South Africa a pariah amongst nations. It is perceived as unique: unique in its problems, unique in its attempted solutions, often also unique in the social evil of the apartheid system by which it sustains its peculiar racial and cultural circumstance. If it were not for the present antagonism and reciprocal defensiveness South African history could be seen as matching another common sequence. As a colony of Britain she became a dominion and finally independent. South Africa was more bedevilled than most by circumstance, but the bilingualism of Canada and its attendant cultural antagonisms are some equivalent of the South African situation where Afrikaans battles through legislation for survival against the world dominance of the English language. South Africa's treatment of its indigenous peoples is different from Australia's policy towards its aborigines in quantity rather than quality, for although Australia has proportionally so much more manageable a 'native problem' it has still reacted on the South African pattern. The importation of Chinese and Malays to compound an already confused racial situation is analogous to the immigration of labour from the East into East Africa or the West Indies.

This is not to defend South Africa by the 'and you're another one' principle of adolescent verbal conflict, but to begin to remove from South Africa that stigma of historical uniqueness that does not permit us to view the development of its literature (or probably, though this is a larger question, its history) by appropriate analogy with other national experience. After all, it is possible to tell the story of American and South African settlement and colonialization in remarkably similar terms. The American history of settlement in the mid-seventeenth century, the division over slave-owning and the subsequent covered wagon migrations which provoked battles with the indigenous population, the war for independence against the colonial power, can all be duplicated from the experience of South African history. Any overview must then allow for similarities as well as for the ominous differences of social policy.

I shall concern myself with South African literature in English, merely observing in passing that there is a vast literature in the Bantu languages, not only the oral epic poems and tales such as the Zulu historical praise poems but also, more unusually, a particularly rich nineteenth- and twentieth-century written literature printed in the accepted orthographies. The Sotho language has an impressive literature and the work of Thomas Mofolo, particularly the historical novel *Chaka*, is relatively well known in translation. Much of this literature is denied to most readers by the cultural barriers that in the final analysis only anthropology, rather than literary criticism, can breach. It is therefore doubly outside our concern here. There is also a substantial literature in Afrikaans. Only quite recently have its themes and attitudes been liberated from the narrow Calvinistic assumptions of the religious duties of a writer into a true literature of skill and power. Etienne Le Roux is the first Afrikaans writer to have achieved international respect and acclaim with his extraordinary trilogy *Seven Days at the Silbersteins, One for the Devil* and *The Third Eye*. These are remarkable works by any standards; in the context of the claustrophobic spirit of Afrikaans writing they are masterpieces; iconoclastic to the point of revolution.

To understand correctly the structure and history of South African English literature one should begin by judging the writing in the context of the literature of those other countries where white settlers from Britain became the population that formed the old dominions of the British Empire. Such literature begins with the mother country. Not only is this the initial allegiance of the settler politically and socially but, in this context more essential, it is also his literary allegiance. His assumption of what literature is derives from England. He is aware that his own writing is part of a tradition: the tradition of English writing. From the standpoint of literary technique he begins with assumptions that can only be modified subsequently by original and unexpected experiences.

The literature of a new country is the gradual forging of a distinctive and separate national idiom out of a remembered and retained tradition. Literature does not achieve its identity by mere geography. It is only after an author adapts both his life and his writing to foreign cultural experience generated by the new environment that specific national elements can be distinguished. The subsequent process of historical literary criticism in these new countries has overemphasized this nationalistic response. It has been based on the need to read backwards, as it were, pursuing the increasingly tenuous threads of specific localization from the certainly national of the contemporary to the nearly colonial of early settlement: the home-grown *versus* the imported. The writing of these settled areas is obviously linked to the literary heritage of England that had originally engendered the authors themselves. This is the inevitable origin. The measure of individuality and thus nationality of a dominion literature is found in the degree to which it opposes and modifies the original literary tradition; a tradition which like other elements of the culture was not left behind in the mother country by the immigrant.

The early writing of South Africa may be seen as such a beginning of a national literature. It takes on the forms and styles of nationhood from the acquisition of a fresh colonial environment. It is only later that it becomes apparent that there will be a specific cast to the South African experience. It will be bedevilled by race and colour problems and there will be a consistent and monotonal theme of a major proportion of contemporary South African writing.

South African literature in English begins as does the literature of Canada and Australia – and of the United States for that matter – with the settler record and the diary. These writers are not necessarily distinguished; our interest is largely a matter of historical curiosity. Two examples might appropriately reflect the beginnings of English language literature in South Africa at the end of the eighteenth century, the chatty letters of Lady Anne Barnard, the wife of the Colonial Secretary, and the poetry of the Scotsman Thomas Pringle.

Lady Anne Barnard's letters have that innocent charm that gushes from well-brought-up English ladies. Some find it delightful, others appalling.[1]

We have now quite settled down at our residence in the Castle, my dear Friend, and I like it very much. I have arranged it as best I can, a few things we brought out with us from old England coming in most useful, and really the effect is very pleasing to the eye. . . .

Strictly speaking, Thomas Pringle was scarcely resident in the Cape long enough to be considered a South African settler, but convention sets him first in the field. It is not an unfair attribution, for in his lines South Africa asserts itself. This is more than merely the borrowing of vocabulary to record the unfamiliar fauna and topography he encountered; rather there can be found the beginnings of specifically South African attitudes both emulated and parodied by later writers. Pringle's most famous poem 'Afar in the Desert' exemplifies both his style and themes. There is the inevitable listing of the quaint local fauna but there is also a real receptivity to the scene.[2]

> Afar in the desert I love to ride,
> With the silent Bush-Boy alone by my side;
> O'er the brown Karroo, where the bleating cry
> Of the springbok's fawn sounds plaintively;
> And the timerous quagga's shrill whistling neigh
> Is heard by the fountain at twilight grey. . . .

From such pioneers to writers of real distinction there is a considerable jump in time. Undoubtedly the first South African writer with a claim to international consequence was Olive Schreiner who published originally under the pseudonym of Ralph Iron. Her novel simply called *The Story of an African Farm*, published in 1883 when she was in her early twenties, is a major work not only because of its intellectual and literary distinction but more essentially because that distinction derives from the African environment.

In the writing of Olive Schreiner there is the impact of originality sustained by a very real talent. As Doris Lessing remarked of it:[3]

I read the novel when I was fourteen or so; understanding very well the isolation described in it, responding to her sense of Africa the magnificent . . . this was the first real book I had met that had Africa for a setting. Here was the substance of truth, and not from England or Russia or France or America . . . but reflecting what I knew and could see.

It draws upon the very spirit of the bare, harsh, parched veldt and makes it not the backdrop of scenery but the participating environment that drives the characters who must work out their hard destinies in the infertile semi-desert.

The story concerns Aunt Sannie, a widowed Dutchwoman, who lives on her farm with Lyndall, a brilliant, fiercely intelligent woman, and Em, a quiet, softer, more obviously feminine type. There is an idealistic young man, Waldo. Their security is invaded by a cruel and smooth-talking swindler, Bonaparte Blenkins, who pays urgent court to Aunt Sannie until he is exposed and driven away. Further disasters bring about the deaths of Lyndall and Waldo. Em, the good one, returns to run the farm with her ideal husband Gregory. The novel itself lacks direction and the characters seem a little contrived in retrospect, but the intensity of the evocation – it is more fierce than mere description in its individual responsiveness – is apparent throughout. As the title suggests it is South Africa that is the centre of this tale, and the characters exist, pursuing their dreams and disappointments, against the commitments that South Africa requires of them. The land is equal participant in the saga, motivating and judging.[4]

The plain was a weary flat of loose red sand sparsely covered by dry Karroo bushes that cracked beneath the tread like tinder, and showed the red earth everywhere. Here and there a milk-bush lifted its pale coloured rods, and in every direction the ants and beetles ran about in the blazing sand. The red walls of the farm house, the zinc roofs of the outbuildings, the stone walls of the kraals all reflected the fierce sunlight, till the eye ached and blenched.

What is apparent from these lines, themselves so typical of this novel, is the interaction of man and land, and the battle which is man's attempted resistance to the land's harsh threatening. It is a continuing duel that demands consistent strength from a man as the remorseless sun battens and burns.

None of Olive Schreiner's later books matched the intensity of this early novel, and the next major stage of South African writing developed in the twenties and early thirties when nationality could be taken for granted. The major writers of this time were William Plomer, Roy Campbell, Pauline Smith and Sarah Gertrude Millan. They drew upon a sense of South African cultural identity, an obligatory association which remained strong whether the reaction was affectionate or antagonistic.

It was Pauline Smith who came closest to the emotions of Olive Schreiner. She shared Olive Schreiner's intense attachment to the veldt and her best stories were collected under the title of *The Little Karroo*. Her characters live their lives, gentle, anxious, industrious, on the bleak soil of the dry centre of South Africa. They learn to love even its dangerous and threatening aspects, finding, 'Even in its cruelty there was a beauty, a sublime fitness and simplicity. . . .'[5] Always in Pauline Smith's tales there is the sense of affinity with the soil of this demanding desert.[6]

> Even the pitiless realities of the drought, which the fading glamour of sunrise revealed, seemed just, and in tune with the sweep of the kopjes, the hum of the poles.
>   This sense of justice, of proportion, of equality, was to Petchell one of the marvels of the Karroo. In some mysterious way the Karroo extracted beauty, rhythm – the rhythm of prose rather than verse – out of all that passed over its veldt.

Smith perhaps more than Schreiner goes beyond the locality to describe people. Schreiner's characters tend to be exotics functioning against the landscape. Smith's are its very product and justification. She can sustain her knowledge of the rather dour and moralistic farmers, yet she always turns back to the geography with which her people must cope. She sees them as people interacting with the bare, hard landscape, the poverty of its keepers matching the ungenerous fertility of the land. The veldt is the background of all her days and is the touchstone of her awareness. 'This grey and desolate region was her world.'[7] No South African writer has so deliberately and consistently reflected a single area of geography and social experience as Pauline Smith. It lends to her work an overall effect; its sum total is more significant even than the tender individual tales she tells.

Plomer, Campbell and their friend Laurens Van Der Post were the first South African writers to establish an unequivocal reputation abroad. It is with these three that the first obvious tension developed between writer and community – that tension which was to be the mainspring of the South African intellectual's attitude towards his country. Now came into the open that division that still remains at the core of South African experience; feelings about race and colour become the persistent theme. Olive Schreiner had treated her native African characters with a casual disregard that matched them with the animals of the farms on which they worked. This was not deliberate but an unconscious sense of their identification with their inevitable landscape. Now there was the recognition, painful and difficult as it always was for South Africans, that these people were human beings. The degree of resentment that this simple enough observation could generate can be seen in the way in which both William Plomer and Roy Campbell, the most able writers in South African letters, were persecuted and virtually hounded out of their country.

There were two literary incidents that triggered this rejection, the response to Plomer's novel *Turbot Woolfe* and a little later the attacks on *Voorslag*, a literary magazine run by Plomer and Campbell in Natal. *Turbot Woolfe* has just been reprinted fifty years after its first publication. It is a tender and shrewd novel, but perhaps its distinction can only be appreciated in the context of our awareness of its pioneer role in the expression of disenchantment with South African racist attitudes. It deals with miscegenation, when a white woman falls in love with an African and marries him. In passing it makes some casual jibes at the work of missionaries in Africa and, more heinously, depicts the whites as cruel, racist, and, more shocking to the South Africans, as cheap, dirty, vulgar, lusting after blacks but savagely denouncing others who proffer even minor kindnesses to them. There is Flesher, who lives only on mealie meal, his face and hands covered with scorbutic sores, and Bloodfield, richer and more capable but with similar evil in his heart. 'Give me a good old criminal lunatic any day, rather than ask me to breathe the same air as Flesher and Bloodfield; I should feel so much more at ease'[8] remarks Woolfe understandably but provocatively.

In condemning these people Plomer chooses to see them as not simply individuals, but a lost cause, 'those who had been broken or beaten or besotted with the almighty violence of Africa.'[9] It is the power of Africa that devastates settlers. Plomer's final painful message is set out simply enough no matter how enormous its implications:[10]

Do not allow yourself to believe that because South Africa is painted red upon the map and has at present a white population of a million and a half, it is a white man's country. It is nothing of the sort. It can never be anything but a black, or at least a coloured man's country.

It was the recognition of this fact that undoubtedly sent him on his travels. He went, driven too by the antagonism his views had stirred, first to Japan and then to England, where he is now established as a distinguished man of letters, his South African origin half forgotten. He has only once briefly returned.

A similar local anger drove Roy Campbell from the country. This time the trigger was the challenge asserted by a new literary magazine founded by Campbell and Plomer called *Voorslag* (whiplash). Their intention is clear enough from its title. Its aim was to flog sensibility into the apathetic South African populace. Campbell, a vehement man, was capable of writing verse that excoriated with its satiric force. He was happily willing to savage the land of his birth. This did not make him popular. New nations are notoriously sensitive. His poem 'The Wayzgoose' begins:[11]

> Attend my fable if your ears be clean
> In fair bananaland we lay our scene
> South Africa renowned both far and wide
> For politics and little else beside.
> Where having torn the land with shot and shell
> Our sturdy pioneers as farmers dwell,
> And twixt the hours of strenuous sleep, relax
> To shear the fleeces or to fleece the blacks.

His long satiric poem continues in this vein, its occasional wit matched by an acid criticism verging on the vindictive. Campbell's scathing review of South African society was an open spurt of that antagonism to South Africa that motivated a number of writers and other liberal intellectuals, reflecting their demonstrable dualism between love for the beauty and delight of this land and anger and resentment at the political direction that it had taken. This attitude reaches its culminating force twenty and thirty years later, but it is important not to forget that Campbell was so much more than this bitter, sardonic man. He was a major lyric poet and his inspiration is rooted in the country of his birth. The weakness of his later work in exile may derive from his sense of loss at being detached from his home soil.

No one has written poetry of greater fervour than Campbell as he reflects his land, its animals and its peoples. His best poems have been often enough anthologized: 'The Zebras' with its surging sheen of visual movement, 'The Serf' with its intelligent compassion for the ultimate relationship between peasant and earth, and 'Zulu Girl', where the description of the African mother feeding her baby takes in aeons of experience linking the human with the geographic landscape.

Campbell left South Africa one of the first of so many literary exiles. It is possible to interpret his poem 'Rounding the Cape' as a recognition of the consequences of this departure. Addressing Admastor, spirit of the Cape, he calls[12]

> Farewell, terrific shade! though I go free
> Still of the powers of darkness art thou Lord:
> I watch the phantom sinking in the sea
> Of all that I have hated and adored.

The painful division within the South African writer's attitude has never been more openly expressed.

Alan Paton's *Cry the Beloved Country* is probably the only novel from South Africa that has found a substantial international readership. In a way the high visibility of this novel is unfortunate. Paton's second novel, *Too Late the Phalarope*, displays far greater skill in its delineation of character and a greater subtlety in its analysis of the psychological complications inherent in South African colour discrimination. Paton's short stories, published as *Tales from a Troubled Land*, deriving largely from his own experience as an administrator in a reform school for delinquent boys, are superior. They balance compassion and shrewdness in a way that avoids the sentimentality that hovers at the fringes of even so moving a work as *Cry the Beloved Country*.

Cry the Beloved Country concerns an African priest who goes to find his son in Johannesburg, where he has fallen in with bad companions. He learns the boy has committed murder, and worse, the murder of a young white whose life was dedicated to helping the African people. More than this, he was the son of the generous landowner back in the priest's own village. Nevertheless, while each father copes with his personal and separate despair, there is enough love remaining so that the white man can still give the priest the money to rebuild his church and build a dam to aid the village. The pain rests in the awareness that both must live contemplating the disasters for which South Africa's racial tensions must be held responsible.

Nothing in this rather Dickensian plot prepares one for the tone of affection that suffuses this novel. The language is rich and evocative. The diction takes on a biblical lilt most apparent in the English version of Zulu that the author employs for his Africans' conversation. The opening lines are famous and familiar, but they are fine examples of Paton's prose at its most lyrical. Again, it is clear that it is the South African landscape, in this case the lush, tropical hills of Natal rather than the sparse desert of Pauline Smith's veldt, that has inspired these loving lines.[13]

> There is a lovely road that runs from Ixopo into the hills.
> These hills are grass-covered and rolling, and they are lovely
> beyond any singing of it . . .

On other occasions the landscape does more than establish the tone of the scene; it also becomes the evidence of the emotional purpose events will unleash. The threat in the skies seems to match that gathering storm that will fall upon the unhappy country.[14]

> And over the valley the storm clouds were gathering again in
> the heavy oppressive heat, so that one did not know whether
> to be glad or sorry.

There is a tremendous amount of Christian compassion in this book which is suffused with a true idealism, and yet, and it is undoubtedly a fact more to our discredit than blame to Paton's generous heart, it seems a little improbable today. The situation has degenerated so fast that the book's implicit Christian optimism seems sadly questionable. Tolerance and charity now can seem mere evasiveness; white kindness becomes guilt.

This cynical attitude may also dictate a present-day judgment of *Mine Boy*. Significantly, this is the first book to be considered that is written by a 'non-European'. This novel by Peter Abrahams was the prototype of what has somewhat unkindly been stigmatized as the 'Jim goes to the city' story. It concerns a noble and innocent young African, Xuma, who goes to Johannesburg and finds work in the mines. He lives in the ghetto, sharing hardships, and meets two women, Eliza, educated as a teacher, and a rather innocent yet amiable servant woman, Maisie. During his work underground in the mines Xuma encounters prejudice and cruelty but also kindness and sympathy. The characters are stereotyped; each good person is carefully matched by a weak or bad one. It is hard to find believable so much kindness and tolerance. Although Eliza has a small part she remains in the memory because with her there is that visceral antagonism that Abrahams seems anxious to placate.[15]

> I want the things of the white people. I want to be like the white people and go where they go and do the things they do and I am black. . . .

Against the background of this painful but ultimately hopeless discovery the ending seems something of a gesture. It is benign in the manner indeed of Paton, assuming that it is the brotherhood in the human heart that is the source of redemption. This is not, of course, wrong; merely optimistic to the point where, regrettably, our credulity becomes strained. Although one can advance neither political nor literary alternatives, the decision becomes almost theatrical. Against the evocation of the horror of day-to-day living, the white man's response seems inadequate and limited. 'You must think as a man first. You must be a man first and then a black man.'[16] Such an argument is simultaneously true and irrelevant. This thought is at least sufficient to impress Xuma: 'Now he understood . . . one can be a person first. A man first and then a black man or a white man.'[17]

It is too easy to be somewhat snide about sentiments such as these. We may become overly cynical, but after all there is a level, deeper than political activism, at which both Paton and Abrahams are absolutely right. It is others who have lost sight of the absolutes of human compassion in the face of social violence.

Soon after this, Abrahams left South Africa for good. Nothing Abrahams was to write later added any more effective statement about the situation. Recent novels include *This Island Now*, an interesting study of political intrigue in an imaginary island in the West Indies (where he is now resident), and an attempt to write a South African thriller, *A Night of Their Own*. It seems unlikely that Abrahams will now write a good new novel of South Africa. Nevertheless, his achievement may not only be measured in the quality of his own writing. He stands at the beginning of a line of non-European writers ultimately more consequential in their productivity than Abrahams himself.

A major African writer is Ezekiel Mphahlele, who became known through his impassioned autobiography *Down Second Avenue*. It recounts the story of his upbringing in the slums of Pretoria. In passing one should note how many South Africans have used the autobiography form. It is clear that this choice of genre displays a significant part of their motivation as writers. They need to tell the world of the experiences they have suffered. There are several good autobiographies, such as Tod Matshikiza's *Chocolates for My Wife* and Bloke Modisane's *Blame Me on History*.

It is Mphahlele's work which has the greatest pretension to literary skill because its quality is less circumscribed by its subject matter. What is noticeable is the honesty and affection of the tone. Total despair is artificial, a distortion of true memory. Even in the harshest childhood there are moments of joy and humour and success. Against the ugly encounters with the police and the developing recognition of the racial restrictions under which the family lives, there are a series of cheerful cameos. People and events remembered from the young boy's slum world are both truly and affectionately conceived.

The most personally revealing aspect of this book is the discussion of the writer's awareness that he was going to have to escape from South Africa in spite of his obligation to the struggle for social revolution. In this country there is always 'the spur', which demands unreasonable intensity of the writer.[18]

> That's the trouble: it's a paralysing spur; you must keep moving, writing at white heat, everything full of vitriol; hardly a moment to think of human beings as human beings and not as victims of political circumstance.

With a comment that incisively judges South African writing today in all its literary and social implications, Mphahlele observes:[19]

> I'm sick of protest creative writing and our South African situation has become a terrible cliché as literary material.

This is a frightening yet totally honest appraisal of the impact of racial politics on the South African writer.

The Penguin anthology *South African Writing Today* includes works by the current most able South African 'black' writers. There is Lewis Nkosi, editor, journalist and intellectual, and Richard Rive, whose powerful short story 'The Bench' has become one of the archetypal tales of apartheid at work. Other writers are Cam Themba, Casey Motsisi, Bloke Modisane and Nat Nakasa. Most of these found two early sources of publication. There was the famous *Drum* magazine, a new development as a popular African magazine neither intellectual nor patronizing, and the Johannesburg literary journal *Classic*, which remains the most important outlet for African writers in South Africa.

These writers draw deeply upon their experience, just barely synthesizing it into story rather than anecdote. There are incidents from the street where the daily battle for survival pits wits and optimism against the police and laws of the city. The characters appear helpless in the face of arbitrary power. They are sometimes driven by frustrations to doomed opposition. Yet sometimes they gain a sense of victory, at least within the context of their own standards which measure defiant survival as the ultimate conquest.

The single writer in this vein who is demonstrably the most able and the most representative is Alex La Guma. Technically, under the South African colour spectrum, La Guma is 'coloured'. His stories are set in the 'coloured' quarter of Cape Town, the infamous District Six. His stories are highly realistic and their characters are set amongst the cheap cafés and bioscopes, the shabby streets and bars of non-European Cape Town. There is violence and squalor, and yet a stoicism and a kind of jaunty determination set in the face of violence and disaster.

Ugly disintegration and poverty is the texture of his life. His world is a vicious one. The police are a threatening presence and occasionally intrude their official power, but the violence is deeper in its causation than any simple battling against the law; the poor can be equally cruel to each other. Violence is endemic in that society that the nation has created by its policies. La Guma's vision is a harsh one – it is also a brilliant one.

La Guma is an intense writer and a deeply committed political man. The balance between these two things is not the easiest to maintain. So far, La Guma's indignation is harnessed to technique, and his stories for all the denunciation that they contrive are substantial art as well as inspired propaganda.

The white writers of the present generation who are internationally known are Jack Cope, Dan Jacobsen, Nadine Gordimer and, although not truly a South African, Doris Lessing. Perhaps the work of Nadine Gordimer can exemplify them. Their attitudes are inevitably liberal in cast. No matter their precise political affiliation, the normal humanity of the artist makes it inevitable that they will have a more broadly compassionate attitude to people than permitted by the pigmented assessments of government policies. Each of the above has in some manner been harassed by banning of books or restrictions on movement. Jacobsen and Lessing now live in London but Cope and Gordimer remain in South Africa, still drawing their themes from the daily experiences which surround them.

Nadine Gordimer is a major short-story writer. She has that scrupulous dispassion, that sharp intimacy of observation, that marks the finest writers. Although her stories primarily concern South Africa, they are intimate and personal as much as political. South Africa merely adds that occasional sharp edge to a human situation that is in itself explosive, providing the particular circumstances; more than background yet less than motivation.

One of her most brilliant stories has the ironic title 'Which New Era Would That Be?' It exemplifies the way that the universal attitude is given specific urgency by the locale of its participants. Jennifer Tetzel, a young girl, liberal, literary, involved, is desperately anxious to show her broad-mindedness, her social ease and awareness. Her boyfriend takes her to visit two Africans he knows. The tension of the colour situation imposes its own logic. In spite of everyone's determination to remain free from its taint, it is precisely this liberal determination to be above the colour bar that makes the situation such a disaster.

The situation revolves around Jennifer's desperate desire to understand, to be other than birth and colour genetics had defined her. She is intelligent enough to see the ugliness of the colour divisions yet she seems incapable of perceiving that it is only part of the general intolerable nature of the society that nurtures it. The whites sometimes want so hard, so eagerly, to show that they are not of the oppressors, that they have tolerance and understanding. But the African knows the artificiality and the inadequacy of the premise on which such attitudes rest.[20]

> He knew the type well. . . . These women – oh, Christ! – the women felt as you did. They were sure of it. They thought they understood the humiliation of the pure-blooded black African walking the streets only by the permission of a pass written out by a white person. . . .

The important thing is not of course the incident, which is minimal as in many fine stories, but the opportunity it provides for Gordimer to investigate human reactions confronted with the South African social *malaise* which inevitably traps everyone. There is no correct response; this is its emotional cancer. Whether you go along with its bigotry or over-react and insist on fallacious standards of equality as irrational and dreamlike as Jennifer's, you are equally trapped. Gordimer scalpels them all: the bigots, the indifferent and the liberals. Even while she does it so surely, she knows that she too is part of this social *mélange*, and her writing continues to probe with intimacy and shrewdness and with sympathy.

A new significant dramatist is Athol Fugard. His international reputation was made with *The Blood Knot*, a brilliant, rather claustrophobic, analysis of brothers whose pigmentation straddles the South African colour line. The theme brought reprimand from the government, for censorship is endemic in contemporary South Africa and the list of banned books stretches more extensively than the papal list of old. But Fugard survives. He is energetically developing a theatre in which he directs and acts. His recent play, *Boesman and Lena*, was a tremendous success in South Africa. It is a powerful and finely wrought play which may prove to be too deeply tied into the culture to achieve the wide international audience that appreciated the ready universality of the symbolism of *The Blood Knot*. *Boesman and Lena* is a brooding play about a couple who live in the wretched squatter slum areas of the Cape and a lost, silent African, both helpless and threatening. They are always moving and searching for some improbable place of settlement until it is seen that life itself is this meaningless circular perambulation. Symbol has become reality and there is no end which could be set up as a possible terminal objective.

The talents in poetry are perhaps average rather than hugely distinguished, yet Guy Butler, Ruth Miller, Perseus Adams, Sydney Clouts and the caustic satires of Anthony Delius are worth a very serious reading. The difficulty both for them and for this discussion is that the more effective their poetry is in its intimacy and introspection, the less recognizably South African are their themes and intentions. So their work can be defined as South African largely through our separate knowledge of the nationality of its author. Nevertheless, it is instructive to discover that even in poetry where the attention is ostensibly elsewhere, there is the sudden twist that determines national attitude, making a regional discovery out of a personal one; a response that finds the local in the universality of human introspection. Guy Butler, for example, in 'Myths', 'reading Keat's *Lamia* . . . beneath a giant pear tree buzzing with bloom', must contemplate the apparent paradox in this European experience that is his national heritage. He observes:[21]

> Yet sometimes the ghosts that books had put in my brain
> Would slip from their hiding behind my eyes
> To take on flesh, the sometimes curious flesh,
> Of an African incarnation.

In a similar way Sydney Clouts's rather jaunty incident of a young boy christened Roy because 'He'll command' finds the South African reality different from the myth.[22]

> I dreamt of a sceptre; I cried and I cried
> Till rock and shore were divorced.
> Division incarnate! An unhappy role!
> My country has given me a flint for a soul.

Compared with the numerous African writers of prose there are few African poets. In spite of the significance of the oral poetic tradition it would appear that in the contemporary situation the motivation of the writers is decisive in their choice of genre. Many South African writers come close to the documentary technique or set their literary art at the service of social and political creeds. This is evident in the extraordinarily realistic vignettes that make their short stories a genre of surpassing popularity. But there are two major poets who manage to allow their authentic voices as artists to be uncorrupted by the temptation of the simplistic needs of political rhetoric.

Dennis Brutus is well known abroad as an activist. He was

jailed in South Africa and forced to go into exile. His urgent commitment to political service does not prevent his poetry being lyrical, wry, sometimes even metaphysical in its rich ironies and complexities. There is inevitably the statement of the dangerous world in which he lives:[23]

> the siren in the night
> the thunder at the door
> the shriek of nerves in pain.

Yet for him there is also the possibility of tenderness and understanding surviving, for there is love to set against the violence, personal feelings to challenge political allegiance.[24]

> ... You pressed my face against your womb
> and drew me to a safe and still oblivion,
> shut out the knives and teeth; boots, bayonets and knuckles:
> so, for the instant posed, we froze to an eternal image.

It is the 'eternal image' which the South African writer seeks to capture. It is one of the burdensome disabilities of his time that the eternality which he is forced to contemplate is one of social horror and political disaster.

A most significant new talent was discovered recently, when the first collection of the poetry of Oswald Mtshali, *Sounds of a Cowhide Drum*, was published. This book, published by the editor of *The Purple Renoster* Lionel Abrahams, is an amazingly accomplished collection. Its spirit comes from the very heart of Johannesburg, where the poet works as a messenger.

Mtshali's poetry is not declamatory, but verse that flowers around the effectiveness of his inspired imagery. Again and again the eye and the mind are caught by the explosive originality of the perception that Mtshali brings to his work. In the first poem of this collection he begins:[25]

> The rays of the sun
> are like a pair of scissors
> cutting the blanket
> of dawn from the sky.

Yet he is not a man who uses the beauty of the scene to avoid the hardships of his life. He represents a human background to the white world, ignored but threatening in his omnipresence.[26]

> I am a faceless man
> who lives in the backyard
> of your house.

He sees himself not only as that faceless African but as a poet, the embryo of his spirit ready to raise itself out of circumstance and make its poetic affirmation.[27]

> Look upon me as a pullet crawling
> from an eggshell
> laid by a Zulu hen,
> ready to fly in spirit
> to all the lands on earth.

That is an impressive decision and it is one not inappropriate for so many South African writers caught within the nets of their country's politics. They seek true affirmative human and humane compassion in a land which often expressly denies outlet to such emotions. Yet they live and survive and write with a rich energy that is perhaps paradoxically the more charged because the moral statement of the artist must be made again and again in this country in the face of antagonistic government edicts. Humanity must be reaffirmed, and survival is a measure of a victory both literary and personal. As Brutus's lines declare,[28]

> Somehow we survive.
> And tenderness, frustrated, does not wither . . .
> boots club on the peeling door . . .
> but somehow tenderness survives.

CHAPTER NINE

THE UNITED STATES
Bruce King

In 1820 a British critic, Sydney Smith, asked 'who reads an American book?' Two centuries of settlement of North America had produced no literary classics. It is not until the nineteenth century that we can speak of genuine achievement, and even then the first important writers of the period, James Fenimore Cooper (1789–1851) and Edgar Allan Poe (1809–49), are more significant for what they represent than for having produced classics. Cooper's 'Leather-Stocking Tales' show how Sir Walter Scott's historical romances were changed by American writers into an examination of national myths; as the land becomes settled Cooper's inarticulate hero flees westward from the restrictions of society and civilization towards the freedom of an ever-receding frontier. Unfortunately, Cooper did not write well, and his novels are perhaps less important as literature than for what they reveal about the American imagination. When significant writing did begin in the nineteenth century, it came hot and fast: Emerson, Thoreau, Hawthorne, Melville, Whitman. By the middle of the century one can speak of a distinct tradition of American writing with characteristics and qualities of its own.

While the American writers of the early nineteenth century are aware that they are the heirs of the Puritan colonial settlers and of eighteenth-century rationalism, they are more directly influenced by the European Romantic movement. There is in American writing of the period the same rebellion against reason, common sense, scientific thought and the imitation of the past. Poe's complaint 'To Science' is representative. American writers begin to see themselves as outcasts, loners, sensitive souls in personal communication with the divine. Romanticism, however, takes an extreme form in the United States. Since the colonial period there had been a myth of the New World as a paradise in which man could be reborn as an unfallen Adam free from the injustices of Europe. Continuing immigration, the presence of the frontier and the consequences of the War of Independence prevented society from gaining a rigid hold on the individual. The dream of the New World as a land of freedom was intensified in the nineteenth century by the opening of the Midwest for settlement and by Jackson's presidency (1829–37), which inaugurated an era when the democratic masses and the frontier spirit seemed triumphant over the conservative Eastern establishment. Such hopes were supported by an intellectual tradition, deriving from the colonial period, of following one's inner light and conscience. America was thus ripe for the Romantic belief in man's innocence and natural potential. The history of American literary culture is largely a continuation of the discussions, arguments and disagreements which grew up around this optimistic view of man.

The place to begin is with Ralph Waldo Emerson (1803–82). Emerson is not a major writer, but the major writers of his age and later generations often can be seen in relation to the assumptions which underlie his essays and lectures. Emerson is unconcerned with the past, society or others. Each life, each day is a new beginning; each individual is the centre of the universe and the world is mirrored in his thought and soul. The individual must become conscious of his relation to nature and to the divine. The ego must expand to fill the universe and embrace the world; in realizing his divinity the individual will achieve union with the spirit of life which animates the world of nature.

In 'The American Scholar' Emerson speaks of every man as a student. Scholarship is 'Man Thinking'. The mind examines the world of nature, by which Emerson means the objective world of which we are conscious, and learns

> that he and it proceed from one root; one is leaf and one is flower; relation, sympathy, stirring in every vein. And what is that root? Is not that the soul of his soul?

The individual learns that nature and the soul are related. Its beauty is the beauty of his own mind, its laws are the laws of his own mind. The greatness of nature is the measure of the attainments of his consciousness. All men are potentially great. Greatness does not necessarily come from action, rather it comes from the way we perceive and how we alter the perceptions of others. There are no barriers to the mind; each mind is an unbounded empire.

Emerson's philosophy is part of the egalitarian spirit of his age and of the American dream of a new, unfallen land in which all can be equal and great:

> the same movement which effected the elevation of what was called the lowest class in the state, assumed in literature a very marked and as benign an aspect. Instead of the sublime and beautiful, the near, the low, the common, was explored and poetized.

If men learn to believe in themselves, think for themselves, and see themselves as part of the divine spirit which animates the universe,

> A nation of men will for the first time exist, because each believes himself inspired by the Divine Soul which also inspires all men.

Emerson's belief in the divine possibilities of the individual still remains with us, as does his concern with the way consciousness can penetrate through the many particularities of existence to find some universal spirit by which we are animated and related. The emblematic quality of particularities, itself a development of Puritan symbolism and allegorization, will often find expression in American literature. Another theme we find in Emerson is the desire to return to some child-like or edenic state of innocence, when the world still seemed fresh and there was no distinction between reason and intuition since the divine nature of a thing was immediately understood. We can see Emerson's influence on Henry David Thoreau's (1817–62) *Walden: Life in the Woods*, where the descriptions of nature are hieroglyphics in which a scene partakes of a spiritual significance.[1]

> A field of water betrays the spirit that is in the air. It is continually receiving new life and motion from above. It is intermediate in its nature between land and sky. On land only the grass and trees wave, but the water itself is rippled by the wind. I see where the breeze dashes across it by the streaks or flakes of light. It is remarkable that we can look

down on its surface. We shall, perhaps, look down thus on the surface of air at length, and mark where a still subtler spirit sweeps over it.

Emerson's Transcendentalism influenced the poetry of Walt Whitman; it was treated sceptically in Hawthorne's *The Scarlet Letter*, and its consequences were profoundly explored by Melville.

While Nathaniel Hawthorne (1804–64) is a finer writer than Cooper, his novels have similar faults of bad dialogue, flat characterization, and an artificial style. It is not until Mark Twain that an American novelist achieves a natural prose style. *The Scarlet Letter* is set in seventeenth-century Massachusetts. A woman commits adultery, gives birth to a child, and refuses to identify her seducer. Her husband discovers that a respected local preacher is guilty. He becomes the sick preacher's doctor and by keeping him alive prolongs the torments of guilt. After years of suffering the preacher is saved from mental and spiritual damnation by publicly revealing his crime. *The Scarlet Letter* is a romance using the Puritan heritage of allegory and symbolism during an age when Emerson's Transcendentalism rebelled against Puritanism. At the market place where Hester Prynne is made to appear wearing her letter A, as punishment for her adultery, 'her beauty shone out, and made a halo of the misfortune and ignominy in which she was enveloped'. The letter itself is elaborately embroidered in gold thread and appears a work of art and imagination. Her attire she 'had modelled much after her own fancy'; it expressed 'the desperate recklessness of her mood'. In contrast to the laws of Puritan society, art grows out of freedom, sin, and the mind in isolation reflecting upon its experience; the letter 'had the effect of a spell, taking her out of the ordinary relations with humanity, and enclosing her in a sphere by herself'.

If Hester is an eloquent voice for woman's right to live a full emotional life, her husband represents the demonic aspects of pure intellect. In using his arts to discover the preacher's guilt he experiences a joy like Satan's 'when a precious human soul is lost to heaven'; but his emotion differs from Satan's in its 'wonder' at what he has seen. As is shown by many of Poe's stories, Romantic writers often portrayed the conflict between intellect and feeling in terms of stealing another person's heart or inner self through observation and analysis. Such 'wonder' is, however, also that of the artist looking on the richness of the world rather than personally participating in it. He is unlike Hester, who makes her scarlet letter reflect 'her own fancy'. Many American writers, such as Henry James, will return to the problem of the intellectual who observes, rather than experiences, the rich possibilities of life.

Hawthorne's descriptions often have emblematic associations. Hester and her child might remind 'a Papist' of 'the image of Divine Maternity', but

> Here, there was the taint of deepest sin in the most sacred quality of human life, working such effect, that the world was only the darker for this woman's beauty, and the more lost for the infant she had borne.

Hawthorne is exploring extreme views of reality, seeing people and things as embodiments of varied and often conflicting ideas. As often happens in American literature, contradictory interpretations are offered. Hawthorne even gives several possible explanations of the improbable events which take place at the conclusion of the novel.

Hawthorne both alludes to the democratic forces of his day in praising the 'multitude' and shows that society is built upon psychic repression. Colonial Puritan society accomplished 'so much, precisely because it imagined and hoped so little'. He is good at implying contrasts between the American dream of freedom and such realities as slavery and the economic view of man. When Hester goes to the Governor's mansion she is met

> by one of the Governor's bond servants; a free-born Englishman, but now a seven years' slave. During that term he was to be the property of his master, and as much a commodity of bargain and sale as an ox, or a joint-stool.

Hawthorne shows the individual in opposition to society, the self-realizing Transcendentalist imagination in opposition to the Puritan repression of emotions. He does not, however, resolve the issues he raises; American writers will often examine such problems without finding any solutions.

The greatest work of mid-nineteenth century America is

Herman Melville's (1819–91) *Moby Dick*. It has a disorderly, rambling structure, reminiscent of such later Renaissance works as Burton's *Anatomy of Melancholy*, which intended to encompass every aspect of its subject. The many quotations prefacing *Moby Dick* suggest various possible significances of whales and whaling. They range from the biblical and allegorical to the practical and realistic. What will be told in the novel can be interpreted in many ways. Melville's prose creates a world of varied and contradictory meanings. His tone ranges from arch irony to the tragic and comic. Biblical allusions, echoes of Elizabethan drama, folk humour, obscure words, whaling jargon, sexual imagery and mocking exaggerations exist side by side in a rich and yet angular style revealing a mind both concerned with and sceptical of spiritual realities. Such an inflated style is common in American literature, where the perceiving self, rather than others or society, is often the object of concern.

Ishmael, the narrator, wishing to get away from civilization, signs on a whaling ship commanded by Captain Ahab. Ahab is no longer interested in the commercial results of whaling; he is obsessed with revenging himself on Moby Dick, a white whale who has destroyed his leg. Although clearly mad, Ahab has heroic energy and vision, which carries the crew along with his obsession. They journey around the world seeking Moby Dick.

The ocean is Ishmael's equivalent of Huck Finn's Mississippi or, in Cooper's novels, Natty Bumppo's wilderness. On the sea he hopes to achieve freedom and spiritual self-realization. But when Ishmael meditates on the various symbolic and mythic significances of water, he finds that such romantic dreaming is dangerous self-love:[2]

> Surely all this is not without meaning. And still deeper the meaning of that story of Narcissus, who because he could not grasp the tormenting, mild image he saw in the fountain, plunged into it and was drowned. But that same image, we ourselves see in all rivers and oceans. It is the image of the ungraspable phantom of life; and this is the key to it all.

Ishmael views the world emblematically; he claims that things are 'full of meaning'. For example, Father Mapple when seen in his pulpit 'signifies his spiritual withdrawal for the time, from all outward worldly ties and connexions'. Ironically, Father Mapple's sermon warns against withdrawing from the world, and is applicable to Ishmael:[3]

> And if we obey God, we must disobey ourselves; and it is in this disobeying ourselves, wherein the hardness of obeying God consists.
> With this sin of disobedience in him, Jonah still further flouts at God, by seeking to flee from Him. He thinks that a ship made by men, will carry him into countries where God does not reign, but only the Captains of this earth.

Captain Ahab's attempt to revenge himself on Moby Dick is the tragedy of the romantic mind obsessed by reality. Ahab's madness is Emerson's Transcendentalism perverted. The whale is for him emblematic of an unjust God or of a world without meaning:[4]

> All visible objects, man, are but as pasteboard masks. But in each event – in the living act, the undoubted deed – there, some unknown but still reasoning thing puts forth the mouldings of its features from behind the unreasoning mask. If man will strike, strike through the mask! How can the prisoner reach outside except by thrusting through the wall? To me, the white whale is that wall, shoved near to me. Sometimes I think there's naught beyond. But 'tis enough. He tasks me; he heaps me; I see in him outrageous strength, with an inscrutable malice sinewing it. That inscrutable thing is chiefly what I hate; and be the white whale agent, or be the white whale principal, I will wreak that hate upon him. Talk not to me of blasphemy, man; I'd strike the sun if it insulted me.

The romantic narcissist turns demonic when faced by the indifference and hostility of nature.

Moby Dick, as seen by Ishmael, acts the role of a vengeful God of the Apocalypse, punishing man for his presumptions: 'Retribution, swift vengeance, eternal malice were in his whole aspect.' He rams the ship, sinking it; all those, except Ishmael, who followed Ahab's obsession drown. Ishmael uses as a life-buoy a coffin his friend Queequeg had made and is eventually rescued by a ship symbolically named *Rachael*. In such a symbolic novel we are right to see pagan Queequeg as a sacrifice, whose natural goodness and love enable Ishmael, like Jonah, to return to the world to fulfil his duty.

The writer who carried Emerson's ideas furthest was Walt Whitman (1819–92). His poetry was meant as autobiographical, a 'Song of Myself', but it is not autobiographical in the usual sense of the word. It records how he saw himself, a representative personality, a common man, of the new American democracy:[5]

> I celebrate myself, and sing myself,
> And what I assume you shall assume,
> For every atom belonging to me as good belongs to you.

His poetry speaks of life as an open road along which one journeys meeting other kindred souls, other pioneers who are living fully and experimentally. It is a world without the usual social and personal defences, in which comradeship is assumed, and the horizons unlimited:[6]

> I tramp a perpetual journey, (come listen all!)
> My signs are a rain-proof coat, good shoes, and a staff cut
>   from the woods,
> No friend of mine takes his ease in my chair.
> I have no chair, no church, no philosophy,
> I lead no man to a dinner-table, library, exchange,
> But each man and each woman of you I lead upon a knoll,
> My left hand hooking you round the waist,
> My right hand pointing to landscapes of continents and the
>   public road.

Exploration of one's self is followed by discovery of one's relation to others through visionary experiences of nature, companions, the nation and universal brotherhood. (Perhaps because American literature focuses upon 'frontier' situations it seldom examines society or romantic love in any depth.) In attempting to overcome his isolation and encompass the phenomena of the world, Whitman does not, like Emerson and Thoreau, deny the body for the sake of the spirit; there is no Puritan sublimation of the sensual. The poems are filled with sexual imagery and suggestions of free love. It is as if Emerson's Nature has become other bodies and personalities through which one can become part of the universal spirit. If the self is divine, others are divine, particularities of experience are divine, the nation is divine; there is no differentiation and discrimination. In 'Song of Myself' such experience is sometimes expressed in vague, mystical generalizations. The self-conscious ego seems unbearably vain and can too easily label the ordinary as sublime. Whitman was aware of this; his boasts are often modified by playful ironies. There is often self-mockery and an awareness of the absurdity of claiming to embody universal truth: 'I dote on myself, there is that lot of me and all so luscious.'

In Whitman's poetry the elect nation of the Puritans has been translated into a frontier democracy. America is God's country, in which men can fulfil themselves unhampered by restrictions. Whitman's style is meant to express this vision. It is colloquial to the extreme, incorporating slang, jargon, journalistic phrases and coinages; the language of poetry has been democratized and made closer to prose. Despite its democratic intention, however, it is a made-up language, artificial and literary, sometimes ugly, sometimes beautiful. Its cadences are often biblical, there is much use of repetition and parallelism. It is meant to be spoken and, like Emerson's lectures, shows the importance of public oratory in nineteenth-century America. Whitman's free verse, seemingly formless stanzaic structures and apparent lack of sequential thought are appropriate to his visionary and democratic hopes.

In subject as well as style Whitman's poetry attempts to achieve the egalitarianism of the common man. It accepts all, often simply naming and enumerating, as if listing were to make relationships and give meaning. Whitman aims at being unselective; since in the modern world high culture excludes the masses, it is necessary to create a new culture based on the masses. The poems are meant to be a bible for this new religion of democracy. All of life has a value: 'Each moment and whatever happens thrills me with joy.' There is no sense of the past; there is only now and the future. The modern descendants of Whitman are such writers as William Carlos Williams and Allen Ginsberg, who find in his free verse, openness to experience and egalitarianism an answer to what they regard as the life-denying qualities of established, hierarchical, Europeanized culture.

The book which has rivalled *Moby Dick* as the most important

American novel is Mark Twain's (1835–1910) *The Adventures of Huckleberry Finn*. Ernest Hemingway spoke of it as the beginning of American fiction and said nothing superior has been written since. *Huckleberry Finn*, indeed, looks like a break from the tradition of allegorical, metaphysical romances; it offers us a world which is recognizable, familiar and very American in detail. The story is set in the Mississippi Valley before the Civil War. Huck Finn is a young boy caught between the advancing civilization of the East Coast as it pushes west and the decaying frontier tradition as it degenerates into drunkenness, violence and small-town cruelty. Faced by a choice between remaining with his drunken father or being 'civilized' by some well-intentioned old ladies, he runs away to live by hunting and fishing. The passages in which Huck feels at ease floating on the river beneath the stars bring to mind many similar descriptions in American writing where the hero, having fled society, experiences harmony with nature.

The Mississippi Valley had been looked upon as the second hope for America. If the East Coast after independence did not produce an egalitarian society where all men were free and equal, then Eden would have to be created in the Midwest. Such a state of innocence, however, is a dream. American history includes the massacre of the Indians, the legalization of Negro slavery, and continuing discrimination against those of other races. Huck's escape is paralleled by that of Jim, a Negro slave. Although Huck initially accepts his society's belief that a Negro slave is mere property, he helps Jim to escape. Their voyage down the river, which for Huck is a return to the freedom of the frontier, is for Jim an attempt to reach the state of Illinois where he would be legally free. The friendship which develops between Huck and Jim, like that of Ishmael and Queequeg in *Moby Dick*, shows the natural universal brotherhood of men of different races. Significantly, both friendships occur outside the boundaries of society.

Early in the novel Huck rejects the Widow's claim that he must help people and not think about himself. He regards it as another aspect of the repressive civilization to which he is being asked to conform. Twain, however, is introducing a contrast between a formally taught and a personally experienced moral education. Huck has not been corrupted by society; with his untutored innocence and goodness he naturally makes the right moral choices. Faced by the prospect of Jim being returned to slavery, he values his friendship over the laws of society:[7]

> 'All right, then, I'll *go* to hell' – and tore it up.
>
> It was awful thoughts, and awful words, but they was said. And I let them stay said; and never thought no more about reforming. I shoved the whole thing out of my head; and said I would take up wickedness again, which was in my line, being brung up to it, and the other warn't. And for a starter, I would go to work and steal Jim out of slavery again.

The irony, of course, is that Huck fulfils the Widow's injunctions to perform spiritual charity, although he believes he is damning himself by breaking society's laws. His wish to be at ease under the stars proves impossible; responsibility for another person brings him into contact with society. There is no Eden along the Mississippi; civilization continually intrudes with its selfishness, cruelty and cultural pretensions. At the end of the book, Jim now free, Huck speaks of once more fleeing:[8]

> But I reckon I got to light out for the Territory ahead of the rest, because Aunt Sally she's going to adopt me and sivilize me and I can't stand it. I been there before.

But there is no hope for such innocence. Huck cannot escape civilization; 'the rest' will soon catch up.

Twain created a natural and colloquial prose based on the characteristics of American speech. His prose economically, directly follows what is thought and seen; observation is exact without being self-consciously precise. Words, syntax, descriptions and rhythms seem spontaneous. Twain avoids euphemisms, balanced cadences and consciously correct grammatical constructions. His tone is informal, unpretentious, and includes the sceptical attitudes of the man in the street towards culture and society. We need not worry about Huck's illiteracies, dialect forms and occasional cuteness. Many American writers will attempt to achieve such naturalness and understatement in their own prose. Yet Huck's language is not flat. Indeed, it creates a personality as large as that of Whitman, Ishmael or Ahab. It is an instrument for registering impressions of reality upon the mind and shows the mind's response to the world around it. In this, it reminds us of the rhetorics of Emerson, James or even Wallace Stevens.

With Henry James (1843–1916) we enter the realm of the modern novel with its close observation of character and society and its self-conscious artistry. His fiction shows what can be done with the use of point of view; his complex prose sensitively implies the emotions and feelings of his characters, creating their perspective on events, recording their impressions. Often the narrator is himself significant and his sensibility becomes an additional focus of the reader's interest. Many of James's novels and stories treat of Americans in Europe or Europeans in the United States. Often the American sets out to explore the Old World only to be victimized by it. If American innocence is baffled or betrayed among the complex social and moral conventions of Europe, the betrayer is sometimes an American who has accepted Old World values. A feature of some novels is an American observer, perhaps representative of the writer, who follows the hero's or heroine's progress with admiration, while being inhibited from actively participating in life. Despite James's international subject matter and sophisticated handling of narrative, his heroes and heroines are the descendants of those self-reliant, free Americans envisioned by Emerson and Whitman. They are innocents unhampered by social conventions, who go forth to experience the world. They are later day Puritans who renounce conventional success for some higher ideal.

In *The Portrait of a Lady*, James offers us another American who attempts to live fully. Isabel Archer is taken from a small American town to England by her aunt. She turns down an offer of marriage from an enlightened and agreeable English nobleman. Her cousin, Ralph Touchett, impressed by her unconventionality, arranges to have a large sum of money put at her disposal. He wishes to observe how she will live when resources are available for her to live up to her imagination. She marries a disagreeable American aesthete who makes her miserable. When offered the chance to escape by Caspar Goodwood, a former American suitor, she returns to her husband and a future of unhappiness.

Isabel Archer could be a later day Transcendentalist:

she had an unquenchable desire to think well of herself . . . one should be one of the best . . . should move in a realm of light, of natural wisdom, of happy impulse, of inspiration gracefully chronic.

She has, however, notions that to live fully she must suffer. 'I can't escape unhappiness,' she tells the English lord. 'In marrying you I shall be trying to.'

Despite his realistic settings, James is working within the tradition of American romance and allegory. Such names as Isabel Archer, Ralph Touchett and Caspar Goodwood are suggestive, as is Gardencourt, the Touchett English country house. When Goodwood attempts to rescue Isabel, he says: 'The world's all before us – and the world's very big.' The claim that the world is 'all before us' recalls Adam and Eve's expulsion from Paradise at the conclusion of Milton's *Paradise Lost*.[9] After he kisses her, Isabel flees from him: 'She had not known where to turn; but she knew now. There was a very straight path.' The biblical echo is obvious.

If Isabel Archer can be said to be an Emersonian heroine seeking to realize herself through experience, she is subtly undermined by James's irony. Long before Caspar Goodwood offers her the whole world she had already shown her predilection for the solitary pleasures of the imagination:[10]

> At this time she might have had the whole house to choose from, and the room she had selected was the most depressed of its scenes. She had never opened the bolted door nor removed the green paper (renewed by other hands) from its sidelights; she had never assured herself that the vulgar street lay beyond.

It is also suggested that when Isabel runs back to the house along the 'straight path', it is away from Goodwood's masculinity: 'it was as if he were pressing something that hurt her':[11]

> His kiss was like white lightning . . . it was extraordinarily as if, while she took it, she felt each thing in his hard manhood that had least pleased her, each aggressive fact of his face, his figure, his presence, justified of its intense identity and made one with this act of possession.

James often implies that the spiritual dramas felt by his characters may have a psychological explanation. His art, like that of Hawthorne, offers material for varied interpretations.

Many of the best writers of the first half of the twentieth century were conservative and distrustful of democracy. They rejected the American tradition of Romantic optimism. Despite the desire for classicism and order, American literature remained, however, Romantic in tendency, using many of the same philosophical and moral themes, in a similar highly rhetorical and emblematic style, as the nineteenth century. (Even Hemingway's flat prose, modelled on Twain's realism, is highly rhetorical in its repetitions and stylized ellipses.) The description of particularities, however, has changed its symbolic function; it now reveals a world lacking spiritual design or purpose. American writers still focus on the individual consciousness, often in isolation from society, but the individual no longer seems capable of moral grandeur.

Although T. S. Eliot (1888–1965) gave up his American citizenship and settled in England, many British writers have argued that his work does not belong to their national tradition and that its style and content are foreign. The frame of reference in which his mind works is, I think, within the Emersonian tradition. Some similarities are the concern with the supposed separation of thought and feeling in the modern world and the desire to see the natural world simultaneously in its physical and spiritual aspects. Eliot's Symbolist style with its need for an 'objective correlative' in which to ground emotions can be said to be influenced by the Puritan-Transcendentalist heritage of seeing the natural world as emblematic or as a mirror of the individual's consciousness.

While Eliot's use of French Symbolist techniques – themselves influenced by Edgar Allan Poe's poetic theories – appeared a new direction for English poetry, they are in keeping with the American poet's tendency to see the world as analogous to his own feelings. 'The Love Song of J. Alfred Prufrock', *The Waste Land* and 'The Hollow Men' offer broken images of a sterile world felt by the consciousness rather than a reality that is necessarily present to others. There is the familiar American expansion of the ego by what Emerson, in 'The Poet', called the 'externization of the soul'; but ironically in Eliot's verse the mind projects its inhibitions upon the world:

> Let us go then, you and I,
> When the evening is spread out against the sky
> Like a patient etherised upon a table.

'Prufrock' reveals a mind in which the desire to experience life more fully is inhibited by a self-consciousness which undermines vitality, faith and action:

> I should have been a pair of ragged claws
> Scuttling across the floors of silent seas.

Eliot, like Whitman, means the personal to be representative and inclusive of the culture. *The Waste Land* reflects the feeling of emotional and spiritual sterility which followed the First World War; its fragmented, chaotic form is representative of the break-down of European culture. In contrasting the present with the past, Eliot suggests there are timeless, universal rituals which are the basis of culture and which it will be necessary for the modern mind to rediscover if there is to be rebirth. This is an Emersonian atti-tude towards history, in which the viewer treats the past as similar to a series of great pictures in a museum, the relevance of which depends upon his perspective and needs. Unlike most American writers, Eliot decided that the mind's need for self-realization in the world could be achieved through accepting some external, rather than subjective, order or belief. The religious conversion recorded in 'Ash-Wednesday' shows a mind which has disciplined itself to Christian belief, but which has not yet experienced the spiritual blessing which, it is hoped, will eventually result.

Eliot, I think, is in the line of American writers who both reflect and dislike the dominant culture of Emerson and Whitman. His intense concern with order and the Western cultural heritage might be seen as a reaction against American mass democracy and romantic optimism. The supposed impersonality of his poems is a reaction against Whitman's 'Song of Myself'. Whitman's influence on Eliot can be seen in the structural use of repeated phrases and images, the making of a poem out of moments of intensity, and the attempt to create a new poetic idiom for the age. That Eliot recog-nized the lasting influence of his American background can be seen from 'The Dry Salvages', where his religious and philosoph-ical concerns are translated into themes, images and a style meant to recall Whitman, Twain and Melville.

After Eliot the most important American poet of the century is Wallace Stevens (1879–1955). Although Stevens was influenced by the French Symbolists, he is an heir of Emerson's romanticism. His poetry is mainly concerned with the mind's perception of reality, or what Emerson called 'me and nature'. He sees the mind as creative and faced by the need to find significance in the external world. Stevens, however, cannot accept any spirit, vital force or God which would bring harmony to the chaos of existence and link man to his environment. Lacking belief in a central myth, the poet must create new fictions about the mind's relationship to the world. The new myths, however, are unlike those of the past in that they are essentially descriptions of man's imagination. Thus, while it is necessary to elevate the spirit by offering new romantic possibilities of the mind's god-like role, there remains an essential tragic flaw; belief has been replaced by a self-conscious awareness of the processes of perception. The poet knows that the world is absurd and any meaning he gives it is his own creation. There is nothing behind the mask of reality, not even an angry God.

Stevens's early poetry is rich in colour, imagery and sound. He is a hedonist of sensation, enjoying the diversity of the world he perceives, while knowing it is disorderly and without purpose. Language in itself has become a pleasure to be exploited in place of belief. The poet is isolated, in meditation, a Platonist attempting to rise to the one and the beautiful while knowing that such ideals do not exist. In 'Invective Against Swans' the contrast between reality and the soul in meditation is made explicit. 'Behold, already on the long parades / The crows anoint the statues with their dirt'; but 'the soul, O ganders, being lonely, flies / Beyond your chilly chariots, to the skies'.

In most poems reality wins. In 'The Plot Against the Giant' odours, colours and sounds 'will undo him'. In 'Metaphors of a Magnifico' three different ways of viewing the same experience are offered with the refrain that this is an old song that will not declare itself. The poem ends with simple images of pure sensation as the mind, having been teased by fancy out of thought, loses interest in its quest for the meaning of existence. In poem after poem the mind rises to offer alternative views of reality only to end defeated. However, the effort has in itself been a pleasure and gives life meaning. The excuse for such mental hedonism and the dandyesque playing of roles is that life without the powers of the imagination is worthless.

In Stevens's poetry the style stands out in high relief. The introspective, self-centred mind confronting reality seems to create a world of its own from style, almost as an assertion of itself. The lack of romance in the real world is made up for by exotic diction. The wind is called 'vocalissimus'; the moon has a 'porcelain leer'; revolutionaries are 'Hairy-backed and hump-armed, / Flat-ribbed and big-bagged'. There is a 'palais de justice of chambermaids'. 'Above the forest of the parakeets, / A parakeet of parakeets prevails, / A pip of life amid a mort of tails.' Stevens's style is often ironic, mocking and close to self-parody.

In such long poems as *The Man with the Blue Guitar* and *Notes Towards a Supreme Fiction*, various strategies for coping with reality are explored and dialectically set against each other to show the power of the mind finding solace in the activities of consciousness and meditation. In his final volume, *The Rock*, there is, for American literature, a rare serenity. Nothing has been mastered, but the effort has been worth while. If the world cannot be reduced to thought, it has no meaningful existence beyond human perception. Man and his environment are linked; they are mutually dependent upon each other for relevance. It is the recognition of this fact which is the final mythology of the modern world. If these poems are less brilliantly ornamented and imaged than the early works, there is a compensating mature acceptance of our condition which is strangely satisfying.

The two major American prose writers after Henry James are Ernest Hemingway (1896–1961) and William Faulkner (1897–1962). Faulkner's novels are richer than Hemingway's, both in their surface texture and in the moral complications they raise. The plot of *Light in August* is unwieldy and confusing; the effect, as in *Moby Dick*, is of mass and weight rather than clarity. It has an elaborate structure and does not follow the ordinary sequence of time. It is narrated by a variety of characters, and most of the events are set in the past. By delving into the past, Faulkner shows that his characters are victims of history. Slavery was a sin damning successive generations to live by continuing injustice, hate and fear. Indeed the racial problem appears symbolic of man's fallen nature. As the result of the northern victory in the Civil War and the racial hatreds carried over from slavery, the South is a fragmented society of uprooted, isolated individuals, held together by fears and obsessions. Religious beliefs are felt with rigid fanatical intensity, killing rather than liberating the spirit. There is no love, only puritanical repression.

Faulkner's novels mix allegory with realistic settings and modern fictional techniques. As the novels of Twain and James show, American realism often masks the spiritual and symbolic. Many of the descriptions in *Light in August* are as emblematic as anything in Hawthorne. For example, Hightower's 'mute chair evocative of disuse and supineness and shabby remoteness from the world, is somehow the symbol and the being too of the man himself'. The characters in the novel have a representative significance which makes them symbolic. Joe Christmas's life has been determined by Southern history. Left at an orphanage on, ironically, Christmas Eve, he grows up believing he is part Negro. He runs away from the fanatic Presbyterian farmer who adopted and raised him without love. Through his wanderings he hopes to define himself; instead he becomes more conscious of his hatred of others and himself. Not knowing his past, unwilling to accept his fate, he cannot be at peace – he can be neither white nor black. His apparent freedom is a burden. He is certainly not the natural man – free of the burden of the past – who the American imagination hoped would arise in the New World.

Whereas most Northern writers wish to deny the relevance of history, Faulkner shows the South imprisoned by its past. Joanna Burden is a descendant of a Northern abolitionist, Calvin Burden, and heir to the New England Puritan tradition. Representative of the victors in the Civil War, she lives in the South where she is unwanted and unhappy. Although emotionally repressed, she becomes Joe Christmas's mistress and discovers sexual desire. Believing him to be black, she sees him as an abstraction, not a real person. She cries in her ecstasy 'Negro! Negro! Negro!'. He in turn makes love to her as if it were revenge on the white race. Having been taught that the black race is damned by God and that her burden includes working for its salvation, she attempts to make Joe pray. Infuriated by this infringement on his freedom – and perhaps remembering his puritanical childhood – he murders her. Gale Hightower, obsessed by the romantic myth of the Old South, lives solely in his fantasies. He is betrayed by his wife, loses his church ministry, and appears to be unmanned. Although he wishes to stand outside his time and meditate on history, he cannot avoid involvement; the consequences of the past affect everyone. Joe Christmas is castrated and killed in his house.

If hope exists in *Light in August*, it is represented by Lena Grove. The novel begins with her journeying in quest of the father of her child:[12]

> backrolling now behind her a long monotonous succession of peaceful and undeviating changes from day to dark and dark to day again, through which she advanced in identical and anonymous and deliberate wagons as though through a succession of creakwheeled and limpeared avatars, like something moving forever and without progress across an urn.

The allusion to Keats's 'Ode on a Grecian Urn' strengthens our sense of Lena's journey as mythic and eternal. She is the unchanging, essential South, perhaps the eternal female. She brings renewal into the fallen world by giving birth to an illegitimate child who will replace Joe Christmas. At the novel's end she enjoys being on the road, seeing the world, and does not yet wish to return to a settled life in a backward provincial community. We are reminded of Huck Finn sailing down the Mississippi or Thoreau's life in the woods; there is a similar idealization of unsophisticated experience as being in harmony with nature.

Faulkner's prose is in keeping with the complexities of the novel's subject matter and structure; an inflated rhetoric expresses an incantatory vision. The sentences are long and involved. The style is repetitive and filled with biblical echoes. Words are piled up, with colloquial expressions sitting alongside strange abstract terms. Faulkner's own narrative voice, in using Southern American speech cadences, is influenced by that region's tradition of oral folktales. The author appears to be the voice of the South, sharing its intensely religious vision. He sees man as fallen, corrupt and predestined towards tragic failure. The histories of his characters and their families are scattered throughout his novels and it is often necessary to piece together their pasts to understand how the sins of the past have doomed the present. Such mythmaking seems to be part of the American tradition: Cooper's frontier, Hawthorne's New England, Whitman's open road, Twain's Mississippi.

American literature consists of journeys, quests, escapes and private visions of reality. From the nineteenth century to the present, writers or their main characters seek unobtainable freedom, in the forest, abroad, or on modern highways. This tradition continues and has spread around the world through the so-called youth or counter culture. The querying of the validity of such a view of life also continues to find expression in American writing. One reason for reading American literature is that it contains the fullest and most articulate examination of a dominant cultural influence on the modern world.

CHAPTER TEN

THE WEST INDIES
Kenneth Ramchand

'The third important event in our history,' writes George Lamming in *The Pleasures of Exile* (1960), 'is the discovery of the novel by West Indians as a way of investigating and projecting the inner experiences of the West Indian community.'[1] Only two years after the publication of Lamming's remark, the still-born West Indian Federation was finally pronounced dead. Since then, Guyana, Jamaica, Trinidad and Barbados, the larger territories of the English-speaking Caribbean, have become independent nations. If, in spite of the island nationalisms that have arisen we can continue to recognize a West Indian community, it is the persistence of certain common features in the arts in general and in the literatures of the now separate nations in particular that contributes most to the sense of a unity. For, because of the literature, the process described by Lamming as having begun in exile continues among readers and writers in the different islands:[2]

> It is here [in London] that one sees a discovery actually taking shape. No Barbadian, no Trinidadian, no St. Lucian, no islander from the West Indies sees himself as a West Indian until he encounters another islander in foreign territory. It was only when the Barbadian childhood corresponded with the Grenadian or the Guianese childhood in important details of folk-lore that the wider identification was arrived at. In this sense, most West Indians of my generation were born in England. The category West Indian, formerly understood as a geographical term now assumes cultural significance.

It is in this light that Lamming's *In the Castle of My Skin* (1953) ✓ is the first West Indian novel. Novels of childhood or novels with substantial portions dealing with childhood are prominent in West Indian writings.[3] All of these accept the proposition that there is or ought to be a connection between the child and the adult; most of them either consciously or unconsciously suggest a parallel between the childhood of the individual and the formative stages of a society. It is not difficult to understand the prevalence of such novels of childhood in the West Indies, for most of the writers were growing up in the 1930s and 1940s, a period of marked social change. Seeing themselves as formed or deformed by the society, the authors are very much concerned in the novels with a close examination of the emergence of that society. *In the Castle of My Skin* is at once a novel about growing up and a novel about changes in society. It evokes the particular childhood of the boy G. in a society we cannot help recognizing as Barbados; but, armed with the discovery of his West Indian-ness, Lamming deliberately arranges and presents the life around G. in such a way as to impress the essential features of a typical West Indian boyhood. The group of boys, Bob, Trumper, Boy Blue and G., live in a rich imaginative world of gossip, rumour and speculation about life, history and adults; a world, too, of ritual and adventure in nature, at times elaborately conceived but always sensuously enjoyed. The narrative 'we' of this sometimes difficult novel alternates between the 'we' of the unified boys' world, and the 'we' of an ordered community of villagers.

Lamming's fictional village rests on the converted ground of an old sugar estate in the eyes and under the shadow of the White Landlord's castle. Between the fixed worlds of villager and landlord is a physical and psychological territory patrolled by those displaced persons, the village overseers, who are 'fierce, aggressive and strict' towards their fellow villagers, and inhibited by their burdened consciousness of the Whites. From the early description of the structure of the village and of the attitudes of its three main groups to one another, it is clear that Lamming wants to make his fictional village representative of a West Indian society whose institutions, values and mental attitudes reflect and perpetuate the consequences of slavery, the plantation system and colonial rule. Nowhere does the novel touch upon the realities of the colonial situation more sensitively than in its tracing of the progress and proliferation of the overseer type moving through the professions, the civil service and the labour movements, on the way to political power and another betrayal of the people. At the end of *In the Castle of My Skin* the White–Black scale, the principle of order in the village, has been disrupted. A consortium of Black business-men headed by the ex-schoolmaster and popular leader Mr Slime buys over the estate from the landlord and evicts the puzzled villagers from their holdings. The old man Pa, who has lived in the village longer than anyone else, is to go to the almshouse, and the boy G., considering all these changes and his own imminent setting forth to another island, knows 'in a sense more deep than simple departure, I had said farewell, farewell to the land'. The narrative 'I' which becomes dominant at this point in the novel is both the awakening product of childhood's passing, and the con-fused, alienated individual at the end of an order. Separated now from boyhood and from the village, he becomes that familiar character in West Indian writing, the exile searching for a new stability and root.

Social realism as a mode and commitment as a value were established in the late 1920s and in the 1930s in the work of 'the *Beacon* group' whose most distinguished literary figures were Alfred Mendes and C. L. R. James.[4] Since that time authors from the West Indies have continued to be concerned with analysing and interpreting their society's ills. The angles from which the different writers approach, their moods and attitudes, and their degrees of success vary, but certain features are common, regard-less of island of birth: the social and economic deprivation of the majority; the pervasive consciousness of race and colour; a sense of a lack of history or history to be proud of; the cynicism and uncertainty of the native bourgeoisie in power after independence; and the absence of settled values or values instinctive to the lives of the majority. *In the Castle of My Skin* is the first West Indian novel not only because it is the first by an island writer to be consciously projected as a West Indian novel, but also because it contains, either as themes explored in depth or as issues floating in the world Lamming creates, almost every significant theme and direction in West Indian writing. Some of these themes also appear in the poetry of Edward Brathwaite (b. 1930), and they lie behind the emotions in the poems of the Guyanese Martin Carter and the St Lucian-born Derek Walcott (b. 1930). Walcott's

'Laventville', for example, burns out of the deepest compassion for those lives 'fixed in the unalterable grooves of grinding poverty'. But Walcott's poem moves beyond the expression of a socio-economic plight to an awareness of something in the mentality of the earth's wretched symbolized in the attitudes of Blacks at a christening ceremony:[5]

> . . . The black fawning verger
> his bow tie akimbo, grinning, the clown-gloved
> fashionable wear of those I deeply loved
>
> once, made me look on with hopelessness and rage
> at their new, apish habits, their excess
> and fear, the possessed, the self-possessed. . . .

And from this awareness of mimicry in the islands, Walcott's poem moves to a closure that dwells on a sense of stasis and cultural destitution:

> Some deep, amnesiac blow. We left
> somewhere a life we never found,
>
> customs and gods that are not born again,
> some crib, some grill of light
> clanged shut on us in bondage, and withheld
>
> us from that world below us and beyond,
> and in its swaddling cerements we're still bound.

Other writers do not seem to be so sure that the 'customs and gods' are not born again, for with the failure of the social revolution in the West Indies there has been, since the late 1960s, a marked movement in the literature away from a straightforward expression of social themes to an exploration of the possibilities of cultural revolution. Like everything else in the West Indies this has not been separable from race. At the end of *In the Castle of My Skin*, G.'s boyhood companion returns from the United States with a self-assurance and a message that the artistic hero cannot help being affected by:

> 'You know the voice?' Trumper asked. He was very serious now. I tried to recall whether I might have heard it. I couldn't. 'Paul Robeson', he said. 'One o' the greatest o' my

people.' 'What people?' I asked. I was a bit puzzled. 'My
People', said Trumper. . . . 'Who are your people?' I asked
him. It seemed a kind of huge joke. 'The Negro race,' said
Trumper.

West Indian man's search for 'something to cradle his deepest
instincts and emotions' (which Lamming's novel discovers to be
the next stage after the disruption of the all-defining White–Black
scale) has become much less tentative in the poetic trilogy of
Edward Brathwaite.

In *Rights of Passage* (1960), Brathwaite expresses the social and
cultural dispossessions of the New World Negro; *Masks* (1968) is
a record of a return journey to Africa by a West Indian Negro,
and a dramatization of an intellectual survey of African history
and traditional culture; in *Islands* (1969), Brathwaite satirizes
Christianity and other European institutions as well as the imita-
tive culture of the West Indian middle class, attempting at the
same time to demonstrate and invoke as a viable alternative the
African culture and religion in the islands. A greater knowledge
and understanding of African history and culture, the trilogy seems
to say, will not only remove the self-contempt of the Negro, it will
stimulate the racial memory and help to bring about a recognition
of elements of that culture still functional in West Indian society,
and help to create a proper measure of the intimate bearing that
heritage ought to have upon the discovery and creation of an
authentic identity for the West Indian.

Commentators on Brathwaite's poetry notice his flexible use of
dialect and dialect rhythms, his incorporation of the rhythmic
language of African drums and rituals, and the kinship of his
poetry to music, particularly jazz and calypso; explanations of the
structure of the long poem are then followed by an explication of
the schema and content of the trilogy. But Brathwaite is a more
complicated figure in his own poems, and, in surprising ways, a
better poet than he appears to be. The assumption that the trilogy
is a long poem gives a false impression of optimism, and, at the
same time, makes it difficult for us to see the poet's changing
relationship to his work from volume to volume as a crucial issue.
Rights of Passage seems a highly autobiographical poem about what
it is to be a sensitive, British-educated, middle-class West Indian
Negro intellectual who has studied history, travelled to Europe

and lived in Africa only to return and find 'Jack Kennedy invading Cuba'; he learns that the poor have not felt the virtue of independence since 'our island's leaders' have become selfish and exploiting. The systematic satire of West Indian institutional life and mimicry that we find in *Islands* does not, in terms of perception, go beyond its source in *Rights*; Brathwaite's concern for 'the supporting poor', and the exploration of their 'silence' are given full scope in *Islands*, but they are already present in *Rights*; and the literal and psychic journeys into African culture and history we find in *Masks* are implicit in the Prologue and Epilogue to *Rights* and in the memory-of-Africa motif that runs through the poem. In *Rights of Passage* the poet is still discovering his themes and feeling his way exuberantly into the varieties of language open to him. If it seems less controlled than the two succeeding works, this is only so by contrast with the cohesion lent to *Masks* by its traditional material, or with the rhetorical control of language that comes with having virtually discovered an ideology, as in *Islands*. *Masks* and *Islands* demonstrate a growing technical skill but suffer from a lack of spontaneity. When, however, particular sections escape the author's expository stance, a growing concern with the artistic process and with the figure of the artist in society expresses itself; or a clash of perspectives deepens or undermines the racial/historical persuasions; or certain poems ('The Forest', 'Sunsum' in *Masks*, 'Leopard', 'Anvil' in *Islands*) reveal more ambivalences or confusion than the surface rhythms or the overt doctrine of the work would have led us to expect. The sense we have in *Islands*, indeed, that we are constantly on the point of arrival but must always make 'one more incision' is the most cheering evidence that poetry refuses every so often to be led by the poet's conscious determinations.

The response to Brathwaite has been phenomenal. For the first time in the West Indies poetry has become popular, and the poet a cult figure. What real increase in the number of people reading poetry this implies, and whether there has been any improvement in the reading of poetry among the literate, it is difficult to say. But the publication of Brathwaite's work has at last brought poetry to the attention of the West Indian populace as something directly related to their lives. This event is as important in its way as the revolution that has taken place in the language and in the subject matter of West Indian poetry. For although there have been poets and poetry in the West Indies since the turn of the century, there is a sense of unreality about the earlier productions. The novelists could become known and have their works published by journeying to the metropolis in the 1950s and 1960s, but the poets had to remain at home, feeling their way slowly out of traditional forms and out of limited notions of what poetry is for and what is fit subject matter for the poet. If tone in poetry can be taken to include the communication of an attitude to self, to language and craft, to one's raw material and to the readers, then early West Indian poetry has no tone or an extremely naïve and sentimental one. The influence of the West Indian novel from exile in liberating West Indian poetry from its air of unreality cannot be properly gauged but it cannot be ignored.

The same literary magazines[6] which encouraged the prose writers in the 1940s and eventually directed them to London stimulated the poets too.[7] Many poems published at this time confirm that factors usually associated with the rise of a distinctively West Indian novel were also at work in the poetry. The introduction of social realism and social protest in the poetry of the late 1940s and the 1950s relates to the work of the earlier mentioned *Beacon* group in Trinidad in the previous decade when social realism was established as a mode. E. M. Roach could write not only the controlled and distanced dialect of 'Ballad of Canga', but also the direct indictment of 'I am the Archipelago':[8]

> I drown in the groundswell of poverty
> No love will quell. I am the shanty town,
> Banana, sugar cane and cotton man;
> Economies are soldered with my sweat.

Dialect had been used before, but mainly for comic and satiric purposes. It was the social consciousness of the period that ennobled the popular speech, revealing in it, just as it was doing in the novels, those possibilities that have come to spectacular and various fulfilment in Brathwaite's poetry and in the flood of new poetry appearing in the magazines of the late 1960s.[9] So in 'Carnival Rhapsody'[10] Knolly S. La Fortune could invoke the drums through the dialect, and relate both to the desired social revolution. It is in the late 1940s and in the 1950s then that we can see West Indian poets looking at the world around them not for Nature, Beauty, Truth and Life, but in a quest for meaning – the meaning of a people's life and struggles in a social and historical context, and meaning at the same time in terms of their relationship to a landscape between which and themselves technology has not yet created forgetful walls.

By far the outstanding poet of this period is the Guyanese Martin Carter whose *Poems of Resistance* (1953) contains the stark declamation of 'I come from the Nigger-yard of yesterday' as well as the magnificent 'University of Hunger' in which, as in Carter's better poems, social and historical themes are given depth and intensity by inner vision and dream; and in which dialect rhythms subtly lose themselves only to give muscle to the verse:

> is the university of hunger the wide waste.
> is the pilgrimage of man the long march.
> The print of hunger wanders in the land
> The green tree bends above the long forgotten
> The plains of life rise up and fall in spasms
> The roofs of men are fused in misery.
>
> They come treading in the hoof marks of the mule
> passing the ancient bridge;
> the grave of pride
> the sudden flight
> the terror and the time.

If West Indian poetry seems to come of age in Carter's *Poems of Resistance*, we can trace its whole process of evolution in the long career of Derek Walcott. Since 1962 Walcott has had three collections of poems and a book of plays published abroad. Before all this he had published locally, and at his own expense, three booklets beginning with *25 Poems* (1949).[11] From first to last the following constantly changing elements are in his work: the sensuous evocation of landscape and seascape – threatening to be something merely lush at first but gradually yielding simile; continuing as a source of metaphor and progressively declaring the plain but rich natural symbols for the poet's inner and outer worlds. Then, there is an early involvement with ideas about existence and human life which develops into a capacity for thinking in poetry, and which, in combination with a flow of images that move beyond logic or conscious reasoning, makes him the most sensuously thinking poet in English at the present time. Next in Walcott's poetry we find an intense preoccupation with his own feelings, particularly the sense of aloneness and of how a man must school himself to cope with life and the final desolation:[12]

> Your death was a log's entry,
> Your suffering held the strenuous
> reticence of those
> whose rites are never public,
> hating to impose, to offend.
> Deep friend, teach me to learn
> such ease, such landfall going,
> such mocking tolerance of those
> neat, gravestone elegies
> that rhyme our end.

Another Walcott concern is an obsession with his craft, a willingness to be led by the poem on the one hand, and a search for the appropriate style on the other. This obsession takes him from conscious and unconscious verbal echoings in the early poetry to deliberate references and allusions later, to poets engaged with similar experiences. Finally in Walcott's poems we find a continual dedication of himself to his craft and of his craft to the exploration of his own personality, and then, with no little diffidence, a devotion of both to the society which has shaped him.

Although such poems as 'A Far Cry from Africa' and 'Return to D'Ennery, Rain' (*In a Green Night*), 'Laventville' (*The Castaway*) and Part III of *The Gulf* are directly about large social issues, Walcott's themes can appear, on anything less than an intelligent reading, too private or too unrelated to matters of great concern. But it is the poet's constant awareness of the socio-economic and cultural plight of the islands that drives him again and again to those themes of love, loss, grief, death and friendship. For it is these that make up the human response to the challenges of history and environment:[13]

> Upon this rock, the bearded hermit built
> His Eden:
> Goats, corn crop, fort, parasol, garden,
> Bible for sabbath, all the joys
> But one
> Which sent him howling for a human voice.

Even those who respond at once to its music, however, sometimes find it difficult to understand all of Walcott's poetry. The difficulties are more than just a question of the language being used, yet criticism tends to be directed at this poet for not writing sufficiently in the language of the people. At first sight there may appear to be something in such a charge. But to understand how unjust that criticism is it is necessary to take note of a major phenomenon in the West Indian literary situation.

West Indian literature would seem to be the only substantial literature in which the dialect-speaking character is the central character. This feature reflects a new and defining event in writing related to the West Indies – the centrality of the Black character and the illumination of an hitherto obscure and stereotyped person. In eighteenth- and nineteenth-century writings about the West Indies, Negroes appeared as comic or pathetic figures; whenever the writers attempt to make them speak, one becomes aware of two unrelated voices – the narrating voice of the British or American author, and the voice of a character speaking what the authors seek to project, with varying degrees of accuracy, as 'Negro English'. West Indian authors, writing in the twentieth century, are the educated products of the dialect-speaking group, so they have a familiarity with the dialect and a competence in the standard English of their education. As West Indians have no other language, it is not surprising that their two languages are influencing each other all the time. This process has been accelerated in the work of the West Indian novelists in two main ways.

The West Indian novelist has made the dialect a subtle enough instrument to express the consciousness of the Black character, and, obviously, he has drawn upon the patterns in his standard English to do so. The most extreme form of this is the literary dialect V. S. Reid invented for the narrator of *New Day* (1949). At the same time, however, the sound system of the dialect penetrates the standard English of the narrative sections of West Indian novels, so that we misunderstand their tone very badly if we do not imagine these sections as being spoken with a West Indian voice. The results of this closing of the gap between the two languages may be observed in Samuel Selvon's *A Brighter Sun* (1952). Selvon was the first West Indian writer to use dialect as the language of introspection, and he has gone so far as to use dialect as the language of narration in a more daring and direct manner than Reid. In this extract from *A Brighter Sun*, Tiger's consciousness is not presented exclusively in dialect, but we have an ideal illustration of how, with the mutual influences of dialect and standard English upon each other, three elements – authorial comment, reportage of a character's thoughts, and the character's actual words – modulate smoothly into one another as has only been possible in West Indian writing with the emergence of the native West Indian author of peasant origins:[14]

> When Urmilla and the baby were asleep he looked up at the roof and felt revulsion for his wife and child. They were to blame for all his worry. If he were alone he could be like Boysie, not caring a damn. He would go to the city and get a job – not just an ordinary job, like how Boysie used to work in a grocery, but something bigger. He would even go to school in the night and learn to read and write. Right here in Baratoria he could have gone to school, but everybody would laugh at a big married man like him going to class with a slate and pencil. Even little Henry could read and write a little. Every time he thought of that Tiger winced as if he had been slapped in the face. True, Joe himself couldn't write, and he had said he could live without it. But he was no old man, to resign himself to a poor life, killing out his body in the fields, spending so much money to buy some kind of special food Rita had told Urmilla was good for the baby. Look at Sookdeo, he argued, you think I want to be like he when I get old? Is only old age that I respect in him. All he could do is read and drink rum. When I learn to read, you think is only *Guardian* I going to read? I going to read plenty books, about America and England, and all them places. Man, I will go and live in Port of Spain; this village too small, you can't learn anything except how to plant crop.

The West Indian poets have learnt from the novelists how to modify and exploit the resources of the dialect. Brathwaite has carefully built upon its rhythmic qualities; Walcott introduces it much less emphatically. But no Walcott poem, however 'sophisticated' the English, makes sense unless we hear it as coming from a West Indian speaking voice.

The criticism that Walcott takes a limited view of dialect is sometimes linked with the feeling that he is not interested in the West Indian dialect-speaking groups. Walcott has remained free from the idealization or Africanization of the West Indian masses now fashionable in the West Indies.[15]

> We recognised illiteracy for what it was, a defect, not the attribute it is now considered to be by revolutionaries . . . The folk knew their deprivations and there were not frauds to sanctify them.

The long introductory essay to his collection of plays is a moving revelation of his commitment to his art and to a West Indian community; in the plays themselves we see him creating the West Indian social world, placing the peasantry at the centre, and making exciting use of folklore and oral tradition, music, dance and the popular speech. The plays have been ignored in recent assessments of Walcott's work, but Walcott the poet is inseparable from Walcott the dramatist: a profound dialogue and balance exist between the presences and problems explored in the social worlds created in his plays and the darker internalizations of his poems. While tired new voices have been drumming about 'the folk', 'the folk language', 'folk culture', and 'bringing theatre to the people', Walcott has been demonstrating over the last twenty years how a serious artist whose primary interest is imaginative rendering converts these self-indulgent abstractions into art.

To a large extent, West Indian drama is Walcott's plays, and the growth of numerous drama groups in the different islands participating in the production of plays good and bad is a growth Walcott's own activities have certainly stimulated and been intended to stimulate. In *Ti-Jean and his Brothers*, Walcott combines animal fable and West Indian folklore with a recognizable social setting to produce a work of great charm and political relevance. But there is only space here to glance at his latest effort, *Dream on Monkey Mountain*. In a production note to the play, Walcott advises:

> The play is a dream, one that exists as much in the given minds of its principal characters as in that of its writer, and as such, it is illogical, derivative, contradictory. Its source is metaphor and it is best treated as a physical poem with all the subconscious and deliberate borrowings of poetry.

The ape-like charcoal burner, Makak, has visions of a white woman, identified with the moon, who encourages him to see himself as a great African king. His delusion releases him from a crippling self-contempt and turns him into a faith-healer. From this point, society begins to press in. Moustique, a companion who capitalizes on Makak's growing reputation as a saint, is killed by a mob let down by the discovery that he is impersonating the old man for private gain, but not before Moustique insults them for their own continuing pathetic longings and manipulability. With Moustique's death, Makak's delusion is over but he is now trapped in his role of king in the dream of the mulatto officer Lestrade, whose peculiar kind of ambivalence ('Lestrade, the straddler') now takes up our interest. Lestrade, who was previously the pompous officer of British rule, now becomes the servant of the African plenipotentiary, and drives Makak to behead the White apparition that has plagued both their souls:

> She is the colour of the law, religion, paper, art, and if you want peace, if you want to discover the beautiful depth of your blackness, nigger, chop off her head! ... She is the white light that paralysed your mind, that led you into this confusion. It is you who created her, so kill her! kill her! The law has spoken.

After the beheading, the action returns to the cell where Makak has been spending the night in the care of Corporal Lestrade. Cured of his self-contempt and freed of the compensating self-delusion, but convinced of the need for a new start, Makak now assumes his real name, Felix Hobain, and is about to return to his hut on the mountain:

> The branches of my fingers, the roots of my feet, could grip nothing, but now, God, they have found ground ... Other men will come, other prophets will come, and they will be stoned and mocked and betrayed, but now this old hermit is going back home, back to the beginning, to the green beginning of this world.

Dream on Monkey Mountain is an expression of the longing for fulfilment that lies behind the dream of ancestral grandeur, and a compassionate but unsentimental analysis of the psychic disturbance of colonized man. It is a warning against seeing the African phase in the West Indies as more than a corrective moment; more importantly, it brings into our contemplation of who is the West Indian the consciousness that no answer to our particular question can be satisfactory unless it also takes into account the ultimate question 'What is man?' Walcott's play is a valuable complement to those ideas associated with Brathwaite's trilogy.

For Brathwaite's turning to Africa, and the feeling that his message is mainly directed towards the descendants of Africans in the West Indies, may seem to be bringing to fulfilment a view that V. S. Naipaul sought wrongly to apply to writers published before 1962: 'Most have so far only reflected and flattered the prejudices of their race or colour groups.'[16] West Indians comprise people of Amerindian stock, descendants of Europeans, descendants of Africans, descendants of indentured labourers from India, China, Portuguese Madeira, and various mixtures from all these – a reflection of successive waves of migration into the Caribbean over a period of three hundred years, and of the process of fusion that has been taking place in the region sometimes in spite of conscious attitudes. Although it is natural that West Indian writers should find the raw material for their imaginings in the social or racial groups with which they are most familiar, one way of seeing the society has been to regard all the immigrants as being shaped into West Indians, whatever their place on the White–Black scale, by a common history and experience and contact in the island environment.

Brathwaite's way of looking, however, is part of a new exploration which sees the West Indies as an area of plural cultures, the cultures corresponding more or less to racial groups. By recognizing and reviving the suppressed culture of the majority, it might be possible to find a way out of mimicry of European cultures, and shape a Creole society whose culture will reflect the ways of seeing and feeling of the majority more truly and democratically than an existing pattern which carries biases determined by the plantation system and colonial rule. In Jamaica and Barbados where descendants of Africans are in the majority by far, Africanization can be seen as part and parcel of the social revolution. But there are difficulties with respect to Trinidad and Guyana where descendants of Indians make up half the population, and where, if one concentrates on the socialization process there is a great deal in common between ex-slave and ex-indentured servant, but where a theory of cultural pluralism, designed to redress imbalances in the White–Black scale, unhappily accentuates and creates divisions between the two socially and economically Black groups in the society. A discussion of Naipaul's *A House for Mr Biswas* in this context is useful. This novel strikes at the Indian illusion of being a group with a preserved Hindu culture, and takes the common-history view of West Indian society. It refutes Naipaul's own view quoted above, for it shows how possible it is to write with great particularity about a specific group in West Indian society without writing for that group, and without writing so exclusively about the group that the West Indian-ness of their experience is denied.

A House for Mr Biswas spans a period from about the beginning of this century up to the years immediately following the Second World War – so, in a sense, it is a historical novel. It takes the form of fictive biography beginning with the inauspicious birth of Mr Biswas in an obscure village, and ending with his death in his own house in the city, forty-six years later. Few West Indian novelists have Naipaul's capacity for the sustained feat of character-ization in depth that *A House for Mr Biswas* is, and none is able to create with such seeming ease so convincingly alive a context of people and things. The life and achievement of Mr Biswas are interpreted and explored against a dense and changing back-ground – the dissolution over three generations in the colonial context of the old way of life of the Tulsis, a rural Indian family into which Mr Biswas came to be married. Towards the end of the novel, the Tulsis shift from their traditional stronghold at Arwacas in a late attempt to make a new life, on a cocoa estate recently acquired from a retreating French Creole ownership. The Tulsi matriarch does not survive the move, and the clan has been turned inwards for too long to be able to cope with the changing times; with the passing of the old authority, opportunism and individual-ism break out in the clan. The closing chapters of *A House for Mr Biswas* are set in a house in Port of Spain where families of Tulsi daughters and their appendages live as separate economic units, thrusting the children forward in the colonial scramble for education. But the Tulsis are not just the human background against which we explore Mr Biswas's history, nor is their process of change and dissolution itself the subject matter of the novel. Mr Biswas's strivings for a house of his own may be interpreted as every man's struggle to lay claim to a portion of the earth on which he walks. His resistance to being absorbed into anonymity by the Tulsi leviathan may be seen also as a human response to the depersonalizing forces in the modern state. Yet *A House for Mr Biswas* points a decided contrast between the late opportunistic individualism of the uncharted Tulsis on the one hand, and the spiritual character, on the other, of Mr Biswas's faithful struggle for independence, and for his individuality, against the in-sucking pull of that unfeeling and indifferent household.

In *A House for Mr Biswas*, Naipaul is far from flattering the descendants of Indians who form about half the population of his native Trinidad, and whom he castigates in a non-fictional work as[17]

a peasant-minded, money-minded community, spiritually static because cut off from its roots, its religion reduced to rites without philosophy, set in a materialist colonial society.

What has not been properly recognized is that he is writing about an experience of acculturation that has been going on among the different immigrant groups in the islands for over three hundred years:[18]

But to see the attenuation of the culture of my childhood as the result of a dramatic confrontation of opposed worlds would be to distort the reality. To me the worlds were juxtaposed and mutually exclusive. One gradually contracted. It had to; it fed only on memories and its completeness was only apparent. It was yielding not to attack but to a type of seepage from the other.

In *The Mimic Men* (1967), Naipaul has written the most searching West Indian novel about the confrontation of communities, but in *A House for Mr Biswas*, which is set in an earlier period, it is the process of seepage that is being exploited. The Creole Trinidadian world is involved in the very conception and structuring of the novel.

The novel comes to a climax in Part Two which is set significantly in Port of Spain where, having resisted Hanuman House's pull towards regression, Mr Biswas toils to make his mark in the larger Trinidad society. *A House for Mr Biswas* is a gradual revelation of the fraudulence of the Hindu culture the Tulsis would like to believe they retain, and of the restlessness of the descendants of Indians in the New World. Mr Biswas's heroism lies as much in his rejection of the specious comforts of Hanuman House as in his faith as a West Indian in the Creole future his author can only just grant as a possibility.

The Prologue and Epilogue to *A House for Mr Biswas* remind us that Naipaul is regarded as the prophet of West Indian historyless-ness and hopelessness. In his sensuous awareness of the natural world, his metaphysical bent, and his disregard for the usual conventions in the novel (time, character, social realism), the Guyanese Wilson Harris (b. 1921) is the direct opposite of the writer from Trinidad. In the ten years since *Palace of the Peacock* first appeared, Harris has produced a further ten volumes of fiction. The most recent of these (*The Sleepers of Roraima*, 1970 and *The Age of the Rainmakers*, 1971) take the form of fables or short stories, and they draw upon myths and legends of the vanish-ing Caribs and Arawaks, thus reflecting the persistence of Harris's interest in coming to terms imaginatively with the Caribbean past and all its peoples, as well as the artist's experimental willingness to invest in the appropriate form. Harris is well aware of the meeting of cultures and peoples in the Caribbean, and of the bitter consequences of slavery and colonialism, but in novel after novel he explores this broken world as one holding exciting possibilities for the creation of more balanced social structures and for the bringing into consciousness of suppressed and unconscious ele-ments in the obscure person. Few can doubt the integrity of the author's one long endeavour, and fewer still can have failed to be moved by the force of his imaginings. The conviction indeed has been growing slowly that Wilson Harris is one of the most signi-ficant writers in English in this century. But the evasiveness of all of us readers and critics, when it comes to stating exactly what Harris is trying to say or do, has given undue emphasis to the feeling that there is something misty around the corners, an architecture and logic we cannot definitively comprehend or analyse.

While it is true that there are areas in Harris's work that continue to defy both analysis and comprehension, its central concerns are so cogently presented that the allegations of obscurity and irrelevance can only be explained as the result of impatience. *The Secret Ladder* (1963) is probably Harris's least difficult novel to read: it contains a central character whose process we can follow in much the same way as we might follow in a conventional novel;

its events develop out of a familiar literary situation – an experience of disorientation in an isolated place; and the story unfolds in a straightforward and chronological manner. Russell Fenwick, a government surveyor, is the leader of a crew who have come to chart the wild upper reaches of the Canje river. Fenwick's mission is the first stage in an irrigation project designed to take water to the rice and sugar-cane areas on the coast. He meets opposition from a small village of fishermen, descendants of runaway slaves; this primitive community distrusts the agent of science and technology, and they are jealous of their autonomy which Fenwick as a government officer also seems to threaten. To add to these troubles Fenwick finds that during the long dry spell which has delayed the work of the surveying party the men have begun to get restive, but for some obscure reason they will not bring their discontents to him. Fenwick himself finds the confrontation with the jungle disconcerting. He begins to question his being and his roles, in a vague way at first, until he meets the old man, Poseidon, the head of the Canje village, and this meeting brings home to him that the authority he now wields must be sensitized and refined by a more profound and imaginative understanding of responsibility before it can be effective, and before he, Fenwick, can find himself as a person. When the novel draws to its close, the conflicts between the government surveying party and the backward villagers come to a fortuitous end: the old man, Poseidon, is accidentally killed by Bryant, who loves him; and the villagers, who believe that two of their number have killed Fenwick, regard their leader's death at the hands of one of Fenwick's men as retribution. They take to confused flight. So the theme of the integration of science and technology into the modes of feeling of a primitive community is left hanging (it comes to brilliant fulfilment in Harris's *Tumatumari*); and while the recurrent West Indian problem of we (the people) *versus* them (authority) is here given its most searching exploration in West Indian fiction from the perspective of authority, little has been made to register in the consciousness of the villagers. Fenwick recognizes the achievement of the villagers in first wresting their freedom, and then holding it against the forces of government and capitalism on the coast. But he also sees that that freedom has not been used, has grown static because the villagers are trapped in the attitudes of the past and will allow no influence from historically antagonistic quarters.

That Harris does not lead these themes to a resolution, and that he does not show the villagers changing, are not signs of incompetence. The characters in Harris's fiction are ultimately agents through whom a vision is being expressed, so the revelation of a set of complexities in a situation does not seek to encourage a continuation of an interest in the lives of the characters as if they were people down the street. The fictional beings fulfil their function and are allowed to fade. The changes that are to take place occur in the consciousness of the reader, who is really Harris's main character. It is in this light that we must also understand Harris's handling of Fenwick's relationship with the crew. With the end of the survey, the crew are to return to the coast, but without any resolution either of the conflicts within themselves as Fenwick's subjects or of their attitudes to his leadership. As the crew depart and the villagers take to flight, the reader is brought in the final moment to Russell Fenwick dreaming that 'an inquiry into the dramatic role of conscience in time and being' had ended, and hearing 'the echoes of annunciation' sounding the promise that 'in our end is our beginning'.

It is here we can see that the novel's revelations have their dramatic impact on Fenwick's consciousness, and that one way of looking at these matters is to see them as externalizations of the process of Fenwick's awakening in conscience and consciousness. Fenwick is a middle-class West Indian with a refined upbringing and mixed racial ancestry, and *The Secret Ladder* is an exploration of his relationship to the masses and to an African heritage he had previously despised or ignored, certainly never come to terms with. The position of authority in which Harris places Fenwick is the ground from which notions of the fulfilment of the person, and the creation of new social and political structures, are shown as inter-related. But first of all, Fenwick must die to his old life and to his old conception of himself through developing a capacity for response to the deepest human needs in the community and in his buried self. When Fenwick tries to win the confidence of the villagers, Jordan fiercely advocates the calling in of the jungle police; and when the surveyor tries to establish a relationship of trust between himself and the crew it is Jordan who warns him of the hazardous territory he is entering upon, urging him to return to the safe politics of the past. Jordan is the type of faceless middle man politician and local administrator whose belief in order pro-

vides great support to the *status quo*. There is no greater drawback
to the creation of a new society and a genuine humanism in the
West Indies, and no West Indian novelist has seen and portrayed
him with his desensitizing comforts and in all his blighting
cynicism as Harris has.

With the casting off of Jordan, and the casting out of the
Jordan within himself, Fenwick is ready for a new start. And
here Harris leaves him and seems to feel that the awakened reader
can leave him too. It is in Harris's handling of the theme of
command and self-command, authority and responsibility in this
novel that we find the most far-reaching treatment of that central
issue in West Indian writing today, the one that attracts Lamming,
Naipaul, Walcott and Brathwaite too – the relationship of the
sensitive, educated West Indian to the West Indian people (whether
we call them 'mass', 'folk', 'Africa' or 'peasantry'). It is the most
liberating treatment of that problem because Harris sees it in all
its complexities as a problem about the creation of a society and
the discovery of an authentic personal existence; it is liberating,
too, because Harris does not prejudice the issue with a camp-
building doctrine of his own. Like the self-taught Trinidad
novelist, Michael Anthony, in *The Year in San Fernando* (1965),
Harris sees the hopeless historyless chaos as one out of which
growth and new beginnings are possible:[19]

> I remembered walking through the short-cut in the heat of
> the dry season when the tall trees among the houses had been
> stricken and barren-looking, and had not caught my eye at all.
> I remembered seeing the mango – so sensitive to heat – and
> their leaves had been shrivelled up and their barks peeled, as
> if they had surrendered and could take no more. I remem-
> bered the cedar too, one of the giant cedars, and I had even
> looked at it and thought how much firewood there was here.
> But all these trees had sprung to life again, with the rains,
> and were so rich in leaf now, it was unbelievable. But I had
> seen this myself. And now I watched the great cedars sending
> even more branches into the sky of the town.

NOTES

Introduction

1 Chinua Achebe, *A Man of the People,* Heinemann, London, 1966, p. 54.
2 A. D. Hope, 'Australia', *Collected Poems,* Viking, New York, 1966, p. 13.
3 W. B. Yeats, 'The Circus Animals' Desertion', *Collected Poems,* Macmillan, London, 1950, p. 392.
4 James Joyce, *A Portrait of the Artist as a Young Man,* Penguin, Harmondsworth, 1960, p. 203.
5 *Ibid.,* p. 189.
6 *Ibid.,* p. 251.

Chapter One   Australia

1 'Colonial Hunt' is taken from *Sydney Gazette,* 16 June 1805. Reproduced in *Bards in the Wilderness,* ed. Brian Elliott and Adrian Mitchell, Nelson, Melbourne, 1970.
2 *My Country* first appeared in the London *Spectator* in 1908. Its light has now somewhat faded but it had a powerful popular appeal in its day and is still repeated.
3 See A. B. Paterson's *Collected Verse,* Angus & Robertson, Sydney, 1947; Henry Lawson's *Collected Verse,* vol. I, ed. Colin Roderick, Angus & Robertson, Sydney, 1967.

4 A reprint of this work, ed. C. Hadgraft, was issued by the Jacaranda Press, Brisbane and Melbourne, 1962.

5 Correctly titled *His Natural Life*, this version is available in the Penguin reprint, ed. S. Murray-Smith, 1970. The title *For the Term*, etc., dates from 1885 and applies to the revision first printed in 1874. It is the version most commonly seen.

6 A reprint of this novel, issued by the Melbourne University Press, appeared in 1955.

7 *Settlers and Convicts: Recollections of Sixteen Years' Labour in the Australian Backwoods*, by an Emigrant Mechanic (Alexander Harris), London, 1847, was reprinted, ed. Manning Clark, by Melbourne University Press, 1953; with new foreword, 1964.

8 *Geoffry Hamlyn* is available in the World's Classics series. Sam Buckley is the young hero of this novel.

9 *Such is Life* was published, as a book but not in the columns of the magazine, by the *Bulletin*. It was much revised and in the course of reworking it Furphy separated out the substance of two later but still related works, *Rigby's Romance* and *The Buln-Buln and the Brolga*, neither of which, however, reached publication in his lifetime (1843–1912). Reprints: *Such is Life*, Cape, London, and Angus & Robertson, Sydney, 1944; *Rigby* and *Buln-Buln*, ed. G. Turner and K. Gilding, respectively, both in Seal Australian Fiction, Rigby, Adelaide, 1971.

10 The *Bulletin*, a Sydney weekly, began publication in 1880 and was very influential, especially from around 1890–1910.

11 See *Joe Wilson and His Mates, Bulletin* stories collected in 1901. Included in *The Stories of Henry Lawson*, 3 vols, ed. C. Mann, Angus & Robertson, Sydney, 1964.

12 The phrase is Furphy's, contained in a letter to J. F. Archibald, 4 April 1897, his first approach to the *Bulletin* on behalf of *Such Is Life*.

13 'Gum trees, ferns, prairies, plains – about here at least; though Australian scenery may be described as a rule to be *toujours gum.*' Letter of Marcus Clarke to Cyril Hopkins, undated. See Brian Elliott, *Marcus Clarke*, Clarendon Press, Oxford, 1920, p. 60.

14 A reprint of *Poems 1913* was issued by Sydney University Press in 1972.

15 This piece is among the selections from Kenneth Slessor in *Poetry in Australia 1923*, Vision Press, Sydney, 1923. Slessor's *One Hun-*

dred Poems, Angus & Robertson, Sydney, 1944, was re-issued with two additional poems in 1957.

16 See Slessor's *One Hundred Poems, ibid*, and see R. D. FitzGerald, *Forty Years Poems*, Angus & Robertson, Sydney, 1965.

17 See *ibid*. 'Edge' appeared first in the collection *Moonlight Acre*, 1938.

18 'The Damnation of Byron' is dated 1934 in A. D. Hope's *Collected Poems 1930–1965*, Angus & Robertson, Sydney, 1966.

19 'The Return from the Freudian Islands' is dated (in the same volume) 1942.

20 'Envoi' was contributed originally to one of Rex Ingamells's *Jindyworobak Anthologies* (1940). See James McAuley's *Collected Poems 1936–1970*, Angus & Robertson, Sydney, 1971.

21 The trilogy consists of *Australia Felix* (originally entitled *The Fortunes of Richard Mahony*), 1917; *The Way Home*, 1925; and *Ultima Thule*, 1929. The original title is now applied to the work as a whole.

22 See *Joe Wilson* and *Joe Wilson's Mates*. Both collections are in the second volume of *The Stories of Henry Lawson*. A paperback collection which includes both is *Henry Lawson, Selected Stories*, Seal Books, Rigby, Adelaide, 1971, introduction by Brian Matthews.

Chapter Two   Canada

1 'Variations on Strachan' in John Robert Colombo, *John Toronto*, Oberon Press, Ottawa, 1969, p. 12.

2 See the Introduction to William Kilbourn (ed.), *Canada: A Guide To The Peaceable Kingdom*, Macmillan, Toronto, 1970.

3 George Woodcock, 'An absence of Utopias', *Canadian Literature*, no. 42, Autumn 1969, p. 5.

4 *Ibid.*, p. 3.

5 Eli Mandel, 'Introduction', *Contexts of Canadian Criticism*, University of Chicago Press, 1971, pp. 13–14.

6 'Conclusion', Carl Klinck (ed.), *Literary History of Canada*, University of Toronto Press, 1965, p. 824. This essay is reprinted in Frye's collection of essays on the Canadian imagination, *The Bush Garden*, Anansi, Toronto, 1971.

7 'The narrative tradition in English Canadian poetry', *The Bush Garden*, p. 146.

8 Edward McCourt, 'Roughing it with the Moodies', in A. J. M. Smith (ed.), *Masks of Fiction*, McClelland & Stewart, Toronto, 1961, p. 90.

9 *Roughing It In The Bush*, New Canadian Library, McClelland & Stewart, Toronto, 1962, p. 227.

10 Clara Thomas, 'Journeys to freedom', *Canadian Literature*, no. 51, Winter 1972, p. 18.

11 'Afterword', *The Journals of Susanna Moodie*, Oxford University Press, Toronto, 1970, p. 62.

12 Margaret Atwood, *Survival*, Anansi, Toronto, 1972, p. 34.

13 All references to Purdy's poetry can be found in his *Selected Poems*, McClelland & Stewart, Toronto, 1972.

14 William Morton, 'The northern frontier: key to Canadian history' from *The Canadian Identity*, reprinted in William Kilbourn (ed.), *Canada : A Guide To The Peaceable Kingdom*, p. 283.

15 All references to Isabella Valancy Crawford's poetry can be found in her *Collected Poems*, William Briggs, Toronto, 1905, reprinted by the University of Toronto Press, 1972.

16 Thomas Haliburton, *The Clockmaker*, New Canadian Library, McClelland & Stewart, Toronto, 1958, p. 148.

17 Robertson Davies, *Stephen Leacock*, McClelland & Stewart, Toronto, 1970, p. 28.

18 Robertson Davies, *The Manticore*, Macmillan, Toronto, 1972, p. 98.

19 *Ibid.*, p. 99.

20 *The Loved And The Lost*, Laurentian Library, Macmillan, Toronto, 1970, p. 32.

21 Robertson Davies, 'The poetry of a people', in Andy Wainwright (ed.), *Notes For A Native Land*, Oberon Press, Ottawa, 1969, p. 98.

Chapter Three   England

1 Thomas R. Edwards, *Imagination and Power*, London, 1971.

2 Henry James, *Autobiography* (ed. Frederick W. Dupee), London, 1956, p. 548.

3 *Ibid.*, p. 560.
4 *Ibid.*, p. 563.
5 *Ibid.*, p. 271.
6 *Ibid.*, p. 564.
7 *Ibid.*, p. 549.
8 S. T. Coleridge, *Biographia Literaria*, XV (ed. Shawcross).
9 *Table Talk.*
10 J. B. Broadbent, *Some Graver Subject*, London, 1960, p. 26.
11 *Ibid.*, p. 56.
12 Letter to S. T. Coleridge, 19 April 1808.
13 Letter to E. H. Handley, 4 October 1830.
14 *Letters* (ed. M. B. Forman), 3rd edition, London, 1947, p. 108.
15 *Ibid.*, p. 147.
16 F. R. and Q. D. Leavis, *Dickens the Novelist*, London, 1970.
17 G. Santayana, *The Life of Reason*, vol. 4, London, 1905, pp. 82–3.
18 F. R. Leavis, *Education and the University*, London, 1943, pp. 118–19.

Chapter Four India

1 *Hindustan Times*, 17 June 1972, p. 6.
2 The Writers' Workshop, Calcutta, 1969.
3 Indian poetry in English is considered to have begun with Henry L. Derozio who died in 1831.
4 *Panjab University Research Bulletin*, III, 1, April 1972, p. 172.
5 K. Markandeya, *The Coffer Dams*, New York, 1969, p. 168.
6 R. Rao, *Kanthapura*, New York, 1963, pp. vii–viii.
7 R. Rao, *The Serpent and the Rope*, London, 1960, p. 1.
8 *Ibid.*, pp. 72 and 301.
9 *Ibid.*, p. 169.
10 *Kanthapura, op. cit.*, p. 109.
11 *The Serpent and the Rope*, p. 37.
12 *Ibid.*, p. 394.
13 The first four lines of the Sanscrit quotation are as follows:

Etat tad eva hi vanaṃ punar adya dṛstaṃ
yasminn abhūma ciram eva purâ vasantaḥ
āranyakāç ca grhiṇaç ca ratāḥ svadharme
saṃsarike ṣu ca sukheṣu vayaṃ rasajnāḥ.

14 *The Serpent and the Rope*, p. 397.
15 *Ibid.*, p. 340.
16 *Ibid.*, pp. 287–8.
17 *Ibid.*, pp. 359 and 361.
18 *Modern Indian Poetry in English*, p. 304.
19 *Ibid.*, p. 104.
20 *Ibid.*, p. 177.
21 *Ibid.*, pp. 172 and 173.
22 *Ibid.*, p. ix.
23 *Ibid.*, p. 5.
24 *The Golden Treasury of Indo-Anglian Poetry*, New Delhi, 1970, p. xxxvi. Sri Aurobindo published only one book of poems before 1900. The point at issue, of course, is not the chronology of publication but the 'modernity' of what was published.
25 *Ibid.*, pp. xxxviii–xl.
26 *Modern Indian Poetry in English*, pp. v–vi, p. xxxiii.
27 *Ibid.*, p. 169.
28 *The Golden Treasury of Indo-Anglian Poetry*, pp. 94–5.

Chapter Five   Ireland

1 Daniel Corkery, *Synge and Anglo-Irish Literature*, Dublin and Cork; London, 1931, p. 1.
2 Terence de Vere White, *The Anglo-Irish*, 1972, p. 38, remarks that he was asked to write this book, the history of the Anglo-Irish, 'on the assumption that they are dead'. He sees the period of the Anglo-Irish as co-terminous with the Protestant ascendancy established after the victories of William of Orange to which he gives an end in the period 1916–21, 'which saw the end of British rule and with it the end of Protestant ascendancy' (p. 19).
3 *Ibid.*, p. 21.

4 Jonathan Swift, *Prose Works*, ed. H. Davis, vol. 2, 1939, p. 120; vol. 12, 1955, p. 273.
5 See *ibid.*, vol. 9, 1948, p. 262.
6 'Nescio', *Irish Book Lover*, 21, 1933, p. 64.
7 See Swift, *op. cit.*, vol. 4, 1957, p. 279.
8 See Mackie L. Jarrell, 'Jack and the Dane', *Fair Liberty was all his cry*, ed. A. Norman Jeffares, 1967, p. 339.
9 See Conor Cruise O'Brien's sympathetic study of Burke in *The Suspecting Glance*, London, 1972, pp. 33–49, particularly for his appreciation of Burke's Catholic ancestry.
10 See Christina Colvin, 'Two unpublished MSS by Maria Edgeworth', *Review of English Literature*, 8, 1967, pp. 53–60.
11 This is included in *Uncollected Prose by W. B. Yeats*, ed. John P. Frayne, London, 1970, which contains most of Yeats's reviews and articles for 1886–96.
12 See F. S. L. Lyons, 'The twilight of the big house', *Ariel*, vol. 1, 1970, pp. 110–22, who remarks 'to be born in a country and to grow up to love it, but never fully to possess it, never completely to belong to it, may create not just great literature but also unhappy men and women'.
13 Frank O'Connor, *The Backward Look*, 1967, pp. 225–30.

Chapter Six   Kenya

1 Bernard Fonlon, 'African writers meet in Uganda', *Abbia*, 1 February 1963.
2 Taban Lo Liyong, 'Can we correct literary barrenness in East Africa', *East Africa Journal*, December 1965, p. 10.
3 *Ibid.*
4 Okot p'Bitek, *Song of Lawino*, East African Publishing House, Nairobi, 1966.
5 Okot p'Bitek, *Song of Ocol*, East African Publishing House, Nairobi, 1970.
6 Joseph Buruga, *The Abandoned Hut*, East African Publishing House, Nairobi, 1969.

7 Okello Oculi, *Orphan*, East African Publishing House, Nairobi, 1968.
8 Okello Oculi, 'Interview', *BaShiru*, University of Wisconsin, Autumn 1970–Spring 1971.
9 James Ngugi, *The River Between*, Heinemann, London, 1965, p. 1.
10 Eustace Palmer, *An Introduction to the African Novel*, Heinemann, London, 1971, p. 19.
11 Ngugi, *op. cit.*, p. 174.
12 *Ibid.*, p. 175.
13 James Ngugi, *Weep Not Child*, Heinemann, London, 1964, p. 43.
14 *Ibid.*, p. 119.
15 Leonard Kibera and Samuel Kahiga, *Potent Ash*, East African Publishing House, Nairobi, 1968.
16 Godwin Wachira, *Ordeal in the Forest*, East African Publishing House, Nairobi, 1967.
17 Charity Waciuma, *Daughter of Mumbi*, East African Publishing House, Nairobi, 1969.
18 Leonard Kibera, *Voices in the Dark*, East African Publishing House, Nairobi, 1970.
19 R. C. Ntiru, 'The notion of modernity in African creative writing', *East Africa Journal*, vol. viii, no. 10, October 1971.
20 Grace Ogot, *The Promised Land*, East African Publishing House, Nairobi, 1966.
21 Cited in Henry Kimbugwe, 'Grace Ogot: the African lady', *East Africa Journal*, April 1969, p. 24.
22 Grace Ogot, *Land Without Thunder*, East African Publishing House, Nairobi, 1968.
23 James Ngugi, *The Black Hermit*, London, Heinemann, 1968; *Three Plays*, East African Literature Bureau, Nairobi, 1971.
24 James Gatanyu, *The Battlefield*, East African Publishing House, Nairobi, 1967.
25 Robert Serumaga, *A Play*, Uganda Publishing House, Kampala, 1968.
26 John S. Mbiti, *Poems of Faith and Nature*, East African Publishing House, Nairobi, 1969.
27 R. C. Ntiru, *Tensions*, East African Publishing House, Nairobi, 1971.
28 Lennard Okola, *Drum Beat*, East African Publishing House, Nairobi, 1967, p. 14.

29 James Ngugi, 'Towards a national culture', *East Africa Journal*, vol. 8, no. 11, November 1971, p. 17, and published in Ngugi's collected essays *Homecoming*, Heinemann, London, 1972.
30 R. C. Ntiru, *loc. cit.*, p. 33.
31 Cited in *ibid.*, p. 26.
32 *Ibid.*, p. 27.
33 *Ibid.*, p. 30.
34 Cited in *ibid.*, pp. 28–9.
35 *Ibid.*, p. 33.
36 Charles Mangua, *Son of Woman*, East African Publishing House, Nairobi, 1971.
37 Eneriko Seruma, *The Heart Seller*, East African Publishing House, Nairobi, 1971.
38 Cited in Ntiru, *op. cit.*, p. 31.

Chapter Seven   Nigeria

Except when otherwise indicated the editions referred to here are Heinemann's African Writers Series for fiction, and Oxford University Press's Three Crowns Series for drama. The place of publication is London, except when otherwise indicated.

1 Joseph Jones, *Terranglia: The Case for English as World-literature*, Twayne, New York, 1965, p. 23.
2 *Modern Poetry from Africa*, ed. Gerald Moore and Ulli Beier, Penguin, Harmondsworth, enlarged and revised edition, 1965, p. 122.
3 *Ibid.*, pp. 121–2.
4 J. P. Clark, *A Reed in the Tide*, Longmans, 1965, p. viii.
5 D. O. Fagunwa, *Ogboju Ode Ninu Igbo Irunmale*, Nelson, 1950; Bello Kagara, *Gandoki*, reprinted by Gaskiya, Zaria, 1952.
6 Amos Tutuola, *The Palm-Wine Drinkard*, Faber, 1952, p. 40.
7 Chinua Achebe, 'The role of the writer in a new nation', *Nigeria Magazine* (Lagos), no. 81, 1964, p. 160.
8 Amos Tutuola's other works are also published by Faber: *My Life in the Bush of Ghosts* (1954), *Simbi and the Satyr of the Dark Jungle*

(1955), *The Brave African Huntress* (1958), *Feather Woman of the Jungle* (1962), *Ajaiyi and his Inherited Poverty* (1967).

9 Gerald Moore, *Seven African Writers*, Oxford University Press, 1962, pp. 39–57.

10 *The Palm-Wine Drinkard*, p. 25.

11 Chinua Achebe, *Arrow of God*, 1964, p. 55.

12 Chinua Achebe, 'The novelist as teacher', *New Statesman*, 29 January 1965, p. 162.

13 Chinua Achebe, *Things Fall Apart*, p. 182.

14 *Ibid.*, p. 181.

15 *Arrow of God*, p. 260.

16 Chinua Achebe, *Girls at War and other stories*, 1972.

17 See, for example, Oyekan Owomoyela, 'Folklore and Yoruba theatre', *Research in African Literatures* (University of Texas at Austin), vol. 2, 1971, pp. 121–3.

18 Wole Soyinka, 'Towards a true theatre', *Transition* (Kampala), no. 8, 1963, pp. 21–2.

19 Wole Soyinka, *Five Plays*, 1964, p. 82.

20 Wole Soyinka, *Madmen and Specialists*, Methuen, 1971, p. 63.

21 *Ibid.*, p. 36.

22 *Ibid.*, p. 36.

23 *Ibid.*, p. 76.

24 *A Reed in the Tide*, p. 30.

25 Soyinka's preface to *A Shuttle in the Crypt*, Rex Collings and Eyre Methuen, 1972, p. vii.

26 *A Reed in the Tide*, p. 2.

27 Molly Mahood, 'Drama in new born states', *Présence Africaine*, Paris, 32, vol 60, 1966, pp. 23–39.

Chapter Eight   South Africa

1 C. M. Booysen (ed.), *More Tales from South Africa*, Cape Town, 1967, p. 21.

2 G. Butler (ed.), *A Book of South African Verse*, London, 1959, p. 4.

3 Postface in O. Schreiner, *The Story of an African Farm*, New York, 1968, p. 274.

4 *Ibid.*, p. 18.
5 A. D. Dodd (ed.), *More Short Stories*, Cape Town, n.d., p. 3.
6 *Ibid.*, p. 3.
7 C. M. Booysen (ed.), *Tales of South Africa*, Cape Town, 1963, p. 61.
8 W. Plomer, *Turbot Woolfe*, London, 1965, p. 73.
9 *Ibid.*, p. 117.
10 *Ibid.*, p. 134.
11 R. Campbell, *The Wayzgoose*, London, 1928, p. 7.
12 R. Campbell, *Selected Poems*, London, 1968, p. 16.
13 A. Paton, *Cry the Beloved Country*, New York, 1948, p. 3.
14 *Ibid.*, p. 256.
15 Peter Abrahams, *Mine Boy*, London, 1963, p. 89.
16 *Ibid.*, p. 237.
17 *Ibid.*, p. 248.
18 E. Mphahlele, *Down Second Avenue*, New York, 1971, p. 199.
19 *Ibid.*, p. 199.
20 D. Wright (ed.), *South African Stories*, London, 1960, p. 66.
21 R. McNab (ed.), *Poets in South Africa*, Cape Town, 1958, p. 11.
22 *Ibid.*, p. 23.
23 D. Brutus, *Sirens, Knuckles and Boots*, Ibadan, Nigeria, 1963, not paginated.
24 *Ibid.*
25 O. Mtshali, *Sounds of a Cowhide Drum*, New York, 1972, p. 3.
26 *Ibid.*, p. 61.
27 *Ibid.*, p. 43.
28 D. Brutus, *Sirens, Knuckles and Boots*.

Chapter Nine   The United States

1 Henry David Thoreau, *Walden: Life in the Woods*, Merrill, Columbus, 1969, p. 205.
2 Herman Melville, *Moby Dick*, Modern Library, New York, 1944, p. 4.
3 *Ibid.*, p. 60.
4 *Ibid.*, p. 236.

5 Walt Whitman, 'Song of Myself', *The Collected Poetry*, Funk & Wagnalls, New York, 1968, p. 62.

6 *Ibid.*, p. 108.

7 Mark Twain, *The Adventures of Huckleberry Finn*, Penguin, Harmondsworth, 1966, p. 283.

8 *Ibid.*, p. 369.

9 James's use of Milton's 'The World was all before them' was anticipated by Hawthorne in *The Scarlet Letter*, where it is similarly used in connection with Hester Prynne's decision to accept her punishment for adultery: 'It may seem marvellous, that, with the world before her . . . free to return to her birthplace, or to any other European land . . . this woman should still call that place her home, where, and where only, she must needs be the type of shame.' (*The Scarlet Letter*, World, Cleveland, 1967, p. 76.)

10 Henry James, *The Portrait of a Lady*, Kelley, New York, 1970, vol. I, pp. 30–1.

11 *Ibid.*, vol. II, p. 436.

12 William Faulkner, *Light in August*, Random House, New York, 1959, p. 5.

Chapter Ten   The West Indies

Unless otherwise indicated, the place of publication of books referred to is London.

1 George Lamming, *The Pleasures of Exile*, 1960, p. 37.

2 *Ibid.*, p. 214.

3 Of special interest are: Jan Carew, *The Wild Coast*, 1958; Geoffrey Drayton, *Christopher*, 1959; Peter Kempadoo, *Guiana Boy*, 1969; Michael Anthony, *The Year in San Fernando*, 1965, and *Green Days by the River*, 1967; Austin Clarke, *Amongst Thistles and Thorns*, 1965; Ian McDonald, *The Humming-Bird Tree*, 1969; Merle Hodge, *Crick Crack Monkey*, 1970; and Wilson Harris, *The Eye of the Scarecrow*, 1965.

4 See especially Alfred Mendes, *Pitch Lake*, 1934, and *Black Fauns*, 1935; and C. L. R. James, *Minty Alley*, 1936, reprinted 1971.

5 Derek Walcott, 'Laventville', *The Castaway and Other Poems*, 1965.
Walcott's other collections published in London are: *In a Green
Night*, 1962, and *The Gulf and Other Poems*, 1969.

6 *Bim*, ed. Frank Colleymore, Chelsea Road, Barbados: began in
1942; *Kyk-over-al* (1945–61), ed. A. J. Seymour, Georgetown,
Guyana; *Focus*, ed. Edna Manley, Kingston, Jamaica: appeared in
1943.

7 Also important was *Caribbean Voices*, a BBC programme edited at
first by Una Marson, then Henry Swanzy. It ran from 1942 to 1959.

8 E. M. Roach, 'Ballad of Canga' and 'I am the Archipelago', *Caribbean Quarterly*, vol. 5, no. 3, 1958.

9 See *Savacou*, 3/4, 1971, ed. E. Brathwaite, K. Ramchand, A. Salkey,
P.O. Box 170, Mona, Kingston, Jamaica.

10 Knolly S. La Fortune, 'Carnival Rhapsody', *Caribbean Quarterly*,
vol. 5, no. 3, 1958.

11 Walcott's collections before *In a Green Night* are: *25 Poems*,
Barbados, 1949; *Epitaph for the Young*, Barbados, 1949; and *Poems*,
Jamaica, 1952.

12 Derek Walcott, 'Landfall, Grenada', *The Gulf*, 1969.

13 Derek Walcott, 'Crusoe's Island', *The Castaway*, 1965.

14 Samuel Selvon, *A Brighter Sun*, pp. 81–2.

15 'What the twilight says: an overture', introduction to Derek Walcott,
Dream on Monkey Mountain and Other Plays, New York, 1970.

16 V. S. Naipaul, *The Middle Passage*, 1962, p. 68.

17 *Ibid.*, p. 82.

18 V. S. Naipaul, *An Area of Darkness*, 1964, p. 37.

19 Michael Anthony, *The Year in San Fernando*, 1965, p. 147.